THE CLICK
MOMENT

SEIZING OPPORTUNITY IN AN
UNPREDICTABLE WORLD

FRANS JOHANSSON

PORTFOLIO
PENGUIN

PORTFOLIO PENGUIN

Published by the Penguin Group
Penguin Books Ltd, 80 Strand, London WC2R 0RL, England
Penguin Group (USA) Inc., 375 Hudson Street, New York, New York 10014, USA
Penguin Group (Canada), 90 Eglinton Avenue East, Suite 700, Toronto, Ontario, Canada M4P 2Y3
(a division of Pearson Penguin Canada Inc.)
Penguin Ireland, 25 St Stephen's Green, Dublin 2, Ireland (a division of Penguin Books Ltd)
Penguin Group (Australia), 707 Collins Street, Melbourne, Victoria 3008, Australia
(a division of Pearson Australia Group Pty Ltd)
Penguin Books India Pvt Ltd, 11 Community Centre, Panchsheel Park, New Delhi – 110 017, India
Penguin Group (NZ), 67 Apollo Drive, Rosedale, Auckland 0632, New Zealand
(a division of Pearson New Zealand Ltd)
Penguin Books (South Africa) (Pty) Ltd, Block D, Rosebank Office Park,
181 Jan Smuts Avenue, Parktown North, Gauteng 2193, South Africa

Penguin Books Ltd, Registered Offices: 80 Strand, London WC2R 0RL, England

www.penguin.com

First published in the United States of America by Portfolio/Penguin,
a member of Penguin Group (USA) Inc. 2012
First published in Great Britain by Portfolio Penguin 2012
001

Printed in Great Britain by Clays Ltd, St Ives plc

ISBN: 978–0–670–92239–0

www.greenpenguin.co.uk

THE CLICK MOMENT

'With his characteristic clarity, insight, and style, Frans Johansson presents an absorbing account of how randomness, serendipity, and "luck" can be used to enhance success in business and in your own life. A fascinating plunge into the rip tides and cross currents of chance and opportunity that so often affect the course of human achievement' Sir Ken Robinson, bestselling author of *The Element*

'An informed and measured account' *Financial Times*

'A terrific read, smartly researched, full of stories you find yourself repeating to others' *Management Today*

'In a world where random events increasingly rule our destinies, forget logic. Invite chance, then maximize it. With highly engaging and entertaining style, Frans Johansson shows us how' Peter Sims, author of *Little Bets*

'Johansson wonderfully captures the strategy of any startup . . . maximizing click moments and, through them, ideas that change the world for ever' Eric Klinker, CEO of BitTorrent

'Frans Johansson is a master storyteller and one of the most innovative thinkers I know' Teresa Amabile, Edsel Bryant Ford Professor of Business Administration, Harvard Business School, and co-author of *The Progress Principle*

700041608260

ABOUT THE AUTHOR

Frans Johansson is the bestselling author of *The Medici Effect*. Raised in Sweden by his African-American/Cherokee mother and Swedish father, he now speaks to audiences worldwide, from the boardrooms of America's largest corporations to villages in developing countries. He has founded a software start-up, a healthcare firm, a hedge fund, and the innovation firm the Medici Group. He lives in New York.

To my wife Sweet Joy and the
amazing and serendipitous journey
we have traveled together

CONTENTS

THE CLICK MOMENT

INTRODUCTION

Heading into the fall of 2004, ABC was dead last among broadcast television networks. Then, on September 22, something surprising happened and its fortunes changed. That was the night *Lost* debuted. The program came out of nowhere and delivered 18.7 million viewers to the struggling network, making it ABC's most-watched dramatic premier in nine years.

In a world of reality shows, *Lost* was a breath of fresh air. Centering on the survivors from an airliner that crashes on a mystical island, the show seemed like a sure-fire winner. It attracted an incredibly intense fan base that passionately dissected all the clues revealed in each episode. The plot was so intricate that the origin of a "smoke monster" from the first season wasn't revealed until the sixth. Critics and fans agreed that the island's "mythology" and the slow unraveling of its central mysteries made the show great. It must have required an incredible amount of planning to even get on the air.

Except the exact opposite was true. Many of the story elements that *Lost* fanatics loved were ideas the producers thought were too crazy to work. The show, it turns out, was a byproduct of a meeting between Damon Lindelof and J. J. Abrams. At the time, Lindelof was a writer on the modestly successful *Crossing Jordan*, and Abrams was the creator of the popular series *Alias*. Lindelof desperately wanted to write for *Alias*, and after years of trying to make a connection, he received a call from a mutual friend.

"Good news," she said, "You can meet him. Bad news, it's a ridiculous idea about a plane that crashes on an island." The idea didn't come from Abrams, but from ABC executive Lloyd Braun, who became infatuated with the notion of a scripted version of *Survivor*. He asked Abrams to rewrite the pilot, but Abrams declined, agreeing to supervise a writer instead. Lindelof thought the idea was insane, but saw an opening—if he could pitch a few good ideas for this "stupid plane crash" show he could propel himself to a writing position on *Alias*.

During their meeting it was clear to both men that *Lost* would never make it, so they pitched increasingly crazier ideas to each other. Abrams wanted random noises on the island to scare the viewer. When asked what the noises would be, Abrams responded, "I don't know, it's never going to get picked up." But it did. Things happened so quickly that Lindelof didn't have time to write the script. Instead, he handed in a twenty-page treatment, which Braun unexpectedly approved, along with *Desperate Housewives,* which turned out to be the biggest success of the 2004–2005 television season.

For his part, Braun was promptly fired for approving a $12 million television pilot that didn't even have a script for a show idea Michael Eisner, the CEO of Disney (which owns ABC) thought was "never going to work." When Eisner graded all the pilots ABC approved that year, he gave *Lost* a two out of ten. The man who developed the two shows that saved ABC was out of a job before they even aired.

Now, if the world moved in a predictable way, nothing in this story would make sense. In such a world we would expect the intricate mysteries on the island of *Lost* to be carefully planned. In such a world we would expect a successful producer such as J. J. Abrams and an executive such as Michael Eisner to realize that *Lost* had amazing potential. We would expect a writer such as Lindelof to strategize about how to get *on* one of the most influential shows in TV history, not how to get off it. And we would, of course, expect the person who developed *Lost* and *Desperate Housewives* to be rewarded, not fired.

But the world does not move in a predictable way. The story behind *Lost* actually makes a lot of sense. The implications are mind-boggling.

*

This book is about two very simple but highly provocative ideas.

The first one is this: success is random, far more random than we have come to believe. The second is that there are a number of specific actions that individuals and organizations can take to capture randomness and focus it in our favor.

The reason people tend to consider these ideas provocative is because success, we are often told, is a result of strategy, planning, and careful analysis. Luck, on the other hand, is a force that lies outside of our control. This book rejects these conventional perspectives and proposes a useful and compelling alternative.

At first blush, these interconnected ideas may seem at odds. If success is indeed random, how can any actions truly improve our chances? If celebrated companies, such as Starbucks and Google, or small businesses or investments or even one's career and love life all are the result of serendipity, then there is no point in directing our efforts in any particular direction, is there? But in fact, acknowledging the power of random forces does not render us powerless. Quite the contrary.

There are a number of specific actions you can take that will open you or your organization to chance encounters, unexpected strategies, and complex connections, just as there are certain actions that will enable you to capture randomness and seize opportunities. These actions set us up for greatness in an unpredictable world, and I will explore them in detail later in the book.

For now, however, it is enough to know that when you dig deeply into what underlies any personal or corporate success, you will see that one theme repeats again and again: somewhere, at some point, someone got lucky. They experienced a serendipitous encounter, an unexpected moment of insight, or an unplanned culmination of events. There was one instant when fate turned their way, a moment they can look back at and say, *that* was when it started. We all have these *click moments*, as I call them, and it is rather remarkable that we don't give them more of our attention, because they can change our lives.

PART I

AN UNPREDICTABLE WORLD

1

THE MOLDAVIAN THEORY OF SUCCESS

One February morning in 2005 the Moldavian pop star Dan Balan woke up to a ringing phone. It was seven a.m. People didn't usually call him that early, even considering the fact that he was in a Manhattan hotel and trailing Europe by six hours. Half awake, Balan answered and heard a friend on the line. "Dan, Dan, put on the TV, put on NBC," his friend yelled. "The *Today Show!*"

Balan crawled out of bed and turned on the *Today Show.* The hosts were discussing a story about a video that had gone viral. In 2005 "gone viral" was not in the common vernacular, in fact YouTube had just been created. But apparently this video had been seen by millions of people around the world in just a few days—an entirely new phenomenon. Balan wondered why his friend had insisted he watch the show, but then they aired the video. And he knew.

The video was of a somewhat pudgy kid lip-synching into a cheap camcorder with the sound of a heavy dance beat playing in the background. It wasn't a particularly good performance, Balan thought; he had certainly seen better. The song, unusually melodic, was in a strange language. But Dan Balan understood it. He should have—he had written it. Balan's song was getting airtime on the most watched morning show in the United States. It was a remarkable turn of events. In the strangest of ways, Dan Balan had gotten very, very lucky.

*

The world is an unpredictable place. On the face of it, this does not strike most people as a controversial statement. It seems obvious; we experience unpredictability almost every day, from dramatic rises and falls in the stock market to our luck catching a lone cab on a rainy day. However, the import of such a statement is not as clear. If the world is unpredictable, then you can't actually foresee whether your idea, project, or meeting will work out as planned. In fact, it might mean that the plan is outdated before you even start to execute it. And if you can't logically plan your way to success, that must mean that success, when it happens, is a result of something unexpected—of something random.

This idea, however, seems radical to many people. On the one hand, we aren't surprised by the uncertainty of everyday life, but on the other, we believe that success can be analyzed and planned for. It is a revealing paradox. The implications are explosive and they obliterate every commonsense notion we have about strategy and planning. Just ask Dan Balan.

*

In 2004, Balan's pop group O-Zone released a song called "Dragostea din tei." It launched in Romania at the top of the charts and spread like an epidemic through Europe. That summer it became one of the most dominant dance-club tracks in history. Within months the song had been recorded in about a dozen languages and all versions raced up the lists. At one point there were *five* different versions of the song in the

French top-twenty music charts *at the same time*. The song was a phenomenon everywhere—everywhere, that is, but the United States.

At the epicenter of the music universe, O-Zone fell flat. The band signed a record contract with an independent label that didn't seem to have the experience or resources to successfully market the album. And the timing was bad. "Dragostea din tei" came out at a time when techno-based club tracks were ebbing in popularity in the United States. The airwaves were dominated by R&B and hip-hop stars such as Destiny's Child and Jay-Z. The song had no sales to speak of and got very little radio play. The band's promoters decided to focus on their strengths, which, in this case, lay in the rest of the world. They pulled the U.S. marketing campaign and skipped touring the States altogether.

But only a few months later, "Dragostea din tei" came back out of nowhere to conquer the United States. Although it never achieved the same blockbuster status as it had in Europe, the song still climbed the charts without any visible promotional efforts at all. How did this happen? O-Zone's strategy, after all, was to walk away from the American market.

O-Zone's success can be traced to Gary Brolsma, a Staples employee from Saddle Brook, New Jersey. Brolsma was having a quiet day at home, sitting in front of his computer with his headphones on, listening to "Dragostea din tei," lip-synching and making funny expressions. "I was just fooling around, having a good time," he said about that particular moment, "and I recorded it." As a joke, he uploaded the video to a site called Newgrounds, then sent the link to some friends. "They all had a good laugh, and I thought nothing of it."

But some of those friends shared the link with other friends. One click led to another and the video caught on and became one of the world's first truly "viral" videos. I recall catching the link on a political blog that had absolutely nothing to do with music or videos, Romania, *or* Moldavia. Brolsma became known as the "Numa Numa" guy and the video is believed to be the most watched in the history of the Internet, with more than one billion people having seen it. "Dragostea din tei" shot up the dance charts and finally made O-Zone a success in the United States.

9

*

There is no way that Dan Balan could have planned for this. Still, it is tempting to try—which, of course, was the immediate reaction of marketers everywhere. The question was straightforward: how can one create a video that spreads as virally as the Numa Numa guy's? It is only natural to assume that we can simply learn what made *that* video spread . . . and then do just that. But can we ever truly explain and replicate the exact success formula of a video, or the greatness of, say, Starbucks and so many other successful companies and individuals?

The short answer is, *not likely.* True success requires something else. Yes, we *want* to find the recipe—the secret sauce that makes someone break through—but sometimes good things just seem to happen and it's impossible for any of us to truly explain why. If there is a recipe, it is, as we shall see, probably not what you think it is.

Michel Roux saw this lack of "secret sauce" play out firsthand. He is the marketing executive who invented the powerhouse brand for the Swedish vodka company Absolut. Before Roux came on board, Absolut was just another generic vodka. "The bottle was shaped like something you'd find on an episode of *M*A*S*H*. And it had no neck, so it was hard for a bartender to pick it up." Roux and his team were told that the Absolut project was "doomed and we should not get into it," he recalled in an interview a few years later.

But they took on the challenge anyway. They designed a memorable bottle and created an iconic marketing campaign—the one with Absolut bottles decorated with paintings by different artists, such as Andy Warhol and Jean-Michel Basquiat. Roux even created a whole new category of vodka—the premium bottle. These efforts by Roux and his team took Absolut from about one hundred thousand cases sold in 1980 to some 10 million in 2007, making it the third largest spirit brand in the world. Many in the industry consider Roux to be a legend. One day I ran into him at an event where we were both speaking. While on stage he was asked what, exactly, he had done to create such a success. Roux hesitated for a bit before simply saying, "If I knew *that*, I would do it again and again." Indeed, he has not come anywhere near creating such a massive success for any other brand or product.

If you ask someone who has lived the dream—someone like Dan Balan—they will admit in unguarded moments to having absolutely no clue how to press "repeat" on their success. "You can't think of any strategy or any formulas to create a song like "Dragostea din tei," Dan Balan told me over the phone minutes before going on at a concert in Moscow. "It doesn't exist."

And it isn't as if he hasn't tried. As noted earlier, many different versions of the song were recorded, and they all skyrocketed to the top of their respective charts. But why? And why not do it again? "I think it was the words *numa numa* and *maia hi*," Dan mused. "They are so fun to sing that they traverse language and culture." But he can't use those words again for another song. Maybe he could use the same process in creating them? Unfortunately those words, or sounds, were created in an entirely serendipitous way. "We did a sound recording early on to get the beats down and I just invented nonsense words on the spot as a stand-in," he explained to me. Balan expected to change them later. But he never did. When Balan heard the song later, something inside him *clicked*. "It was just the way the song sounded with the nonsense words in them. It just sounded good, so we decided to keep them," he said, and concluded: "Luck made it the way it was."

*

What holds true for individual careers also holds true for organizations. For instance, how did Nike come up with the idea for the first Nike trainer, the shoe that ignited the company's meteoric rise from retailer to global brand? Bill Bowerman, the legendary running coach, was having breakfast one morning with his wife while they discussed a thorny challenge he was grappling with: how to develop a spikeless sports shoe. Then he saw his wife pry a waffle from their six-inch art deco waffle iron. It was a fateful moment as Bowerman, without saying a word, sprinted back to his lab and returned with two cans of chemicals which, when mixed, created latex. He poured them into the

11

waffle iron. Could the small "spikes" on a waffle grip the track without damaging it and also provide comfort to the runner? He poured three more latex waffles and combined them on one shoe. The answer was yes. The experiment worked. That one random moment represented a turning point for the shoe company and allowed the company's CEO, Phil Knight, to build the foundation for an athletic apparel empire.

Then there is Facebook. There are several fortuitous aspects to Mark Zuckerberg's story, but one in particular caught my eye recently. The *Business Insider*, a business news Web site, detailed a surprising instant-message conversation that took place between Mark Zuckerberg and a confidant. It was July 26, 2004. By that time Zuckerberg and his pals had moved to California and begun working on the start-up full time. Facebook had netted almost one million users and was becoming a force to be reckoned with. But the conversation revealed that Zuckerberg believed that a different project altogether was more worthy of his efforts.

`Confidant:` Well you should recover the shares you need to recover legal fees.

`Zuckerberg:` I won't pay the legal fees

`Zuckerberg:` The company that buys us will haha

`Confidant:` Cool hopefully that'll be soon so you can move on and just work on what you want to

`Zuckerberg:` Well it just needs to propel Wirehog

What was Wirehog? It was an application that allowed users of Facebook to transfer files to one another. The founder of what would become a $100 billion company thought the greatest value wasn't in the social connections we make or even the information Facebook could sell to advertisers ... it was in transferring files. Good thing he didn't sell.

*

Randomness, it turns out, is everywhere, and it upends best laid plans over and over again. This may be particularly true in politics, where fortunes can rise and fall in an instant. Take Joseph Estrada, for example. Estrada was one of the Philippines' most respected movie actors and a hero to the poor in the vast island nation. After deciding to run for president in 1998 he won by the largest margin in the nation's history. But only two years into his term, a friend and provincial governor, Luis Singson, delivered a bombshell. He admitted to having personally delivered nearly $12 million in gambling bribes to President Estrada. "He is not just a gambling lord," Singson said. "He is a gambling god. He is the most corrupt person I have ever met."

The allegations sent shock waves through the Philippines. Opposition political and religious leaders demanded Estrada's resignation, but he refused. Nearly two months after the revelations, a contentious impeachment trial began. Estrada's prospects looked grim. A bank executive testified that Estrada had invested nearly $12 million under a fake name, but the real death knell apparently lay inside a sealed envelope. Rival politicians claimed the envelope contained financial documents that proved Estrada's corruption, but the president's political allies successfully blocked opening the envelope. The opposing senators walked out in disgust, and for a moment it seemed as if Estrada's presidency would continue.

But then something unexpected happened—something that Estrada could never have foreseen. Students began gathering at the Shrine of Mary, commonly called the People Power Shrine, in Manila to protest the president. Some of them began texting other students to join in. Something in the messages clicked and the texts spread like wildfire. Over the course of a few days more than 70 million text messages were sent, coordinating a peaceful protest of nearly 700,000 people. After months of stalemate in the courts, it took just eighty-eight hours for the people to succeed in forcing Estrada to resign via a process no one had expected—or predicted—could possibly work.

Just as random events can oust a president from power, so, too, can they propel a politician into the stratosphere. By any usual measure, prior to 2004 Barack Obama would have had virtually no chance at winning the presidency, no matter how talented, intelligent, or strategically minded he was; but a single moment in time changed all that. His keynote speech at the 2004 Democratic National Convention was meant to ensure his victory in the Senate and introduce a new political player to the national scene, but his ringing speech was repeated over the cable news shows and spread virally over the Internet to millions of viewers. Before the speech, the *Philadelphia Daily News* ran the headline, "Who the Heck Is This Guy?" After the speech, the *Christian Science Monitor* called it "the national debut of what could be one of the most exciting and important voices in American politics in the next half century."

When Obama returned to Illinois he found himself campaigning in front of thousands, rather than a few hundreds, and he won the Senate election easily. He began to realize that he might have a shot at the presidency, but he was torn. Obama was incredibly popular, but also inexperienced. Senator Tom Daschle gave him some advice. "I told him that he has a window to do this. He should never count on that window staying open."

That one night changed everything for Obama.

Success in the real world is far less scripted than we usually acknowledge, and filled with unexpected moments that tip the balance. Random encounters, insights, meetings and outcomes dominate the backstories of successful start-ups, fast-tracked careers, long-lasting corporations, and even world-changing artists and scientists. However, such an observation might leave us feeling we've missed something. If the world is so filled with uncertainty, how, aside from hoping for the best, do we consciously strive for greatness?

*

Since our caveman days we have trained ourselves to look for patterns in nature in order to find explanations for what we see and experience. But just because we have found that it makes sense to connect the shapes of clouds with the appearance of rain does not mean that social interactions can be predicted in the same way.

I started thinking about unpredictability and randomness a few years after my first book, *The Medici Effect*, was published. That book examines how and why groundbreaking ideas occur at the intersection of different fields, cultures, and industries. These types of ideas appeal to people concerned with innovation—people working in strategy, R&D, business development, entrepreneurship, and so on. But of course, there are a lot of writers competing for the attention of that audience. Around the same time that my book was published there must have been at least another fifteen new books on innovation alone. How could a first-time author stand out?

One evening, my wife came home from her job as a diversity consultant for JP Morgan Chase. She was very excited. She had just been tasked with finding the "business case for diversity" and realized that the ideas in my book were exactly what she was looking for. Weirdly, we had never made the connection before, but now it seemed obvious. "I honestly think people would want to hear about it," she said. She was right. Before I knew it I was presenting to Steve Black, who at the time headed up the investment banking side at JP Morgan Chase.

That single conversation turned the world on its head for me. Chief diversity officers in corporations around the United States invited me to speak to their CEOs and executives on how to drive innovation. The interest took me completely by surprise; the demand for my ideas went global and allowed me to build a consulting firm based on these principles.

One evening at a client dinner a strategy executive sitting next to me leaned over and said, "Your side-door strategy has been nothing short of brilliant." I frankly had no idea what he was talking about and had to ask him what he meant. "Well," he said, "instead of going to chief innovation officers, heads of strategy, or R&D folks, you targeted chief diversity officers. And through them you got to people like me. Your strategy," he said, "was to knock on the one door that other innovation thinkers did not."

A *side-door strategy*, I thought. It even had a name. To an outsider this must, indeed, have seemed like a brilliant approach. But I knew better, of course. What had very clearly been the result of a serendipi-

15

tous conversation with my wife was construed by others as evidence of my strategic foresight. It was, however, a notion that I could comfortably reject out of hand. I would be hard-pressed to call my *side-door strategy* anything but plain luck.

But this realization immediately led to a question. What if this was the case everywhere? What if all of the well-planned and well-executed "strategies" people have told us about are really the result of unplanned meetings and encounters, random moments and events, serendipity, and plain luck? What if the stories behind companies such as Microsoft or Nokia or the stories behind world-famous authors, index-destroying investors, and breakthrough scientists had a lot more to do with randomness than we thought? What if success or failure is just one unexpected moment away?

Curious, I sent an email to my class from business school to ask them about the role serendipity and luck had played in their lives. Within minutes my inbox was overflowing with responses. Yet, despite this overwhelming admission of how unpredictable our world can be, very few people I talked to had spent much time thinking deeply about how to incorporate what seemed to be a very basic law of nature into their corporate or professional strategy. The reason seemed obvious: randomness defines the part of our lives that we can't control, so how can we rely on it?

My journey now had a clear goal—to incorporate randomness, serendipity, and luck into the heart of execution and strategy. By the time we are done, you should have a new understanding of how to seize opportunity in an uncertain world. The chapters that follow are filled with stories that reveal what really happened to people and companies on the road to success. The point is not for you to follow them exactly, but for us to uncover the role circumstance played in their paths to greatness. Ultimately, we will look at the specific actions you can take to increase your own exposure to serendipity, luck, and random events, and learn how to capitalize on the outcomes that end up working in your favor.

*

So far I have used the words "randomness," "serendipity," and "luck" somewhat interchangeably, even though there are meaningful differences between them. The term random, for instance, has a precise definition within mathematics—one that is quite different from the more colloquial use of the word. As for the words luck and serendipity, they are often used to explain a positive outcome, but the former term implies less control than the latter.

However, these terms all have one thing in common: they all are used to convey or describe unpredictability. They all suggest that something has happened that you could not or did not plan for. For instance, if you plan to meet a person for coffee and then you *do* meet that person for coffee, the meeting wouldn't be attributed to serendipity. If you know that a certain geology book has the answer to a question on minerals you are struggling with, you'd be hard-pressed to call yourself lucky when you find the answer there. Instead, words like random, serendipity, and luck are used when something unpredictable happens. We meet someone at the coffee shop we didn't expect to see. Or we couldn't find the book we were looking for, but stumbled across another one that set us off in a better direction. Likewise, throughout this book I will refer to events that are unexpected, unplanned, or unintended as "random," "serendipitous," or "lucky." In exploring these concepts I have split the book into two parts.

Part 1 examines why the world is so unpredictable. We will look at why we have such a hard time making accurate predictions or effectively explaining the past. We will look at why an overreliance on logic might kill any chance we have for success, and why we don't want to believe that the world is random, even in the face of very strong evidence that it is. We must understand our own biases and limitations in order to incorporate randomness into our lives.

That's where Part 2 comes in. We all want a "cheat sheet" for life, some surefire way to take the lead or push our organization ahead. By the time you get to Part 2, you will see why following a formula for success can be hugely counterproductive. We will look at the specific actions you can take instead to increase your exposure to serendipity,

17

luck, and random events—and how to capitalize on events that look promising.

We will explore three approaches for capturing randomness that represent three ways of thinking about success. The first is *click moments*, which are unexpected yet defining moments in time, such as Bill Bowerman's insight with the waffle iron or Obama's 2004 convention speech. The second is what I call *purposeful bets*, which are actions we take despite our not knowing whether they will work or not, for example, the creation of the pilot for *Lost*. Finally we have *complex forces*. These are unexpected and un-planned-for consequences of actions that nevertheless lead to success, such as the events that ousted President Estrada in the Philippines, or what happened when Gary Brolsma uploaded his lip-synching video of "Dragostea din tei."

It may seem implausible and even unsettling that success is so dependent upon circumstance. Can Microsoft's rise to dominance in the nineties be the result of a click moment? Can the genius of Picasso be attributed to a string of purposeful bets? Can the success of a company, such as Pfizer, be a function of complex forces? Is it possible that what we attribute to foresight, brilliance, strategy, planning, and analysis is actually a function of randomness, serendipity, and luck?

As you will see in the chapters that follow, the answer to these questions is *yes*.

The next question, of course, is: What we can do about it? Before we answer, we must first understand *why* the world works this way. In order to understand that, it makes the most sense to look at the limited pockets of the world where randomness has *minimal* influence. By understanding these exceptions we can tackle what the world looks like for the rest of us. And there are such exceptions—zones where we can better predict how to become successful. As you turn the page you will discover one of them. It is 2,106 square feet in size and located roughly twenty minutes outside of Manhattan.

2

SERENA'S SECRET

There was a moment in the 1999 US Open Women's Tennis Championship Final when Serena Williams could have put away the match and won. She had two match-point opportunities to defeat the current number one seeded female tennis player in the world, Martina Hingis, but had been unable to close it. Now, looking up at the center-court scoreboard in the Arthur Ashe Stadium in Queens, she found herself on the receiving end in a tie-breaker. If she lost this point, the match would go on to a third set, and anything could happen. If she won the point, she would have a chance to serve for her first grand-slam singles title.

To this day Serena is known for her crushing serve. That weekend it dominated the entire tournament, and she notched 62 total aces—42 more than anyone else. But today that power serve was counterbalanced by the nerves of a girl not yet old enough to vote. Despite her overwhelming power, she had committed 57 unforced errors, more than doubling her opponent's 24. But none of that mattered right now. No one would remember the errors if she returned this serve.

Standing on the left side of the court, Hingis rocketed a ball crosscourt. Sensing its arrival, Serena transferred her weight to the balls of her feet. Hingis anticipated a return volley, but Serena returned a forehand down the right side of the court. Hingis could do nothing more than watch the ball bounce past her from a distance. The tiebreaker was even. If Serena won the next two serves she would win the match.

Serena willed the next serve to remain in and pounded the subsequent volleys into the backcourt. Unable to handle Serena's power, Hingis lobbed a ball over the back line. Advantage Williams. The crowd erupted. Over the course of just a few hours they had watched her dominate, then lose her composure, then come within one point of redeeming herself. With the game on the line Serena took a deep breath at the baseline center mark and powered a serve into the left sideline. Hingis defended the ball back, only to see Serena pound a forehand into the opposite side of the court. Hingis could barely return it—and the ball landed just beyond the baseline. The match was over and seventeen-year-old Serena Williams was the winner of the 1999 US Open. She doubled over, clutched her chest, and began to cry and laugh simultaneously. The match would mark the public rise of one of the most formidable tennis players of all time.

*

Serena Williams has, since that moment, dominated the women's tennis circuit. There has been no one who can touch her. The only opportunities afforded her competitors have occurred when she has been injured, but she is always able to come back, climbing the rankings swiftly and playing with remarkable confidence.

In fact, Serena's longevity and ability to stage comebacks is what makes her such a riveting player. She won the 2010 Australian Open and Wimbledon more than a decade after earning her initial Grand

Slam singles title and, despite repeated injuries, she's owned the number one slot on five separate occasions. She is only the fifth woman in history to win four straight Grand Slam singles titles, and the most recent to hold all four simultaneously. With thirty-nine singles and twenty doubles titles, Serena is widely considered to be one of the most accomplished and admired tennis players in history.

How did Serena garner such incredible success? What was her secret? The easy answer is that she possesses a superhuman talent for tennis. She stands above the rest of us in a way that is almost impossible to understand. She is, simply put, born to play the sport. You could almost say that she is one of a kind, but that wouldn't be quite true. Serena has a sister, Venus, who has been almost as good as Serena on the tennis circuit. And that is no accident.

*

When Richard Williams heard in 1980 that Romanian tennis player Virginia Ruzici earned $40,000 in one day for winning a minor tournament, something inside him clicked. He turned to his wife and said: "Let's have more kids and make them tennis players." Venus Williams was born in June of that year, followed by Serena in 1981.

A high school dropout, Richard Williams had no formal tennis training. Instead, he studied books and videos on the subject and became a self-taught expert. When Serena was a toddler, Williams moved his family from Saginaw, Michigan, to the notoriously dangerous city of Compton in Los Angeles County, reportedly because he wanted to expose his daughters "to the ugly possibilities of life" and enhance their competitive advantage. By the ages of three and four, Serena and Venus were practicing two hours a day on the public courts of Compton.

By 1991, Serena's record was 46–3 on the United States Tennis Association's junior tour. In 1995, before she graduated from high school, she turned pro. Two years later, she was already number ninety-nine in the world rankings. Then came the fateful 1999 victory at the US Open when she captured the family's first Grand Slam win.

A few years later, beginning in the spring of 2002, she went on a tear. She pulled off the "Serena Slam," claiming four straight Grand Slam titles and ascending to number one in the world rankings for the first time in her career. Venus has also enjoyed incredible success. She has been ranked number one on three separate occasions and was the first African-American female tennis player in history to reach the top spot. During her career, Venus has won twenty-one Grand Slam titles—more than any other female tennis player currently playing. Except for her sister, of course.

There is almost nothing about this story that seems random. Richard Williams set out to turn his two daughters into tennis superstars. And he did. It certainly seems that he had found some secret formula. So the question here is: What did Richard Williams do to set up his daughter for such success? Are there any lessons we could learn from him? There are—and those lessons are, generally speaking, completely repeatable.

*

In his book *Outliers*, Malcolm Gladwell suggests that the key to success in any endeavor is, to a large extent, not a matter of talent, but rather a result of practicing for a total of about 10,000 hours. If this formula is correct, then it would seem that success *can* be achieved in ways that are entirely predictable. You simply select something you want to be the best at, and then you work very, very hard at becoming just that. You practice much more than anybody else, and this virtually guarantees your place at the top of the game.

This rule certainly seems to hold true for Serena and Venus. They practiced several hours a day from the time they could lift a tennis racket. "My first tennis memory?" Serena writes in her memoir. "People always ask about it, but I'm afraid I don't have one. I just remember playing, all the time." Her father's singleminded determination helped Serena in her early years. Richard would fill a shopping cart with hundreds of tennis balls and the sisters would take turns hitting them over the net—one after another after another. When

Serena grew old enough, she made and kept making personal sacrifices, anything to get more hours practicing tennis. She gave up cheerleading and softball in order to spend early mornings and late afternoons on the courts. After her 1999 US Open win, a jubilant Williams told the *Philadelphia Inquirer* that "I just practiced so hard for this day and now it's really here."

Gladwell based his "10,000 hours" idea on research by K. Anders Ericsson. In the early 1990s Ericsson studied what separates good violinists from great ones—and what separates great ones from the virtuosos. What he found was surprising, and it went against many of our commonly held beliefs about talent. He found that there was no such thing as a "talent" for playing violin. Instead, the number of hours spent practicing was what made all the difference.

Although his subjects started playing at about age five, their practice patterns soon diverged. The group that became the best in their class was practicing thirty hours a week by the time they reached twenty. If you add all of those hours up, you get roughly 10,000 hours worth of focused practice, far more than the 4,000 hours for those who became, for instance, music teachers. Gladwell writes, "The striking thing about Ericsson's study is that he and his colleagues couldn't find any 'naturals,' musicians who floated effortlessly to the top while practicing a fraction of the time their peers did. . . . Their research suggests that once a musician has enough ability to get into a top music school, the thing that distinguishes one performer from another is how hard he or she works. That's it."

Success, painted in this light, does not require winning some random talent lottery. Instead, success is something you cultivate through hard work and intense focus. Many others have supported this view of success. In his 2008 book *Talent Is Overrated*, Geoff Colvin argues that deliberate practice is the key to success. Yo-Yo Ma has spent more time practicing on the cello than perhaps any other person on Earth. Ever. He was a superstar at twenty, and he still is. David Shenk makes a similar argument in *The Genius in All of Us*. He talks about baseball legend Ted Williams, who had an incredible ability to see the ball leave a pitcher's fingers and predict where it would pass over the plate. People simply resigned themselves to the fact that he had unmatched natural ability. Not true, said Ted. "Nothing except practice, practice, practice will bring out that ability."

Richard Williams's approach now seems pretty straightforward, even predictable. Extremely difficult to execute, yes; a ton of work—absolutely. But straightforward, nonetheless. Relentless, dedicated, deliberate practice is the secret. When Richard moved his family a second time, in 1991, from California to Florida, Venus was ranked number one among girls twelve and under, with Serena ranked number one in the ten and under division from the Southern California circuit. He enrolled them in the Rick Macci Tennis Academy until July 1995. "Six hours a day, six days a week, for four years," said Macci of their practice schedule.

That's 7,500 hours right there.

*

The 10,000-hour rule has been used to explain success more generally. Work very, very hard at becoming the best you can in any industry, and you will succeed. And yet despite a tremendous amount of research supporting this notion, it still seems remarkably incomplete. In fact, this approach to success only seems to apply in certain types of activities, such as tennis, chess, violin, and basketball. The rule appears to fall apart in almost all other cases of success.

We can list countless individuals who have become leaders in their fields and industries with little practice or training. Richard Branson launched Virgin Atlantic Airways on a whim, more or less, despite having zero experience running an airline. No 10,000 hours needed. And consider Reed Hastings, the founder of Netflix. Hastings had no video or media experience whatsoever, and yet his company became the number one video-rental business in the United States. Niklas Zennström and Janus Friis, the founders of Skype, had some telecommunications experience between them, but not enough to make them experts. They logged nowhere near 10,000 hours. It is the same story with people from almost every industry and background.

Consider Nintendo executive Shigeru Miyamoto, who is the re-nowned Japanese video-game designer and producer responsible for megahits like Donkey Kong, The Legend of Zelda, and Mario Brothers. Judging by when these games were released, the 10,000-hour rule does not apply here either. Donkey Kong, one of the biggest arcade game hits of all time, was Shigeru's *third* game. That would be like Serena Williams winning the US Open in her first year of playing tennis. And although Shigeru went on to develop several other megahits, he has also had massive failures. In 2011, well *after* he had logged 10,000 hours as a game designer, he designed Steel Diver, which did not stand out in any way. Shigeru didn't need 10,000 hours of dedicated practice to succeed, and when he did reach the critical hour mark, it was no guarantee of success.

So what is going on? Why is it that Serena Williams or Yo-Yo Ma can *predictably* practice their way to success while it is virtually im-possible for the rest of us? How can people with little experience in the video-game industry dominate their field when such a move would have been impossible for, say, Lance Armstrong?

*

In order to fully appreciate this difference we must understand how these types of fields evolve. In all of these cases—the Williams sisters, Yo-Yo Ma, and other prodigious successes—norms have been put into place that prevent these fields from evolving. The rules of the game, whether we are talking about tennis, chess, or classical violin, have remained relatively static for years at a time. If they change, they change very slowly, and often in entirely predictable ways.

The International Tennis Federation (ITF), for example, is the body that governs the game of tennis. It has the primary responsibility for determining the rules and standards of the game. The organization, of which the United States Tennis Association is a member, sanctions the four Grand Slams: the Australian Open, The French Open, Wimbledon, and the US Open.

The ITF created the rules and regulations of the game in 1924 and it has sole discretion to authorize changes and updates. However, it does so very infrequently, and major rule changes have been few and far between. It was once the case that the player serving the ball had to keep one foot on the ground at all times. That rule was rescinded in 1961. The tie-break scenario, in which the players take turns serving until one of them manages to pull ahead by two points, wasn't adopted until the 1970s. More recently, the ITF introduced an electronic review technology coupled with a point-challenge system, which allows a player to challenge the umpire's call after a point. Players have unlimited opportunities to challenge, provided they are right. Beyond those rule changes, no other substantive changes have been made in the rules of tennis.

The standards of the game, also governed by the ITF, have likewise remained constant over time. The court is a rectangle, seventy-eight feet long and, for singles matches, twenty-seven feet wide. For doubles matches, the court is thirty-six feet wide. The court is divided across the middle by a net suspended by a cord or metal cable, which is attached to two net posts at a height of three and a half feet. Balls and rackets are also approved for play under the rules of tennis set forth by the ITF. Changes, such as making the ball a little heavier in order to extend rallies between players, are slight and well discussed before they are adopted.

The rules, standards, specifications, and guidelines of tennis have remained pretty much the same since they were written. The result is that you can predict exactly what the game will look like over the next ten or even twenty years. It's a fixed system that limits creativity and doesn't allow for exceptions, which means you can get to know it inside out and practice your way to the top. There are strengths and strategies, yes, but you can count these on two hands and two feet. According to many coaches, there are just four main styles of singles tennis: serve and volley, aggressive baseline, defensive baseline, and the all-court player. The point is that there is a limit to tennis strategy.

Angle your racket slightly forward to create topspin or slightly backward to create slice. Perfect your serve. Conquer the baseline.

Learn to love the net. Paint the lines. Work on your lob. There are more ways to win, but not infinitely more. With 10,000 plus hours of focused effort beginning at a young age, you can develop one hell of a slice.

Indeed, Serena needed to have ability and the will to win in order to become an elite athlete. There's no doubt about that. But the rigidity in world tennis—because it's all but closed to innovation—is what allows a player like Serena to put more than 10,000 hours of focused efforts toward mastering the well-established rules and to play at the very highest level. This approach to success, then, holds true for any endeavor where society has put in place distinct norms and rules—and where those norms and rules rarely change. The implication is clear. In these types of fields, you can follow a predictable approach to success; Serena and Venus were not just flukes. Perhaps the most convincing example of this principle comes from a field where the rules have barely budged at all—chess.

*

According to Mikhail Botvinnik, three-time World Chess Champion and Russian International Grandmaster, chess is all about the art of analysis. Chess is an intellectually taxing and complex game with scores of possible move combinations. It requires strong critical-thinking skills in the visual-spatial realm. That said, there are a finite number of potential moves and combinations of moves. You can't introduce a new chess piece or teach your pawns to move in different directions—that's against the rules. Therefore, at least in theory, because the options are well established and universally enforced in competitive play, it is possible to search and consider every possible move. The more practice you have, the more familiar you become with the possible moves and combinations. With familiarity and focused effort, considering your options becomes easier and more automatic.

Given that chess has barely changed at all over the past century, it would be surprising if someone *hadn't* figured out how to produce a chess master—it's clearly spelled out in the rule book. The Hungarian psychologist Laszlo Polgar proved that this was possible when he embarked on an incredible social science experiment in the seventies, announcing that his three daughters would all be among the best in the world at chess—and then succeeded in achieving exactly that. His oldest daughter, Susan, became the first woman to earn a Men's Grandmaster's Title through traditional FIDE requirements. At the age of fourteen, his middle daughter, Sofia, stunned the chess world by winning an open tournament in Rome with a performance rating of over 2735, one of the best ever recorded. The youngest daughter, Judit, became the youngest Grandmaster in history at the time, breaking Bobby Fischer's record. She would be ranked the number one woman's chess player in the world for twenty consecutive years. An article in *Psychology Today* describes the Polgar sisters' incredible skill, which increased with each daughter:

> Susan dominated the New York Open chess competition. At 16 she crushed several adult opponents and landed on the front page of The New York Times. The tournament was abuzz not just with the spectacle of one pretty young powerhouse: Susan's raven-haired sister Sophia, 11, swept most of the games in her section, too. But the pudgy baby of the family, 9-year-old Judit, drew the most gawkers of all. To onlookers' delight, Judit took on five players simultaneously and beat them. She played blindfolded.

Laszlo Polgar believes that "geniuses are made, not born" and published a book entitled *Bring Up Genius!* even before he had children. He later married a Ukrainian-born teacher, Klara, who helped him carry out his bold experiment. "I was brought up in an ambience where it was believed that there is no such thing as talent," Susan Polgar told my team one afternoon. "Talent means being able and willing to work hard." The Polgars homeschooled their daughters. "Their education by and large consisted of two or three hours of table tennis each morning followed by seven or eight hours devoted to chess." They studied chess every day. They practiced it hour upon hour.

To succeed in chess, then, you need to know the game cold. You need to play against highly skilled opponents and log enough hours of practice to respond to every conceivable attack. That type of mastery takes incredible dedication, preparation, and skill, as well as parents who will dedicate their lives—and yours—to success. Yes, in chess and tennis and classical violin and any number of other formal endeavors it is possible to develop a winning strategy: through incredible focus and practice you can chart a path to the top.

*

Here, then, is the explanation for why success is predictable for a Serena Williams or a Yo-Yo Ma or a Susan Polgar but random for O-Zone or Nike. Susan Polgar can focus her efforts and practice in a way that no entrepreneur, lawyer, scientist, or even artist can. She is playing the same game over and over again. But the rest of us are playing in a world that is constantly changing and adapting through market forces. In one world, the rules of the game have remained static for decades or even hundreds of years. In the other, the rules of the game change all the time.

This difference is critical in understanding how much randomness, serendipity, and luck is allowed to influence the course of success in various fields. Is there even such a thing as luck in chess? "Well, of course," Susan told me, "there can be a little element of luck, although the more professional the players we are talking about, the less that luck is luck. It is more about many years of experience and preparation and knowledge accumulated."

Here is an example of what she was talking about: "Let's say my opponent sometimes opens a chess game with a King's Gambit. Say that I know this and so maybe I prepare more for that before the game starts. Maybe I spend ten hours. But then he or she ends up using a Ruy Lopez, which is another opening. Well, in that sense I got a bit unlucky. Obviously my opponent knew it was going to be Ruy Lopez because that was his choice. So, that's the sort of luck we are talking about."

This kind of luck is very different from what Bill Bowerman experienced when he connected a waffle iron with a running shoe. It's also unlike the luck involved in having a kid in New Jersey create a worldwide viral sensation involving your song, and different again from the luck an inexperienced politician had in giving a remarkable keynote speech that placed him on the path to become a contender for the presidency of the United States.

We can see the level of random success increase as societal norms around a specific field become looser. Modern professional boxing, for instance, is tightly regulated. Fighters must have regulation gloves and tape, compete in similar weight classes, and win a defined set of matches before they can improve their rank. Fighters cannot use any part of their body except for their arms. Because the strict rules limit creative options, there are only a certain number of combinations fighters can use to win. According to Jason Strout, a trainer at Manhattan's famous Church Street Boxing Gym, boxing is all about mastering the fundamentals: "footwork, defense, basic boxing combinations; a good jab, a good cross, a good hook, and learning how to defend [all of] those." It is, quite simply, impossible for someone to randomly come out of nowhere and become a world champion in boxing.

Mixed martial arts (MMA), on the other hand, is an entirely different contest. MMA is a full-body contact sport that allows the use of techniques and moves from boxing, wrestling, jujitsu, kickboxing, karate, judo, and other disciplines. It's a live-combat cocktail that looks entirely different every single time. It's intense and innovative. The combinations and strategic options are exponentially greater than in boxing. In MMA, inventive ingenues—those not just with strength and guts but also with fresh thinking—can come out of nowhere to beat the best. Experience and even 10,000 hours of practice matter much less when the moves are new every time. Take a guy like Evan Tanner. He did some wrestling in high school. He later went to college, but dropped out. After being encouraged by his friends, he decided to try out MMA at a local tournament and won three fights in one night, including beating Paul Buentello, a future Ultimate Fighting

Championship (UFC) heavyweight contender. Tanner then went on to become a UFC world champion.

You see a similar duality in music. Society imposes a somewhat fixed and intellectually rigorous set of guidelines on the definition and shape of classical music. There is a certain structural integrity that needs to be maintained that suits the genre. Fans, artists, and connoisseurs have expectations about what defines, for example, a cello composition, if it is to fit within the confines of "classical," or serious, music. Experimentation is possible, but you can only take it so far or you've strayed beyond what most would consider a classical composition. Because of that, it is extremely unlikely that someone who is new to the cello can best an experienced musician, let alone a virtuoso such as the great Yo-Yo Ma. Even given a wide creative berth, it takes time to master the structure of the classics, which is why success is always preceded by many years of exacting practice.

The rules for what constitutes hip-hop, on the other hand, are much more fluid, which allows new people to enter the field in unpredictable ways. It is entirely possible, even common, for a young and inexperienced musician to dominate the genre through innovation or because of serendipitous circumstances. Even though their music has few commonalities, Cypress Hill and Lauryn Hill are both considered to be hip-hop stars. So are artists from the Beastie Boys, with the punk attitude and hard-metal guitar licks they brought to *License to Ill* in 1986, to Dr. Dre and his surprising and diverse 1993 album *The Chronic*, to Will Smith, who released *Big Willie Style* in 1997, as well as today's stars like Eminem, Kanye West, and Will I Am. All of these artists became successful in the same genre despite having little in common. Their musical styles and their paths to the top each look altogether different when one compares them.

What drives success in chess is not the same as what drives success in developing a new business model. What drives success in tennis is not the same as what drives success in closing a new deal, or writing a novel. In all of these other fields and endeavors, society allows norms to change at a furious pace. The world at large is, in fact, much more like hip-hop than classical violin, much more like MMA than boxing. In most situations the rules of the game change all the time. And unlike in sports and classical music, they change in entirely unpredictable ways. In such a world, where there are no real rules because the conditions keep changing and evolving, what does it take to succeed? As we will see in the chapter that follows, we can learn by looking at the former titans in industry and the mere mortals that defeated them. We can, for instance, look at Nokia just minutes after the devastating tsunami of 2004.

3

THE NOKIA MYSTERY

On December 26, 2004, at about 8:00 p.m. EST, an earthquake rocked the western coast of Indonesia. It was the third-largest earthquake ever recorded, and the third deadliest since 1900. When the earth shifted, it released the equivalent of a 100-gigaton bomb into the ocean and produced a tsunami ninety feet high. Two hours later the waves hit Sri Lanka, and within hours more than thirty thousand people were dead.

Immediately, millions of frantic relatives and survivors dialed their loved ones, only to get a busy signal. The onslaught of calls had crashed the infrastructure. Tuning in to the radio, listeners were bombarded with information from the government, but the tenuous state of Sri Lankan politics meant fiction often melded into fact. There didn't seem to be a reliable option for Sri Lankans to communicate with the outside world.

During a natural disaster, access to information enables local emergency responders to make better decisions and allows international relief agencies to gauge the severity of the crisis. "Right now, information saves lives, and we want to do our little bit," the film producer Sanjay Senanayake told *Information Week* shortly after the tsunami hit. As the waves reached land, Senanayake was at his home in Colombo, the western capital of the nation. The western region of Sri Lanka was left relatively unscathed, but the eastern portion of the nation was devastated. Senanayake got in his car and began to survey the damage. When he was unable to call his friend, Bombay-based blogger Rohit Gupta, Senanayake decided to try a text message from his Nokia phone. It worked. The telecom infrastructure couldn't handle the heavy call volume, but it could easily transmit a 1–2 kb text message. Over the next four days Senanayake texted Gupta 4,000 times with messages such as:

```
I'm standing on the Galle road in Aluthgama and
looking at 5 ton trawlers tossed onto the road.
Scary shit.
```

Gupta in turn published the text messages on his blog *Tsunami Help*, which was used to disseminate news to journalists and relief workers. "It's proven to be a very effective and fast way of getting information online," he said.

Senanayake's is a story of how technology continues to change the world around us in unexpected ways. And Nokia was right in the thick of it. It was not surprising that Senanayake had used a Nokia phone to do his texting. In 2004, their ruggedness was legendary—one commentator reminisced that he had accidently sent his Nokia phone through the washing machine. At first the screen looked like an aquarium, but after drying for a few hours the phone "worked perfectly." If any phone was going to survive a disaster zone it would be a Nokia. Not only that, but Nokia had the best designs, the strongest brand, the greatest market share, the largest profits and the most efficient operation. In other words, they knew the rules of the mobile phone industry and they dominated the game.

If the mobile-phone industry had hard-and-fast rules—the kind that govern tennis—whatever understanding Nokia had about how to win would stay valid. It would be able to spot challengers a mile away, watching as they learned the rules of the game and improved their performance step by step—the same way you can spot an upcoming star on the tennis junior championship circuit. But, of course, the mobile phone industry is nothing like tennis. Challengers come out of nowhere and everything can change in an instant.

*

By 2007, Nokia had become the Serena Williams of the mobile phone market: big, bold, winning, and the envy of every competitor. The company's market share was more than three times that of its nearest rival, Motorola, and its immense scale allowed it to compete on a playing field all its own. "The company does nearly all its manufacturing in-house," wrote *the Economist,* "designs its own radio chips, is far more vertically integrated than its rivals, and has unrivalled prowess in logistics." Nokia's supply chain was ranked second in the world, beating Toyota, Walmart, and IBM. *Business Week* declared that Nokia's "dominance in the global cell-phone market seems unassailable" and that it "outmaneuvered competitors in lucrative emerging markets." By September 2007, Nokia was the most valued brand in Europe, and the fifth strongest in the world. "If you judge a brand on influence or reach," *Forbes* declared, "Nokia may be the most successful brand in history."

On November 7 Nokia reached a market capitalization of roughly $162 billion. It has not hit that number again since then, and its fall has been relentless. At the time of writing, Nokia's value has dropped more than 90 percent. It is seven years since Nokia phones played a primary role in marshaling information for Sri Lankan tsunami victims and their families. Then, the Nokia brand was relevant and its cell phone was a ubiquitous trailblazer. Today it is more or less

35

viewed as just the opposite—a perspective that is bolstered even by statements from Nokia executives.

When Stephen Elop, formerly of Microsoft, was installed as CEO at Nokia in late 2010, he sent out an internal memo that became an instant Internet sensation. It was referred to as the Burning Platform Memo, and in it Elop did not mince words. "There is a pertinent story about a man who was working on an oil platform in the North Sea," he wrote. "He woke up one night from a loud explosion, which suddenly set his entire oil platform on fire. . . . As the fire approached him, the man had mere seconds to react. He could stand on the platform, and inevitably be consumed by the burning flames. Or, he could plunge 30 meters into the freezing waters." Nokia, Elop claimed, was also standing on a burning platform and, like the oil worker, the company had to decide whether to change or die. "We fell behind," Elop admitted, "We missed big trends, and we lost time. At that time, we thought we were making the right decisions; but, with the benefit of hindsight, we now find ourselves years behind." Whatever rules governed the mobile phone industry in the past, they had all changed—and Nokia had not seen it coming.

It is sometimes difficult to get an accurate fix on what factors push a company off its pinnacle, and Nokia had its fair share of challenges. Samsung, for one, was starting to erode Nokia's market share with its low-cost cell phones. Other Asian competitors came on the scene as well. But in the case of Nokia, the main culprit is not that hard to pin down. The crushing blow was delivered by none other than Apple.

When the iPhone hit the market on June 29, 2007, it started a process that soon backed every other mobile phone manufacturer into a corner. Smartphones, driven by powerful software, became the new growth market. In its first weekend, sales of the iPhone neared five hundred thousand, and by March 2011, more than 100 million iPhones had been sold, making it the fastest selling phone of all time. In the last quarter of 2011 alone, Apple sold 37 million of them. Perhaps most astounding was that, although Nokia led the industry in shipped handsets, Apple commanded nearly 75 percent of the entire industry's profits despite having a market share of only 8 percent. Its launch soon inspired Google, another software developer, to create and release Android, which featured an open platform that allowed manufacturers everywhere to create their own touch-screen mobile phones. Squeezed on all sides, Nokia found itself with less than 2 percent of the industry's profits, putting the former mobile giant in last place.

*

The iPhone completely changed the rules in the mobile-phone market. "The piece that Nokia had spent little time transforming, its operating system," a Nokia executive told me, "became the only thing that mattered." Suddenly, ordinary people with no tech background found themselves engaged in heated debates, comparing the merits of Apple's iOS and Google's Android operating systems. Just two years earlier, no one cared. "The things that once drove purchasing decisions, like cool shapes, sleek designs or eye-popping, fashionable colors suddenly meant nothing," she continued. "Phones became dark, brick-like touch-screen slates. Everything changed overnight." Instead of comparing ringtones, the question of the day became: *Have you downloaded any cool apps, lately?*

My guess is that if you had told an executive at Nokia back in 2006 that in a few years Apple's greatest competitor in mobile phones is Google he or she would have called you crazy. Neither Apple nor Google had any presence in the mobile-phone market at the time, so how could they possibly land in the driver's seat so soon after? It would be like Serena Williams getting creamed by Lance Armstrong in tennis—right after he started playing. Yeah, sure, Lance is a world-class athlete, but he wouldn't have a snowball's chance in hell against Serena even with years of serious training.

But that is exactly what happened in the mobile-phone industry. A company with zero experience swooped in to dominate the market in less time than it takes to earn a law degree. The difference? The rules can change and be changed in the mobile-phone industry. A tennis player could never walk on to the court and change the basic structure of the game, but the rules for competing in the mobile-phone business morph all the time. They are up for grabs. At one point phones were supposed to be robust and sturdy, the next moment they were cool and sleek; then they had to take amazing pictures and play music, and now you have to be able to edit those same pictures while playing a game with your friend on another continent and then hand the phone to your grandmother because she needs to check her Facebook status.

The bottom line is that there are no rigid rules in the mobile-phone industry—or any other industry, for that matter. There might be a few more governmental restrictions in some sectors than in others, but even in a regulated market, such as pharmaceuticals or insurance, the rules of the game are nothing compared to tennis. You have many more options to serve-and-volley your way to success as an insurance company than you do as a tennis player. Want to change your business model with a new online play? Go ahead, try it. If it works, you've just changed the game. The implications of this difference are enormous, because they suggest that in the real world, as opposed to the world of tennis, you have no real clue about what it takes to win at any given time. The rules can change so quickly that success is essentially random. This is true virtually everywhere.

Take the shift from traditional animation to computer animation. Steve Starr had worked at Disney for twenty-six years as a traditional animator, contributing to classics such as *The Lion King* and *Beauty and the Beast*. During his peak years he commanded a salary of $130,000. Then over the span of a few years the success of movies such as *Toy Story*, *Shrek*, and *Monsters Inc.* changed the fundamentals of the field. In 2001, the category of Best Animation debuted at the Oscars. None of the films nominated that year were hand drawn (and only one traditionally animated movie has ever won the award). And in 2002, Starr found himself out of a job and enrolling in classes at community college.

On the other hand, consider Matt Mason. Mason began his career as a pirate-radio and club DJ in London. From there he went on to become the founding editor in chief of the seminal hip-hop and urban lifestyle magazine *RWD*. "Up until this point I had not published *a single article in my entire life,"* Mason told me when I asked him about it. Still, the magazine went on to become the UK's most widely distributed music magazine. That would have been impossible if his world was structured like Serena's. But it isn't. Mason simply decided to change things around. He gave the magazine away for free, but it was supported by lots of ads. This had never been done before in this field, so he could not be sure it would work. But it did work—and there was no rule against trying.

This begins to explain why success is random. If the rules can change at any time, then it is impossible to predict with certainty what strategies and tactics you must use to succeed. It also explains why new entrants can change the game so quickly. New rules mean that anyone can try their luck at something different, something the current players in an industry have never even thought of.

However, the fact that the rules change constantly does not *necessarily* mean that random forces are at play. Maybe the rules change according to some system that can be discerned, if only one is smart enough and perceptive enough to figure it out? The hallmark of exceptional leadership is, after all, the ability to see where the market is heading—to predict future trends and tap into them. Could this explain what went wrong at Nokia? As Elop said in his memo, the company missed key trends. Once Apple unleashed the smartphone and Google followed suit, analysts blamed Nokia for blinking while the world evolved around them.

In April 2008, almost a year after the iPhone's release, Nokia's then CEO Olli-Pekka Kallasvuo said, "The iPhone is a niche product." He was obviously wrong. How could the company miss such a crucial shift in a technology they had all but invented? Is it really that difficult to see what's coming around the corner?

*

In September 1998, Sergey Brin and Larry Page founded Google, a company based on a search algorithm they had developed while they were students at Stanford. But being busy with their PhD studies, it was difficult for them to find the time this project needed. They decided to sell the program for $1 million, and they approached a number of established tech companies with pen in hand. First there was Excite, which balked at the figure. The now-defunct company negotiated the pair down to $750,000, only to have its CEO George Bell veto the deal. Next up was Yahoo, soon to be anointed "winner of the search war" by *Fortune Magazine*. On the cusp of the new millennium, conventional wisdom had it that search on the web was finished. The real money had moved on to web portals. At the time, Yahoo's visitors were increasingly coming to its home page for services such as email and stock quotes; the Google algorithm simply didn't fit Yahoo's business model. So Yahoo, too, passed on buying the fledgling company.

This, however, seems a bit strange. Yahoo was *perfectly* situated to understand the potential of Google. Yahoo was the largest search company in the world; it had the clearest view of market and it was under tremendous pressures to grow. But it was unable to spot greatness. Remarkably, neither were Brin and Page—they obviously weren't able to appraise the massive potential in their own idea if they valued the asset at just $1 million. As it turns out, neither the experts at Yahoo nor the founders themselves were able to predict the success Google was about to garner only a few months later.

Maybe I'm being unfair. Google was barely even a company back then. These were the early days—anything could have happened, and maybe it would have been impossible for anyone to anticipate Google's full potential. But what about four years later, after Google had been around for a while? In the summer of 2002 Yahoo was back. Now *it* was the one asking to buy Google. This time Yahoo offered Brin and Page $3 billion. For the same company. Brin and Page politely declined. Analysts suggested upping the offer to $5 billion. Yahoo's CEO Terry Semel replied, "Five billion dollars, seven billion, ten billion. I don't know what they're really worth—and you don't either," he told his staff. "There's no fucking way we're going to do this!" It is fair to say that the analysts were way off in their estimation. Just two years later Google was worth roughly $150 billion.

As Google's story demonstrates, predicting which person, idea, business model, strategy, or company will become great and which will fail to distinguish itself is like taking a shot in the dark. Even the experts, including the founders and executives—those with the best information and the strongest incentive to know—have a hard time predicting what is going to work. This is not a conclusion made in isolation. The failure of stock pickers and analysts to beat the market, for instance, is well established. And the same thing can be seen beyond finance. Scientific research, for instance, places great value on the peer-review process, in which editors and reviewers try to identify breakthrough studies. The best way to judge the importance of a scientific paper is by looking at how many other scientists have cited it in their work. Remarkably, there is virtually no correlation between the papers expected to become game-changers and the number of citations those papers ultimately garner. Scientific papers predicted to have a huge impact sometimes leave no trace in the field, whereas breakthrough papers are often deemed just passable.

In the late 1980s, in one of the most ambitious studies of its kind, the psychologist Philip Tetlock collected predictions from hundreds of political-science experts who were asked to make judgments on a range of topics, including whether Canada was going to disintegrate or not, what would happen to the post-Soviet states, and whether the EU would succeed. He waited twenty-five years before gauging the accuracy of these predictions. About eighty-two thousand predictions were made and the somewhat stunning conclusion was that the experts fared no better than if they had given each prediction a fifty-fifty chance. The riveting account of Tetlock's research methodology and results are presented in his book *Expert Political Judgment.* It paints a fascinating picture not only of how wrong we can be in trying to predict the future, but also how easily we forget about the times we were wrong in the past.

Given all of this, maybe it's not surprising that Nokia failed to predict the rise of the smartphone, touch-screen functionality, the importance of apps, and all the rest. Maybe success does not come from

41

a logical analysis of an industry's competitive dynamics or from understanding trend lines but from somewhere else entirely. If it had been possible to foresee the rise of the iPhone, companies would have been ready to respond to it. Or disrupt it. If we could have known three years in advance that both Apple and Google would enter and dominate the mobile-phone market, we would have heard as much from the experts. But we didn't.

Here is what Michael Kanellos at CNET, a leading tech site, had to say: "Apple is slated to come out with a new phone. . . . And it will largely fail. . . . When the iPod emerged in late 2001, it solved some major problems with MP3 players. Unfortunately for Apple, problems like that don't exist in the handset business. Cell phones aren't clunky, inadequate devices. Instead, they are pretty good. Really good."

He was not alone in feeling that way. Here is another account, this time from Matthew Lynn at Bloomberg: "Apple is unlikely to make much of an impact on this market . . . the iPhone won't make a long-term mark on the industry." Lynn's opinion was backed up by many other professional market observers. "The iPhone will not substantially alter the fundamental structure and challenges of the mobile industry," said Charles Golvin of the leading analyst firm Forrester Research. Apple's competitors felt the same way. "We've learned and struggled for a few years here figuring out how to make a decent phone. PC guys are not going to just figure this out. They're not going to just walk in," said Palm's CEO Ed Colligan.

No wonder Nokia couldn't find its way. These were the people who understood the industry better than almost anyone else *on the planet*. And they were all dead wrong. It isn't a question of preparation or expertise or intelligence. These people had those things in spades. Instead, the real question is this: If these experts can't figure out what the next logical move should be, then can anyone really expect to do it?

*

There is one thing about all this that still seems strange: success happens all the time. What of the tens of thousands of business successes and failures throughout the course of history? It seems obvious that if we could just study these cases very carefully, we would learn something. There are aspects of success that we can emulate and there are aspects of failure we can avoid. And we should be able to use that knowledge to plan, to strategize, to analyze—ultimately to predict success and not be left in the clutches of randomness.

Take a company like Starbucks. Its founder, Howard Schultz, opened the doors to his Seattle-based coffee chain in 1986. By 1988 Starbucks owned and operated thirty-three stores across North America. In 1992, they totaled 165 stores. Just one year later they added another 107. Then Starbucks stores opened everywhere. By the start of the new millennium there were more than three thousand Starbucks coffee shops across the country, and today there are nearly seventeen thousand Starbucks stores around the world. If you plot this growth out on a chart you will find that in the first five years or so of Starbucks' existence it's growth pattern looks like a flat line, close to zero. But in 1992 the curve bends sharply and shoots north at an incline that is essentially straight up. It is an almost perfect growth curve and so it's only natural to ask: What exactly did Starbucks do to become great?

One commonly held theory is that Starbucks succeeded because of the quality of their product. "Starbucks epitomizes a company that has achieved amazing success by not compromising on quality," Joseph Michelli writes in *The Starbucks Experience*. Most observers agree that Starbucks serves excellent coffee and that it was certainly better than a lot of its competitors' in its early days. But is this really the reason for its success? If so, why haven't Gloria Jean's and Newman's Own experienced similar success? In September 2011 *Consumer Reports* rated both blends significantly higher in terms of quality than Starbucks, and yet neither brand approaches a similar level of success. Not only that, there are countless chains serving food and drinks that are less than great, but they have thrived. This makes one wonder about the "great product" theory.

Others point to Starbucks' willingness to relentlessly launch new products and countless variations of coffee and flavors. There are currently roughly eighty-seven thousand variations of coffee and other products available at a Starbucks store. NPR's Wendy Kaufman argued that all of these products "translated to higher in-store sales and more bottles sold in grocery stores and places like Target." That sounds right. But is it a recipe for success? Burger King, for instance, has over the years introduced new menu options such as Angry Whoppers, and even french fries that are available in your grocer's freezer. Despite its best efforts, the company's market share in fast food declined from 20 percent in the 1990s to under 13 percent today. Even more perplexing, experts everywhere cite Apple's willingness to *decrease* the number of products in its line as a chief reason for the company's spectacular success. Fewer products, but really good ones, seems to be the ticket for Apple—the exact opposite strategy Starbucks chose.

There is a third theory, which says that Starbucks places a high value on employees, paying above-market wages and offering medical benefits even to part-timers. This generates loyalty and saves on training costs—Starbucks' yearly turnover rate is nearly 80 percent less than its competitors. "Starbucks is a smashing success," wrote *Fortune Magazine*, "thanks in large part to the people who come out of these therapy-like training programs." But of course, better wages and benefits is not a fail-safe strategy either. American Apparel also pays its factory employees well above market wages and offers extensive benefits, yet its stock price has hovered right around $1 for years.

Then there is the "Walmart argument." In *Wrestling with Starbucks*, Kim Fellner outlined the traditional ten-step coffee exporting chain. Within that process there are at least three middlemen who package, roast, or process the bean before it reaches the consumer. Starbucks went directly to farmers, eliminating all of these steps. But removing the middleman is one of the oldest tricks in the book and has been employed by a number of business failures around the world. When Levi Strauss & Co. attempted to disintermediate its retail partners by limiting their ability to sell Levi products online, the scheme backfired and the company was forced to reverse the strategy after only a year.

Finally, we have Howard Schultz himself, who told his investors in 1987: "Look, we're going to keep losing money until we can do three things. We have to attract a management team well beyond our expansion needs. We have to build a world-class roasting facility. And we need a computer information system sophisticated enough to keep track of sales in hundreds and hundreds of stores." He makes it all sound like a logistics issue, which is very different from the earlier explanations.

Perhaps it's not about any one of these factors. Starbucks did *all* of these things, and maybe that is what it takes. But that explanation doesn't make sense either. First, we know many companies that have succeeded wildly without having anything remotely close to Starbucks' comprehensive strategy. Facebook has very little in common with Starbucks, and things have gone quite well for them. Subway is different from Starbucks, but it also has thrived. IBM uses different pieces of this puzzle and has succeeded just the same. Second, if the explanation for Starbucks' success is simply that you have to be Starbucks, then there's not much of a takeaway there for other companies.

We want to know how Starbucks became great for one simple reason: we want to learn something from it. Unfortunately, it seems to be extremely difficult to find general explanations as to exactly *why* a company like Starbucks is successful. An enormous amount of research and analysis has been undertaken on the topic. But for all of that research, the success of Starbucks remains, in many ways, as obvious as it remains a complete mystery.

*

We've identified two mysteries, and they are linked. First, it seems impossible to predict which companies or strategies will succeed. Second, once a company does succeed, it is just as difficult to glean any general lessons about why the success happened and how one can repeat it. This helps us understand why Nokia missed the rapid rise of the smartphone. It wasn't that its people were incompetent, but that the rise of the iPhone was completely unexpected. Nokia's past experience

45

in the mobile-phone industry did not necessarily help them see how things were going to change. It also explains why this is impossible in any industry or field where the rules have not been locked down. Everything keeps changing, and in this sense, history never really repeats. Or in the words of the famous British historian Arnold Toynbee, "History is just one damn thing after another."

But this leaves us with a dilemma. We want to know how to be successful and we need to have some sort of plan to make it happen. But if we can't make sense of greatness and if we can't predict success, then what are we left with? It seems that all that remains are random actions and unpredictable outcomes. Is such a conclusion really valid?

If we are to understand why success is so random, we have to understand the underlying mechanisms behind such a world. In the following chapter we will do just that. Why is it, for instance, that we can't use the lessons from the past to create success in the future? Why is it that understanding trends is not a surefire way to become successful? The answer can be found, at least in part, on a sunny meadow in rural Washington, where tensions are rising in dramatic fashion.

4

THE TWILIGHT OF LOGIC

One morning in June 2003, a young woman named Stephenie Meyer woke up from an incredibly vivid dream. The dream consisted of a conversation between a boy and a girl in a beautiful, sunny meadow in the middle of an otherwise dark forest. The boy and the girl were in love with each other, and were discussing the risks associated with that love . . . considering that she was human and he was a vampire. The scene had incredible potential for violence because the boy had a nearly uncontrollable desire to drink the girl's blood.

"I delayed getting out of bed for a while, just thinking through the dream and imagining what might happen next," Meyer recalled. The dream stayed with her all through that morning. "As soon as I had a free moment, I sat down at the computer and started writing so I wouldn't forget it. I wrote ten pages that day, and that night I started imagining where the story would have gone if I hadn't woken up." Over the course of the summer, Meyer kept writing every night. By the end of August she had completed what would become a 498-page book. At this point the boy and the girl had names, of course. Edward Cullen and Bella Swan. And Meyer's story had become a whirlwind of forbidden love, honor, and teenage angst. Still, she had not shown her manuscript to anyone except her sister, who loved it and urged her to try to get it published.

Meyer eventually got in touch with fifteen literary agents. Of those queries, five were ignored, another nine agencies rejected her, and the final reply, from Writers House, expressed interest. What she didn't know at the time was that the encouragement had come from an assistant pretending to be an agent. Writers House eventually signed Meyer on as a client after the assistant brought the manuscript to her boss.

Twilight, as the novel was titled, went on to become one of the best-selling books of all time. Meyer wrote three sequels, and all of them were made into movies that have broken box-office records around the world. To date, her books have been translated into more than fifty languages, and they broke J. K. Rowling's record with the *Harry Potter* series by spending 235 weeks on the *New York Times* bestsellers list. Of those weeks, 136 found her in the number one spot.

Since fiction writing is a field with few rules, it should actually have been possible for Meyer to accomplish all of this with little experience in writing books or telling vampire tales, however strange that may sound. Is that, in fact, what happened?

*

Remarkably it is. Meyer achieved all her success despite having little experience writing books—or anything else, for that matter. Meyer says she loves to write but that she barely wrote anything at all in the six years leading up to the dream that inspired *Twilight*. Her writing had taken a backseat to motherhood. She had never been published, and she did not start writing seriously until the moment she had that dream. She has achieved incredible success without even a fraction of the skill and hard work that someone like Serena Williams has put in.

Some might even argue that Meyer is one of the least-skilled bestselling authors ever. In what is largely a positive review of Meyer's work, *Time*'s Lev Grossman describes her writing style thus: "Meyer floods the page like a severed artery. She never uses a sentence when she can use a whole paragraph. Her books are big (500-plus pages) but not dense—they have a pillowy quality distinctly reminiscent of Internet fan fiction."

Meyer agrees that her prose is mediocre. "It certainly wasn't a belief in my fabulous talent that made me push forward," she says. "I don't think I'm a writer; I think I'm a storyteller. . . . The words aren't always perfect." And as we will see, Meyer had no clue about vampires, either. Yet the *Twilight Saga* has sold over 116 million copies worldwide. It seems to defy logic.

But so do many instances of surprising success and failure. How is a behemoth like Nokia at the top of an industry one year and then struggling to survive only a few years later? How can a marketing pro like Michel Reux create one of the world's iconic vodka brands, Absolut, and then be unable to repeat that success elsewhere? How can someone who has barely written a word for six years sit down and write one of the most successful bestsellers in history?

All these cases seem to imply that relying on past experience, logic, and careful analysis are not the true drivers of success. In fact, they can be major impediments if you are working to innovate ahead of your competitors. We simply can't know how to make things play out in our favor by relying on what has worked in the past. Not only that, we can't even use our understanding of future trends to our advantage.

This last point might seem surprising because, for example, despite the problems Yahoo had in predicting the success of Google, there *are* some trends we can be quite sure of. For instance, as I write this chapter in early 2012, it is obvious that many people will read this book on some sort of electronic device. I can also confidently predict that the

49

elderly population will keep growing in Western countries, the economic development of Africa will in general keep speeding up, the cost of computer memory will keep dropping, and processing power will keep rising. So why don't these insights help me succeed? If we study the data carefully, after all, we should be able to use logic to figure out the best next move. That is what strategy is: rigorous logic applied to data and the competitive landscape to unearth opportunities to dominate. Traditional strategy firms apply this approach with a vengeance. But let's see just how far logic will take us.

*

Ten years ago, if you wanted to guarantee yourself a life of financial security and prestige, one of the surest paths was to become a lawyer. From *Boston Legal* to *L.A. Law* to *Damages*, legal dramas had sailed to the top of the television charts because they illustrated power, a certain moral guardianship, and a measure of wealth. In 1996, the median income for Americans working full-time was about $35,000, while the starting salary for first-year associates at large law firms neared $70,000.

That salary was on an unswerving upward trajectory in part because of the enormous rise of the financial sector. Legal work was associated with multibillion-dollar lawsuits and mergers that were on an even larger scale. Lawyers that worked hard for a couple of years, particularly at the larger firms, could look forward to remarkable compensation, sometimes above $1 million per year, at least once they became partners. It is rare to find a job with such a predictable path to success.

But what happens when it is easy to predict success? With the lure of such obvious benefits, interest in practicing law exploded. In 2009 alone, one hundred and seventy thousand people took the LSAT, the entrance exam for law schools. That's an increase of 60 percent over ten years. During that time, twenty-five new law schools gained accreditation, bringing today's total to 200 in the United States with even more on the way.

From 2007 to 2010, nearly 131,000 newly minted JDs entered the workforce. At the same time, more than ninety thousand positions disappeared. The result: the most depressed job market for new lawyers in history. Just 68 percent of 2010 graduates found a job requiring a license to practice law—the lowest level ever recorded. Many who do find jobs hold temporary positions or do contract work that pays substantially less than in the past. A recent job posting revealed an opening for an entry-level trademark attorney. The pay: $15 an hour. Popular law blogger David B. Lat said, "Legal services are almost like Miami condos . . . It's going to take years to work off the excess supply." As for partner tracks in major law firms, you can just forget about it. In fact, more and more law firms are replacing partner tracks with "career associate" positions. They feature the same level of work, but half the pay and no opportunity to make partner.

Not only that, but with so much money to be made in legal fees, it was inevitable that innovative firms would start looking for opportunities to make the market more efficient. Lawyers teaming up with software companies such as Symantec are changing the rules of the game, replacing entire segments of the legal profession, particularly document discovery, with software. Even small-scale services are being disrupted. Traditionally, if you needed a will or a simple contract drawn up, you could expect to spend hundreds of dollars; now you can download a legally binding contract for less than $25. In addition, straightforward legal tasks such as filings and tax returns are being outsourced to countries such as India.

Going to law school, in other words, is no longer a reliable path to success. The mere fact that it *was* a sure bet ignited a chain reaction that obliterated that certainty. This example offers a clue as to why tomorrow's success stories are hard to predict in fields that change quickly, and why those successes seem so random. If we pursue an approach that we know has worked in the past, we can be certain that competition will be fierce; others will pursue it as well. Whatever advantage we created is eliminated and success is still as elusive as ever. Economists call this the efficient market theory. The theory argues that using almost any readily available information to try and beat the market, is pointless. If the same data is available to everyone at the same time, prices will move too quickly in response to that data for you to realize any gain. You move—but so does everybody else.

There is another, highly counterintuitive point to be made here: your chances of success actually *drop* when you analyze the market and try to predict what you need to do to succeed. Because logic led people to conclude that law school was a great way to become successful, law school became the exact opposite.

We are accustomed to believing that analysis can help us increase our chances of success. We believe that sharp logic is the best guide to greatness. But if the pathway to success is logical, it means that everyone else can find it fast, and that puts the whole approach in question. Take tablet computing, for instance. When Apple released the iPad, it soon became obvious that there was a serious demand for such a product. The tablet computer became one of the fastest selling technology products in history, selling 3.3 million units in its first quarter. It didn't exactly take an Einstein to predict that demand would continue to rise for tablet computers. But so what? Everybody else could see that this was true as well. And within a year, sixty-four companies had developed 102 competing tablets. None of them made any serious money.

*

The faster the world changes, the faster other people or organizations can catch up with you. The speed of discovering and sharing new business practices, marketing campaigns, products, or services has reached a fever pitch. The interconnected universe we are building across cultures, industries, and other barriers makes for a hyperadaptive environment, one in which a logical approach to strategy will fare worse and worse when others can easily copy and adopt successful practices, quickly diminishing their advantage. But this interconnectedness also increases the frequency of serendipitous encounters and unexpected insight and enables far greater rates of innovation.

Together these trends will likely affect all careers and industries; even those we don't think have anything to worry about. Logic told us that traditional animation or law were industries that changed very slowly, but that assumption has been invalidated by recent events. The future does not behave predictably. If we rely simply on logic we will be sideswiped when random change comes our way.

This failure of logic, however, has not prevented us from using it in countless ways to chart a path to success. It is honestly difficult to avoid doing so since other approaches, by definition, don't really make sense. We see this play out in the recommendations and advice we hear from consultants and analysts. On September 15, 2010, Dan Frommer of Gizmodo, a leading technology site, indicated what he thought Nokia's CEO Stephen Elop should do to return Nokia to greatness. First on the list:

1. Make it the company's top priority to be competitive in smartphones.

That, of course, makes sense. Smartphones are where all the growth is happening in the industry and where all the profits are located. Nokia has to be part of that. Suggestions number 2 and 3 are just as logical.

2. Shift the focus from smartphone hardware to software.
3. Pick a single smartphone platform to invest in, and dramatically simplify its platforms across the board.

This is essentially taking a page out of Apple's handbook. That company has made sure its software rocks and it has an incredibly simple product line. Nokia should do the same: have fewer products but make them awesome. The rest of the list is similarly levelheaded, for example suggestion number 7, which says:

7. Figure out what Nokia means to the United States, especially to carriers.

This is something they ignored under earlier leadership and it cost them dearly in the United States.

All of these recommendations are rational. They are, in fact, part

53

and parcel of how a traditional strategy would approach solving this question—it would just be more elaborate, yet still unflinchingly logical. But what these suggestions all do, in essence, is model Nokia after Apple or Android. That's where a logical analysis will push them.

But what did Apple do when they wanted to grow? They did the same thing Nokia did once upon a time: they went for a strategy that was different and unexpected. Yes, today it might seem obvious that Apple would create the iPod and then move on to the iPhone. But back when they did it, it seemed strange and surprising for a company that sold desktops to take on the music industry.

In his book *Good Strategy, Bad Strategy,* UCLA management professor Richard Rumelt mentions a conversation he had with Steve Jobs in 1998 that encapsulates this thinking. "Steve, this turnaround at Apple has been impressive," Rumelt said. "But everything we know about the PC business says that Apple cannot really push beyond a small niche position. The network effects are just too strong to upset the Wintel standard. So what are you trying to do in the longer term? What is the strategy?" Apparently Steve Jobs just smiled and said: "I am going to wait for the next big thing."

Well, my first memory of Nokia was that of their green rubber boots, which, when I was a kid, I used when I went picking mushrooms or fishing. Yes, Nokia made green, Wellington-style rubber boots and for years that was the only way I knew about their brand. In my mind, at least, they went from rubber boots to mobile phones more or less overnight. So why does every recommended answer to Nokia's future have to do with mobile phones now?

What Nokia needs is the next big thing—again. Either they can change the mobile-phone industry in a way that surprises everyone or they change some other industry. If logic is their guide, they are likely to be fighting a pack of competitors; if randomness is their guide, they might be all alone. They might be the innovators again. Which is why I like suggestion number 10 in Frommer's article more than all the other ones combined:

10. Do something magical.

We use that word to describe serendipity or luck, because the magic, in this case, comes when something unexpected happens. Magic is clearly not something you plan to make happen, it is something that happens *to* you. In Part 2, we'll explore how to increase our chances of experiencing this kind of magic.

But if you can't follow a logical approach to achieve success, what can you follow? There is really only one answer: it has to be an approach that is *not* logical, however strange that may sound. Which brings us right back to Stephenie Meyer and *Twilight*.

*

Twilight and its sequels are peopled with vampires, chronicling their lives, their desires, and the lives of their archrivals the werewolves. The books are part of a rich genre of vampire stories dating back to the eighteenth century. But how much did Stephenie Meyer really know about writing a good vampire yarn before she wrote *Twilight*? As I read through the first book (I did it for science) it seemed immediately apparent to me that the answer to this question was, *not a lot.*

Monsters in these types of books usually have a certain number of specific qualities. These can vary, occasionally, but not by all that much. Although the details of the Kraken, for instance, might change (Kraken appeared most recently as a villain in the *Pirates of the Caribbean* films), this octopus-inspired monster is always very, very large, has powerful tentacles, and munches on ships for lunch. The same is true for werewolves; although a few specifics may differ, the disease that leads to becoming a werewolf, lycanthropy, is transmitted through bites. If bitten, you turn into a wolf, or a half-wolf, usually when the moon is full.

Vampires, too, have certain accepted characteristics. But *Twilight*'s undead are very different from the traditional notion of what a vampire is supposed to be. Some readers and critics could barely bring themselves to think of Edward, for example, as a vampire. The most memorable instance of vampires in literature is arguably Bram Stoker's *Dracula*. The story is an epic battle between good and evil, with the

Transylvanian count personifying one of the most terrifying monsters ever to roam the earth. Dracula is enigmatic and mysterious, and most definitely evil. His *Twilight* counterpart, Edward, fails this first test. Like Dracula, Edward feeds on blood, but unlike the count he has renounced human blood on moral grounds. Hold on . . . *moral grounds?*

Yes; and that's just for starters. Here are just a few other differences: 1) Dracula deceives his victims. He not only takes great pleasure in doing so, but he is also damn good at it. Edward is an open book in terms of his intentions and feelings. 2) Vampires have long, pointed fangs. But in *Twilight* they have strong teeth that can pierce, but are normal in appearance. 3) Vampires burn in sunlight. Not Edward and his family: they glitter like diamonds. 4) Vampires need to sleep during the day, often in coffins. Edward and his family don't sleep at all. 5) Vampires in *Twilight* are "basically good, thoughtful individuals who don't want to harm anyone." Dracula, and mainstream vampires in general, are pretty much the exact opposite. 6) When the vampires in *Twilight* are hurt or destroyed, there is no blood or gore involved; instead, they shatter into pieces, like glass.

Perhaps most significantly, vampires have been known to have strong carnal desires. They have been portrayed as having insatiable lusts and the ability to attract the opposite sex, as if they were sex gods. This is true for Stoker's Dracula and also in the novels written by Anne Rice. It certainly is true in the HBO series *True Blood*. But in *Twilight*, in a remarkable reversal that has apparently only heightened the appeal of the books, Edward chooses not to consummate his love with the heroine, Bella. She is the one who wants him—but *he resists.*

Many people consider this last point to be critical. This forbidden love, exemplified by restraint, has been seen as the series' chief driver of success. It epitomizes the sexual tension and confusion felt by teenage girls. Critics and readers also identify many of the other differences mentioned above as important hooks that attract readers.

It would be easy to conclude that Meyer was just very savvy about all of this. Her target audience consists of "tween" and teenage girls, after all, a demographic known to favor a strong hero who is powerfully drawn to protect a heroine. The guy must be sweet and kind but also dangerous and strong. By making her vampires fit this mold, Meyer was able to write a teenage romance instead of a dark novel for adults, with violent and erotic themes. But it wasn't her reasoning ability, per se, that prompted Meyer to make her vampires different.

Meyer disregarded every expectation about vampires because she started writing about them without even knowing what the norms *were*. She didn't have a grand plan. She broke all the rules, in a sense, because she didn't consider them. "It wasn't until I knew that *Twilight* would be published that I began to think about whether my vampires were too much the same or too different from the others," she says. "Of course, I was far too invested in my characters at that point to be making changes . . . so I didn't cut out fangs and coffins and so forth as a way to distinguish my vampires; that's just how they came to me." The only time she studied vampire mythology was when, in the book, Bella's character researches vampires. Meyer was too busy creating her own world and "didn't want to find out just how many rules I was breaking."

Let's imagine, just for a moment, that Meyer had actually stopped in order to logically analyze how vampires are "supposed" to act before she started writing. After all, it is customary to approach a new project or opportunity by analyzing the existing landscape, and then plan accordingly. It's not so far-fetched to think that, with research in hand, Meyer would have concluded that her ideas couldn't really work. If vampires had to sleep during the day, for instance, Edward and Bella could never have been classmates. Much of their early courtship plays out in high school. So maybe she could modify her ideas a little bit? She would keep the storyline of a "dangerous" lover but change Edward from vampire to a boy with a dangerous past? Or maybe Edward could remain a vampire but Meyers would set all the scenes after dark, skipping the whole school bit? Point by point, everything that made *Twilight* such a big success would have to be edited out. By following conventions, her book would have become less and less random with each step—and ever more predictable.

57

If the rules of writing vampire fiction were as rigid as the rules of tennis, *Twilight* would never have been published. Meyer couldn't write well and knew nothing about vampires. Fortunately for her, the rules for writing fiction are wide open. They are not even rules so much as societal conventions that are up for interpretation. The same, of course, is true for mobile phones, coffee shops, and even legal careers—anything exposed to market forces. You need to do something different in order to become successful and rise above the avalanche of competitors. Success in the future defies logic and prediction because it is and must be random.

*

And yet, you could argue that many people and organizations have been wildly successful in a variety of endeavors by following a seemingly logical approach. It is beyond dispute that many successful individuals and organizations have used deep, rational, and logical thought processes to guide their actions. Maybe they analyzed reams of data, developed expertise in a particular area, or executed a well-considered strategy. If the world is truly uncertain and random, how do we explain these types of successes?

Take, for instance, hedge fund manager John Paulson. He works in a field filled with quick-thinking prognosticators who use data from a variety of sources to land on the right side of a bet. Paulson is legendary in hedge fund circles because he made almost $15 billion in one year for his firm when he predicted the coming housing crisis and placed a massive bet against it. In a letter to his clients, Paulson wrote, "When we expressed concern about the mortgage markets, many of the most sophisticated investors in the world, who had analyzed the same publicly available data we had, were fully convinced that we were wrong, and they were more than willing to bet against us." Bear Stearns had more than two thousand employees, none of whom predicted the approaching turmoil with enough confidence to place a bet on it. Paulson, meanwhile, had a staff of only nine, and he figured out exactly what was going on and made a ton of money because of it.

In this case, randomness seems to be nowhere in sight. Paulson had analytical abilities that put him way ahead of his competitors. How did he gain such deep insight?

The best (although not foolproof) way to see if someone has cracked the code of success is to look at whether or not he or she can reproduce their success over and over again. How does John Paulson fare in this regard? He started out on Wall Street amassing shares of companies that were ripe for a buy-out and shorting those with faltering acquisitions. Later, as a hedge fund manager, his results were unexceptional. Judging by his career, Paulson does not appear to be the most likely to succeed by making billions in the housing crash. His career had essentially stalled. In fact, it was a chance phone call in 2004 from a man named Paolo Pellegrini that changed his fortune.

Pellegrini, once a rising star on Wall Street, woke up one day to find himself forty-five and unemployed. He had spent nine years as a vice president at Lazard Frères & Co., but the salesmanship required for investment banking was not his forte. Pellegrini got in touch with Paulson one night to ask for a job. Paulson said yes, and slotted him into a post recently vacated by an associate who left to pursue an MBA.

Paulson knew firsthand how inflated the real estate market appeared to be. He had watched an acquaintance buy a property for $3 million and sell it for $9 million, only to see the second buyer flip it for $25 million. He wanted to bet against it, yet he didn't have the data to back up his hunch. Pellegrini offered to investigate the mortgage market to see what he could find.

A numbers junkie, Pellegrini pored through public data and suddenly found something big. When adjusted for inflation, from 1970 to 2000 home values had increased by just 1.5 percent. From 2000 to 2005 on, they had soared by 7 percent. Prices would have to drop by 40 percent just to return to the trend line, and usually during a correction they dropped far below that. When Pellegrini showed Paulson his chart, Paulson had a true click moment: not only was the housing bubble real, but it was also dangerous. Paulson began to bet against the banks most heavily exposed to mortgage debt. When Lehman

Brothers failed, for instance, Paulson had bet $22 million that it would. That single bet repaid him over $1 billion.

Paulson was savvy to act on Pellegrini's research, and he, along with Goldman Sachs, was one of the few left in the black when the bubble burst. But that doesn't mean that his process for choosing investments was surefire, or even reliable. Had it been reliable, he should have been able to unearth another phenomenal opportunity—but that hasn't happened. Quite the contrary, in fact. In June 2011, Paulson lost nearly $500 million when a company in which he invested was revealed to be a Ponzi scheme. As of January 2012, his Advantage Plus fund was down 52.5 percent. That is a stunningly poor performance, and a far cry from when he delivered billions to his investors.

When you think about it, Paulson's insight was triggered by a remarkable confluence of circumstances, and not easy to replicate. His main data man, Pellegrini, needed to really hit one out of the park, so he agreed to take a position *replacing someone who left to pursue an MBA*, a true step down for a former VP at a venerable investment bank. The chart Pellegrini produced was such a darling for Paulson that he kept it always visible on his desk. "I love that chart," he would say. But if Paulson could find opportunities like that on command, he would have his wall plastered with such charts. Yes, John Paulson is undoubtedly smart, but so was Jesse Livermore, who made $100 million by shorting during the Great Depression. By 1934 he was bankrupt. Paulson may have used logic to arrive at certain insights, but that was not what presented him with the opportunity to beat the market. For that he needed luck.

*

Trading is a tricky business, as is writing novels. The author Stephen King, however, is far from bankrupt. A master at repeating success, to date he has written forty-nine novels. Every single one of them has been a *New York Times* bestseller. His long winning streak dates back to the 1974 of *Carrie*. Pumped up by a movie adaptation, the paperback edition of *Carrie* was a massive bestseller and King became a literary icon. He subsequently published *'Salem's Lot* and *The Shining* to commercial and critical success. Since then, it seems like every new book by King manages to land at the top of the list. While Paulson has been unable to repeat his billion-dollar winning streak, it seems that King has found the formula, and his success goes beyond a statistical aberration. It has been long and sustained. How is that possible, if success is random?

There are, of course, a number of individuals and companies that outperform others for long periods at a time. Coca-Cola and Pepsi, Starbucks and Walmart, General Electric and Ford are just a few examples. Each of these companies has had, at one point or another, a long stretch of remarkable success, longer than one lucky bet alone would produce. Yet Stephen King proves to be an excellent case study because of a remarkable experiment he ran a few years into his career.

The globally known horror author has a blockbuster brand name. This is also true for a small group of other writers who produce mass-market bestsellers, including Danielle Steele, John Grisham, Dan Brown, and J. K. Rowling. There are legions of people who buy every book by one or more of these writers. I will buy every one of John Grisham's books, for instance, despite the fact that I can no longer tell the difference between any of them. Grisham has, to use marketing vernacular, built an amazing brand equity.

But if John Grisham or Stephen King are such brand mavens, then why haven't they been tapped by consumer marketers to "translate" their amazing expertise? Why couldn't they use their know-how and help cultivate iconic brands for companies? That is, brands that would last for decades in the way that these writers' books have? We know that idea seems weird, and for a reason. There is something very specific about King's success and it seems to stem from cumulative advantages and network effects that snowball with each new title.

Once Stephen King achieved his initial success with *Carrie*, it was far easier to do the same with his second book, *'Salem's Lot*. Those bestsellers created the runway for the third. Three in a row, which he managed with *The Shining*, was enough to hook a cadre of lifelong

61

fans. He has a reader base to ensure that new books—assuming they deliver the baseline King experience—will be bestsellers. But what would happen if Stephen King had to start all over again? Let's say he had to change his name. Would he be able to repeat his success based on content alone? It is hard to speculate on something like this, but in King's case we don't have to. Because he did exactly that.

In 1977, a new author by the name of Richard Bachman came on the scene. Born and raised in New York City, the young Bachman left his home for a four-year stint in the coast guard. After his tour, he relocated to rural New Hampshire and opened what became a modestly successful dairy farm. It was about this time that Bachman developed insomnia. Thereafter, he spent his nights writing horror novels. In 1977, he found a publisher and his first book, *Rage*, was released to unspectacular reviews and lackluster sales. Undeterred, Bachman continued to write, publishing four additional books, none of which stood out in a major way. His book *Thinner* came closest to acclaim when one critic said that it was "what Stephen King would write if Stephen King *could* write."

Suspicions kept surfacing, however, that Bachman actually *was* Stephen King. Not long after *Thinner* appeared in 1984, the jig was up. A bookstore clerk named Steve Brown couldn't believe they were not the same person. He tracked down the paperwork for a Bachman book in the Library of Congress and found—you guessed it—Stephen King's name attached to it. Yes, Richard Bachman was Steven King, writing under a pseudonym. It was his attempt to publish more books without diluting the Stephen King brand. At the time, conventional wisdom in book publishing put a one-book-per-year limit on authors. King invented Bachman to work around that limitation.

As a result of that experience, King came to see that his name was what drove sales. It wasn't his skill, per se, neither was it something like a secret recipe that others could use to succeed. Each book he released under his own name sold incredibly well, while each book he released as Bachman was relegated to the remainder bin. In 1986, once the secret was out, King re-released all of Bachman's published works under his real name and they skyrocketed up bestseller lists. The first run of *Thinner* had sold 28,000 copies—the most of any Bachman book and above average for an author. The moment it became known that Richard Bachman was Stephen King, however, the Bachman books took off, with sales quickly reaching $3 million.

In his book *Fooled By Randomness* (and later in *The Black Swan*), Nassim Nicholas Taleb illustrates how it can be very easy to mistake randomness for skill. He shows that people with a recent success, or string of successes, often view themselves, and may be viewed by others, as smart or skilled. But time tells the truth. Often, these same people reveal themselves to be mere mortals and they fail, sometimes spectacularly. Consistent with this is the notion that a so-far "unspectacular" life can turn on a dime and become successful, which jibes with the fact that someone like Meyer can conquer the world of books without any significant writing experience. This is not to say that skill doesn't matter, but it does suggest that a skill set is primarily the way for us to figure out how to focus our time and effort, not how to achieve success. Other random and complex forces are key to understanding the source of someone's success.

Although we will talk much more about complex forces, including network effects, in chapters 11 and 12, it is fair to say at this point that random success, even in an isolated occurrence, can develop, under the right conditions, into a major, long-term success. This, in some ways, is also what a great brand can achieve. Every product Apple releases, for instance, has a better chance to succeed than a product from a lesser-known competitor because it will be noticed by far more people. In addition to brand, being the first to build a virtuous circle of customers, suppliers, and economies of scale goes a long way to sustaining success for years to come. The same is true for, say, Facebook. Even if you or I created a social networking site that was twice as good as this global behemoth, we would still be at a ridiculous disadvantage because Facebook has gained so much traction in terms of brand, customers, and partnerships.

While it may seem that logic was behind King's long reign of success or Paulson's major one-time win, it was really serendipity and complex forces that pushed them over the edge. King's popularity, and the power of his bestselling brand name, has increased with each new book, and he has been able to create a situation whereby his name on the cover is enough to guarantee sales. Like the elusive video-gone-viral and the coveted network effects, King's name is enough—and that's not something we can duplicate. Paulson's success was also a result of serendipity. He took a chance and hired an out-of-work investment banker. That banker handed him a chart one day. It was the gift of a lifetime. You can't predict your way to that type of serendipity. And it is not something we can readily repeat. So, without unexpected click moments or the type of complex forces that magnify an initial advantage, we can't replicate Stephen King's streak or duplicate Paulson's luck. Even they couldn't do that.

The reality is that randomness rules our lives. Somehow we have always sensed this. The person we fell in love with, the deal we closed, the near miss—all of these involved serendipity, luck, and the utterly random. But today everything is changing so fast that randomness is not just a bug, it is the dominant feature in our lives and careers. It has become the defining aspect of success. As we've seen, predictability has plummeted to an all-time low. Whatever plan or strategy we create in advance is sure to be wrong. Instead, success comes from the serendipitous meeting, the random insight, and the lucky bet.

In the second half of the book, I'll introduce several powerful approaches for veering away from logic and conventional wisdom to make the most of random opportunities. But first, we need to take a look at why we are so hesitant to embrace serendipity and randomness in laying out our strategies for success. Why are we so desperate to explain every success as the triumph of the smart over the dim-witted, the disciplined over the unfocused, and the strategic over the willy-nilly? The answer can be found in the aftermath of one deadly winter night in Sweden that seems ripped from the pages of *The Girl with the Dragon Tattoo*.

5

THE CONSPIRACY OF RANDOMNESS

On February 28, 1986, a smartly dressed couple emerged from the semidarkness of the Grand Cinema in Stockholm, Sweden. It was a bitterly cold evening, but the two were enjoying a rare moment of anonymity, talking about the film and about where they might head next. As they walked through the streets a man walked up from behind and, at 11:21 p.m., fired two shots from a Smith & Wesson .357 revolver. The second bullet grazed the woman's back; the first shot hit her companion square in the chest. Lisbet Palme sustained only minor injuries, while her husband, the Swedish prime minister Olof Palme, was declared dead on arrival at the hospital.

The assassination of Palme, a charismatic and highly polarizing leftist figure, shook Sweden to its core. Nearly two centuries had passed since the last similar event in 1792, when a nationalist shot

King Gustav III at the Royal Opera House in Stockholm. The country's citizens considered themselves beyond this type of political violence. Palme had been the country's prime minister for eleven years and had managed to make many enemies, but no one could have envisioned such an end for him. Palme's assassination is, by a wide margin, the most significant crime in Swedish history—and easily its most controversial.

It took a few days for news of the night's singular irregularities to spread, but when it did, it hit like a powerful aftershock. Investigators learned that the prime minister's bodyguards were conveniently off duty on the night he was shot. Several men carrying walkie-talkies were seen in the area around the time of the murder. The police were blamed for a slow response to calls from the scene and it took several hours for them to seal off the country's borders. It kept getting stranger. The prime minister's wife, for instance, was never examined by a physician, and both bullets were found by the public. One was located before the police had a chance to examine the area, and the other bullet was found a day *after* they had examined it inch by inch. It was lying on top of the snow only twelve feet from the spot where Palme had been shot, and was barely deformed. How could the police have missed it the first time around?

A number of potential plots came to light in rapid succession. The one that initially gained traction involved South Africa's apartheid government. A week before the assassination Palme had delivered a keynote address declaring that "apartheid cannot be reformed, it has to be eliminated," reminding the South African government that Sweden's financial support of the African National Congress would continue. At the time of the murder, a South African spy was confirmed to be in Stockholm. Another plot involved a Turkish prisoner who was a leading member of the terror organization Kurdistan Workers' Party (called PKK). Indian arms dealers were likewise implicated in another lead, along with Swedish defense contractors, the KGB and the CIA, and many other organizations whose feathers had been ruffled by the Swedish prime minister. There were soon a dozen or so theories as to who was behind the murder, and the puzzle grew ever more intricate.

But maybe that is to be expected?

*

In 1979 Clark McCauley and Susan Jacques of Bryn Mawr College ran a study in which they asked college students to evaluate the likelihood, based on the headline in a newspaper, that a conspiracy was in play. For example, they were asked to read the following two headlines and decide if a conspiracy—a covert plot planned among partners and secretly executed—was likely:

A MAN SHOOTS AT THE PRESIDENT AND MISSES
A MAN SHOOTS AT THE PRESIDENT AND KILLS HIM

The researchers found that when the president in the fictional headline was killed, people were far more likely to believe it to be connected to a conspiracy than when the would-be assassin missed. That is somewhat curious. Objectively, we know that the successful completion of an assassination does not really hinge upon whether it was the result of a conspiracy or not. It's just that when something major happens—something consequential—we tend to believe that there was a larger plan in place. We want to know that actors were at play in a purposeful way. And this holds true for much more than just assassinations.

It doesn't make sense to us that Starbucks could achieve its extraordinary success without an intricate plan in place or that Google could dominate the on-line world without some sort of carefully crafted strategy. Stated simply, we want to believe that things happen for a reason and also that we should be able to understand those reasons. This holds particularly true in the face of exceptional results. Nokia was absolutely *brilliant* during its dramatic rise to greatness, but plain *stupid* during its dramatic decline. In that light it would be surprising if there were no conspiracy theories put forth after Olof Palme's assas-

67

sination. Our need to make sense of such a tremendous event forces us to find an explanation that matches its scale. And in this case there was one terrifying lead that stood out from all the others—one which, if true, would bring Sweden to its knees.

*

I was in seventh grade during the time of the murder and I got to know a lot of details around one of the most prominent and deeply investigated conspiracy theories—the one that has fascinated Swedes the most. My aunt's husband at that time, Lars Krantz, was a Swedish TV producer and investigative journalist who had been on a bus some blocks from the murder only a few minutes after the shots had been fired. From his seat he saw a man board the bus and then conspicuously step back outside. A few days later Krantz, in an unrelated matter, was covering the trial of an alleged member of the extreme right-wing "Baseball Gang," a fringe group of police officers accused of engaging in vigilantism. Krantz suddenly recognized the officer on trial as the same man who had stepped on and off the bus. The Baseball Gang was known to harbor ill feelings towards the prime minister. Krantz began to put the pieces together; and he realized that he may have actually come face to face with Palme's assassin. He reported his observation to the police, while the very same bus driver independently reported similar suspicions. Both reports formed the basis of what became known as a police conspiracy plot.

According to the alleged plot, a small group of cops that hated Palme's policies had conspired to assassinate him. The idea gained immediate traction in the media and among Swedes, and while not very well defined, it made sense to a lot of people. The police being responsible might explain why Palme had no bodyguards on the night of the murder, why it took so long for an officer to arrive on the scene, and why it took so long to close down the borders. Witnesses had seen the killer touch Palme's shoulder before shooting. Why? Maybe an intense personal dislike would explain that type of behavior—the assassin wanted to see his face before shooting.

Other strange aspects of the case seemed to point to a possible explanation, too. For instance, the head investigator on the case, Hans Holmer, was extremely focused on the Kurdish terror lead, a theory quickly dismissed by most others because there was no evidence to support it. After a while Holmer dropped it, too, but maybe this wild-goose chase had already served its purpose by diverting valuable resources from pursuing the real killer? The police conspiracy plot seemed possible, and to some even probable. My uncle-in-law was in the thick of it, and the more he dug into the stories the more incredible connections he found. Witness testimonies, coroner reports, and the strange behavior of the police during the night of the murder all seemed to point towards a cover-up at a very high level. "This," he would say, pointing towards a large stack of reports, "is a conspiracy." Because there was just no way that this could all be a coincidence, right?

Of course it could, but that notion is highly unsettling for most people. Even if we *know* that a connection is entirely random, we still feel more at ease of we can find an explanation. An accidental meeting at an airport with a friend quickly becomes a sign that we should get together more often. A surprisingly good hire turns into having a good eye for talent. We fall for these connections, even when we know they are not real. Abraham Lincoln and John F. Kennedy were remarkably different people in thousands of ways. But if you consider only their similarities, the commonalities make the hair on the back of your neck stand up. Abraham Lincoln was elected to Congress in 1846. John F. Kennedy was elected to Congress in 1946. Both were presidents of the United States, elected 100 years apart. Both were shot and killed by assassins who were known by three names with fifteen letters, John Wilkes Booth and Lee Harvey Oswald. Neither killer made it to trial. Lincoln had a secretary named Kennedy, and Kennedy had a secretary named Lincoln. They were both killed on Fridays while sitting next to their wives, Lincoln in the Ford Theater, Kennedy in a Lincoln (made by Ford). Both were succeeded by a man named Johnson: Andrew Johnson was born in 1808, and Lyndon Johnson in 1908.

It seems almost unreal when you read it this way. *How is this possible?* is a thought that even the most hardened realist can't help to at least briefly consider. And this is a situation where we *know* the connections are entirely coincidental. But what happens when the situation is a bit less clear? Our desire to avoid falling back on a random explanation is almost overpowering. This is particularly true when we try to explain greatness. Sure, we want luck on our side, but if we achieve something extraordinary, well, it seems unfair that we should have luck to thank. We are more apt to attribute success to brilliance—it just feels better. Our uneasiness with randomness comes into play frequently.

Users complained that early versions of random playlists on the iPod were not random at all. Often the same artist would appear over and over again, or a few songs would be played in the same order in which they appeared on the album from which they were taken. Of course, that's what you'd expect to happen occasionally if the playlist was random, even though it doesn't feel that way. In *The Perfect Thing*, technology writer Steven Levy interviewed numerous cryptology experts and nearly all agreed that the shuffle function was indeed random. "It's completely random. It is absolutely, unequivocally random," said Jeff Rubin, head of the iTunes development team. Despite the consensus, in 2005 Apple debuted "smart shuffle," which allowed users to control just *how* random their shuffle was. "We're making it less random," said Steve Jobs, "to make it feel more random." Now that feels better: controlled randomness. If only we could set the degree to which randomness controls our lives. We crave predictability, hate the idea that success is a function of randomness, and find it very hard to believe in such a notion. How did it ever come to this?

*

Take look at the two star charts below. One has been created randomly and the other has been made by hand. Can you guess which one is which?
The charts were created by physicist Richard S. Muller, who teaches

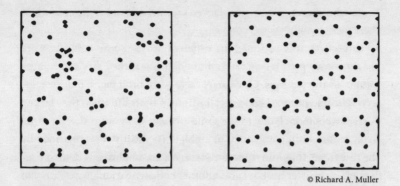

© Richard A. Muller

about the illusions of randomness. Using a computer, he generates completely random locations within a defined area and then assigns each location a "star." When he asks his class to decide which pattern looks more random, most people say the pattern on the right. But that's incorrect—it's the one on the left. Yes, the diagram seems to be full of clumps, groupings, lines, and vacant regions but those categorizations are just a way for us to explain the patterns we see. According to Muller, it's hard for most people to believe that the diagram on the left is the random one. It just looks too planned.

In a series of interesting experiments, University of Texas at Austin researchers Jennifer Whitson and Adam Galinsky found, over and over again, that people tend to find patterns where none exist. In one experiment they showed the participants a video of visual "noise"—essentially TV static—and the participants would discern figures in the random noise. This was most often the case when the subjects sensed a lack of control in their life. In one study, for instance, half the subjects were given feedback on how well they identified images engrained in video, while the other half were told nothing. Those who received no feedback were more likely to spot images in the next experiment, when none existed. Next, participants were told to recall a dangerous situation in their life, and then examine ten pictures that displayed random black dots on a white background. The researchers categorized those who had control over the dangerous situation and

71

those who didn't. Those who lacked control saw more images when there were none.

This effect was repeated in different ways. Some subjects were shown snowy pictures and asked to point out if they saw any images hidden in the pictures. Of course, there were no images, but the subjects who had been asked to recall a time in their life when they lacked control were more likely to see some anyway. They were also far more likely to suspect a conspiracy in ambiguous short stories provided by the researchers. In one story, for instance, an employee is denied promotion right after his boss and another colleague exchange a flurry of emails. Coincidence? Those who had been reminded of a time when they lacked control in their life were much more likely to suspect a conspiracy. It had to be related, right?

Our brains have been designed to perceive order instead of randomness. Pattern perception, for example, is an important component in many of our basic abilities such as memory, sight, speech, and facial recognition. But as useful and vital as pattern recognition may be, and perhaps because of its great usefulness, we constantly find, and feel the need to find, patterns where there are none. It is a fundamental, almost primal attempt to maintain order and find meaning. The reason for this overzealousness in avoiding random explanations stems from some evolutionary advantage.

We've been conditioned over millions of years to make a direct connection between cause and effect, probably because doing so can help us save our lives. Harvard University biologist Kevin R. Foster and University of Helsinki biologist Hanna Kokko used evolutionary modeling to demonstrate that when the cost of believing a false pattern is real is less than the cost of believing the genuine pattern, natural selection will favor the false pattern. For example, they demonstrated that believing that the familiar rustle in the tall grass is a predator when it is only the wind does not cost much, but "believing" the reverse—that a dangerous predator is only the wind—may cost an animal its life.

This research explains why people so easily get caught up in conspiracy theories. We are conditioned to search for similarities, not differences. Millions of college students over the years have argued that a legitimate connection exists between Pink Floyd's legendary album *The Dark Side of the Moon* and the 1939 film classic *The Wizard of Oz*. They claim that if you start the record when the MGM lion roars for the third time, the music follows along with the movie in ways that must be intentional.

The song "Brain Damage" begins when the Scarecrow launches into "If I Only Had a Brain." Moments later he dances in a grassy field as the album blares, "the lunatic is on the grass." The black and white portion of the movie is the exact length of the first side of the album, and the film morphs into color at the moment when the legendary cash registers of "Money" begin clinking. The album's iconic cover image even seems to pay homage to the movie's famous black-and-white-into-color switch, displaying a prism distorting a beam of plain light into color. The smoking gun, however, is when Dorothy places her ear to the Tin Man's chest at the moment the album tails off to the sound of a heartbeat.

Of course, it is also true that, more often than not, the album does not line up with the movie. If there are ten brief connections, there are also ten thousand distinctions and differences. When asked about the linkages, the album's producer Alan Parsons said, "There simply wasn't the mechanics to do it. We had no means of playing videotapes in the room at all. I don't think VHS had come along by '72, had it?" Nick Mason, the band's drummer, calls the assertions "absolute nonsense."

We want to believe that Dan Balan knew what he was doing with "Dragostea din tei" because that would mean we can emulate him. We want to believe that Nokia was dim-witted when it lost its groove because that would mean we can avoid the same fate. And we have a hard time believing that the assassination of a head of state could have been anything but an intricate conspiracy. But none of it is true.

*

After several years of allegations, investigations, and examinations into the various plots and other theories—some likely and others absurd—a small-time criminal and drug addict, Christer Pettersson, was arrested for Prime Minister Palme's murder. He probably had the right gun (although this could never be proven), he had a police record, and he was in the vicinity when Palme went down. There was an issue about possible motive—Pettersson did not seem all that interested in politics and, if anything, he liked the prime minister. Why would he kill the guy? But that did not matter much, because the prosecution had a star witness: Lisbet Palme, the prime minister's wife. She was the only person who had actually seen the killer's face and she identified Pettersson in a lineup. The trial was intensely followed by the Swedish people, and when the guilty verdict finally fell on Pettersson, it was a relief for many.

Still, an odd reaction immediately followed the conviction. People were suddenly saying that the outcome kind of made sense. The idea that the police or any other large organization was behind the murder now seemed far-fetched. It was as if the answers to the mystery surrounding the assassination had been obvious all along. *Oh—Olof Palme was assassinated by a drunk, low-life criminal? Yeah—I knew there was nothing behind those conspiracy theories anyway.* This is a well-explored phenomenon called post-hoc rationalization, and it is one way to explain our unwillingness to yield anything to randomness.

In his book *Everything Is Obvious Once You Know the Answer*, sociologist Duncan Watts takes particular pleasure in showing how humans have a propensity for post-hoc rationalizations. In one interesting example, Watts describes a study by the War Department on U.S. soldiers returning home after World War Two. In his review for *Public Opinion Quarterly*, Paul Lazarsfeld tells readers that one conclusion from the study is that soldiers from rural backgrounds have an easier time adapting to military life than those from urban backgrounds. And, yes, that does make sense. Rural life is less comfortable, requires initiative, and is regimented in ways that match army life. But then Lazarsfeld turns the table on the reader. He was actually kidding. The real result is that soldiers from urban backgrounds fare better. It only takes a minute of reflection to realize that this, too, makes sense. They *should* fare better given more experience with large organizations and dealing with strangers, for instance.

We can, in other words, explain any observation or any outcome by fitting our conclusion to the data. Randomness is not needed because we knew what would happen all along—*but only after it has happened.* I recall the first time I heard about the Ice Hotel, a remarkable tourist attraction located in northern Sweden. Everything in this building is made out of ice—the walls, roof, floors, beds, tables, chairs, even the glasses you drink from. If someone had told me that the idea never worked out I would have nodded my head knowingly. Of course not— the idea is crazy. But that is not what happened. The Ice Hotel has become one of Sweden's largest tourist destinations. Well, yeah, that makes sense, too. It is just crazy enough to work.

The implications of post-hoc rationalizations are huge. They show us that we have an incredibly hard time dealing with the fact that success can be based on randomness. Every day financial pundits tell us why the stock markets moved one way or another. Markets dropped? *There is unrest in Egypt and people are worried about it spreading, which can impact oil prices.* But then the market rallies and we can explain that, too. *Due to a strong showing in the manufacturing sector and positive quarterly earnings, the market saw a sharp uptick by the closing bell.*

In his book *The Halo Effect*, Phil Rosenzweig illustrates how this need to understand what happened can drive us far away from accepting random explanations in favor of detailed, but essentially made-up, explanations. The book lines up example after example in which he shows how explanations for a company's success are highly dependent on how well the company is doing at the moment. If the company is doing great, then it must be doing a bunch of things right. Perhaps it has a culture of empowering its front-line workers? But if the company is doing poorly, there must be a reason for this, too. Maybe it has taken its customers for granted or the management has been too greedy.

Take Cisco, an example Rosenzweig spends quite a bit of time on.

In 1991 John Chambers became the company's new CEO. This marked the start of a growth journey of almost unimaginable proportions. Cisco made history by reaching $100 billion in shareholder value faster than any other company—and it kept rising. It even overtook Microsoft as the most valuable company in the world for a brief period in March of 2000 when Cisco climbed above the $500 billion mark. How did it accomplish such a spectacular achievement? *Fortune* pointed out that Cisco had made "acquisitions a science" by having acquired seventy-three companies of all sizes. Others, such as *Business Week*, pointed towards John Chambers' strong management skills and, specifically, his intense customer focus.

But only a few months later Cisco started declining in shareholder value and soon shed more than $400 billion. It was a stunning reversal of fortunes—and now the business literature pointed out that Cisco never really was the amazing company we'd thought it was. How could it have been? If it had been great, it would never have faced such a sharp drop-off. Instead, we learned, Cisco had actually been arrogant to its customers. John Chambers had allowed a "Wild West culture" to permeate the company. And they got blasted for their undisciplined buying of "unproven start-ups with no profits."

When Cisco is doing great, we can find an explanation for it. When it does poorly, we can find an explanation for that too. Rosenzweig spends much of the book mocking the business literature for this type of reporting, but in doing so he misses an important rationale for this approach. Humans need to make sense of the world around them, and they will accept reasonable explanations to help them do so. Business articles and analyses help us do that—even if the explanations are not correct. But maybe that is not their purpose. We would hate it if someone told us *Cisco is doing well but we are not sure why*. What would be the point of that? Believing that you are, or can be, in control is actually a healthy characteristic in humans, as long as it is not taken too far. It allows us to pursue goals that otherwise might be out of reach and to take chances when we might otherwise have backed off. Feeling that we are in control enables us to take action, plain and simple.

We can now begin to see the contours of a real paradox. Study after study indicates that our power of predicting success is essentially zero. And yet strategy frameworks, business books, and case studies are used now more than ever. Leaders—very smart leaders—rely on these case studies, books, and strategies, so they clearly fulfill a purpose. To say that they are useless is to miss a fundamental need in our journey towards success. How, then, should we think about this need?

Humans are simply not wired to handle the idea that the world is random, despite the fact that it is. This means that any approach we take for achieving success must take this particular human condition into account. In other words, if we want to develop a sustainable approach to reaching success we must *simultaneously* acknowledge that the world is random while retaining some sort of rationale in our approach. I call this the RPS Paradox based on what happens in one of the most peculiar tournaments I've ever come across.

*

Surrounded by a roaring crowd of vacationing college students and a few bikini-clad models, two determined competitors stumbled up on to the stage. Brittany "BK" Kraft, an education major at Eastern Illinois University, was first up. Her opponent, an aspiring physicist from the University of Northern Iowa, was right on her heels. At this, the worldwide Rock Paper Scissors Championship, enthusiasts vied for the right to be named the very best at what the World Rock Paper Scissors (RPS) Society has called "the most elegant and profound of all conflict-resolution processes." The rules are simple: two people face each other, count to three, and then throw down a hand symbol that represents a rock, paper, or scissors. Rock smashes scissors, scissors cut through paper, and paper covers rock. BK stepped to the center of the stage and threw paper three times in a row. Just like that, she found herself the winner of a $25,000 scholarship.

Although a "Paper Scissors Stone Club" was founded in London in 1842, many experts agree that the game dates back to ancient Asia, possibly to the Chinese Han dynasty. But this age-old game, played by kids all over the world, became a modern-day ad-sponsored event following an epic RPS match at a family cabin in northern Canada in 2002. Passionate play ensued between Douglas and Graham Walker and the fists were flying. Afterwards the brothers decided to host what would be the world's first RPS championship.

"We really didn't know how things were going to turn out," Graham Walker told the *Washington Times*. "Really, we would have been happy if 25, 30 of our friends came to drink beer and play for a big prize."

Instead about 250 people showed up, and two years later the tournament had close to fifteen hundred attendees. "That was a bit too much, so we decided to scale it back a bit," Douglas Walker told me one evening. Now most tournaments are smaller (and local), but a vibrant community remains online. In 2004, the Walker brothers published *The Official Rock Paper Scissors Strategy Guide*. Like the rest of the RPS saga, the idea of a "strategy guide" falls somewhere between unlikely and absurd. How is it possible for anyone to seriously count on strategy in a game of chance?

RPS is an intransitive relation, meaning there is no single dominant strategy; every throw can always be beaten by another, and each player has no perfect way of knowing what the other will throw. According to John Haigh, a mathematician at the University of Sussex, "it creates a loop of preferences that has no beginning and no end, defying standard notions of hierarchy. Though each item is better than some other item, it is impossible to define what is 'best.'" Deviating from a completely random strategy "is always dangerous because a superior strategy always exists."

To give you a sense of how that plays out in real life, imagine that you were to play a game at an RPS tournament. You and your opponent are just about to start when you are informed of an interesting (and accurate) statistic: more players tend to choose rock over scissors or paper as a first move—37 percent of them. Now, what should you do with this piece of information? Just how helpful is it? Initially it may appear to be very helpful. If 37 percent choose rock, you should obviously choose paper. Case closed. But hold on . . . your opponent was just informed of the very same statistic. She is obviously thinking the exact same thing. So if *she* chooses paper because she expects *you* to choose rock, you can take advantage of that and get the jump on her if you choose scissors first. Your scissors beats her paper and you win.

Your eyes lock . . . and you suddenly see a hint of a smile creep across her lips. It's very subtle, but she seems to think she is going to win this one. Why? What is she thinking? You realize that she, just like yourself, might have gone one level deeper in this chain of thought. So that means you need to avoid the scissors—she is already way ahead of you. She is probably going to crush your scissors with a rock. Which means you need to use paper. . . . The feeling of an *Inception*-style game of what-ifs starts to unfold. There is no way you can solve this one.

The best approach to winning an RPS tournament, then, is entirely straightforward. Just stay random. In fact, it is easy to show mathematically that randomness is the single best strategy no matter what your opponent chooses to do. It is therefore kind of strange that the World Rock Paper Scissors Society does not actually recommend that a contestant use a random strategy—in fact, they actively advise people to stay away from it. How come? And why is it that none of the winners in an RPS tournament has ever pursued a random strategy?

There is a very simple explanation for this mystery: it turns out that pursuing a random approach is advantageous, but extremely difficult. People are terrible at using randomness as a rationale. It's just too hard for us to execute. Indeed, the RPS world has a plethora of popular game strategies. For instance, the "Rock is for Rookies" approach exploits the fact that novices tend to throw rock as a first move. So you should throw paper. The "Step Ahead Thinking" move capitalizes on the idea that inexperienced players will subconsciously deliver the throw that beats their last one. Therefore, if a player plays paper, his opponent will very often play scissors on the next throw. So that means you should throw rock.

Then there is the "Scissors on First" strategy, which says that most advanced players do not want to throw rock because they know the "Rock is for Rookies" mantra. Instead, they often play paper. When playing an advanced RPSer, therefore, you should lead with scissors to defeat paper. The auction house Christie's employed this approach and won a bid to sell $20 million worth of art. (Yes, Christie's actually played rock paper scissors against Sotheby's.) There are even more advanced strategies, called gambits, in which the contestant selects three throws in advance. Some of the all-time great gambits, according to the World RPS Society, are "Avalanche" (three rocks in a row), "Crescendo" (paper–scissors–rock) and "Paper Dolls" (paper–scissors–scissors).

Really? All this when it's *proven* that randomness rules in RPS? You can do no better than that. Unfortunately, we humans are not biologically equipped to tolerate that type of mindset. What RPS championships show is that even if we *know* that the best strategy is to be entirely random, we still need some sort of game plan because plans motivate us to act. This, in a nutshell, is the RPS Paradox. Even if we know that serendipity matters, even if we know that luck plays a huge part in creating success, we *still* need a rationale to act. And it is at the heart of this paradox that we can gain a new understanding of the ultimate purpose of strategy.

*

The verdict in the Olof Palme case was immediately appealed. But the second time around, the prosecution's hands were tied from using Lisbet Palme's eyewitness testimony. The lineup had been badly botched by the police: the foils—those other guys used to fill up the line—were mostly clean-shaven, while Pettersson looked like he had been picked up straight from the street. The "bad guy" could not have been any more obvious if they had added a British accent. Without the wife's testimony, the conviction was overturned, and the crime was never officially solved.

Many years later, however, Christer Pettersson admitted to the killing, claiming that he had intended to shoot a competing criminal—a man well known to the police whose appearance was similar to the prime minster's. That man owned a similar looking coat and lived in the same neighborhood. Pettersson owed the man a lot of money and waited for him, high on amphetamine, outside the movie theater where he thought he had seen him enter. It was only the day after the murder, when he heard on the news that the prime minister had been shot at that exact same spot, that Pettersson realized what had happened. He waited for the police to come crashing through the door, but they never did.

Pettersson restated this detailed confession in his later years and was even set to confess on live TV decades after the murder, only to change his mind minutes before the show was to air. In a crime where dozens of people and organizations had motive and means, it appears that the assassination may have come down to a case of mistaken identity. Christer Pettersson meant to shoot a fellow criminal but mistook the prime minister of Sweden for the man because of a coat. The lives of a head of state, of his wife, of a nation, and of a small-time drug user stood and fell on that one moment.

Lives twist and turn in the most unexpected of ways. It does not make sense, in a strategic framework, to ignore this basic fact. The faster the world is moving and the more interconnected it is, the less predictable it becomes. By the time you have finished reading this sentence, something may have happened in your organization that will affect its fortunes. Any realistic strategic approach must take that into account. But how do we think intelligently about strategies if there is no way to logically identify the optimal one?

One approach says that because nothing is certain, we must remain flexible. This allows us to react swiftly, based on whatever the environment throws at us. William Fung, managing director of the Hong Kong-based firm Li & Fung Ltd., illustrated this clearly during a recent conversation we had. Li & Fung coordinates the manufacture of goods across more than seventy countries and allows its clients to react at record speed to changing conditions, for example, should they need to create new products or change existing ones. "Because things are lasting shorter and shorter, product cycles are shorter, everything is shorter, so you've got to build a corporate structure that is flexible and is geared for change and rapid change," he explained. Depending on time of year, unanticipated demand, changing commodity prices, competitor response, transportation issues, and so forth, Li & Fung can quickly shift the supply chain to handle much of what the market throws at their clients.

Although this responsiveness is helpful (as we will see in Part 2) it does not solve the underlying problem. Most of us don't want to be purely reactionary, we want to be in control of our destiny. We want to chart a path to success. That is the lesson from the RPS Paradox. And no matter how useful it is to ignore logic and court randomness, we still need to sense some sort of purpose behind our actions—some sort of rationale.

So where should this rationale come from? The surprising implication of the RPS Paradox is that it should come from wherever you need it to come from. Some of us need a plan that makes sense, some of us need a plan that emotionally grips us, others need a plan that speaks to their personal goals in life, and most of us need a plan to coordinate activities and keep our schedule straight. The reason behind the plan is not especially important because you will be wrong anyway. Whatever you need to make the case to act, is fair game.

Can you substantiate your action by using an explicit strategy framework, one that will help convince yourself, your colleagues, your board, or your investors that you are heading down the right path? Fine—do that. This is where I believe the plethora of business books, business case studies, and management tomes can play a useful role. They are a source of inspiration that can get people on the same page so that everyone can move forward. During one of my conversations with Randy Haykin, a venture capitalist in Silicon Valley, he told me that the most important goal of a business plan is to show that a team is moving in some coordinated fashion toward a goal. "The plan itself," he chuckled, "will be outdated within the month."

Then again, maybe you don't care about that sort of validation. Maybe you are more likely to be motivated based on a passionate belief in an idea or a strong gut feeling about a particular course of action. Well, if that motivates you to act, then it is just as useful. There is tremendous value in just getting something done. In fact, in my experience, most start-up investors favor strong passion, drive, and forceful execution over analysis and business plans. Interestingly the exact opposite seems to be true in corporations.

Strategy is, at its core, not about finding "the solution," because success is the result of randomness and serendipity. It is more important that you get moving in some direction, although it does not matter as much exactly *which* direction you take. In the words of Herb Kelleher, founder and former CEO of Southwest Airlines, one of the most successful companies in history, "We have a strategic plan. It's called doing things." The purpose of strategy, in other words, is not to find the right answer, because you will be wrong anyway.

The purpose of strategy is to motivate us to *act*.

That said, some approaches *are* far better at seizing opportunity in an unpredictable world than others. We know that if you use logic to methodically plan your next move, you are more likely to shoot yourself in the foot. Instead you have to intentionally inject randomness into your actions. You have to feel that you know what you are doing while still opening yourself up to serendipity. Then, when you find it—when you hit upon that click moment that brings everything together—you need to be poised to double down on that opportunity.

Part 2 of this book will show you how to do just that.

PART II

SEIZING OPPORTUNITY

6

THE THREE RANDOM MOVES OF
DIANE VON FURSTENBERG

When Julie Nixon Eisenhower left home one morning for a speech she was to give later in the day, she was unaware that she was about to set in motion events that would change the world of fashion forever. The year was 1972 and the scandals surrounding her father, President Richard Nixon, were still far away. If she was worried at all, it might have been about what she was going to wear that day. "I probably averaged two or more speeches or appearances a week," she told me in an email. "I was always looking for clothing that traveled well and felt soft and comfortable, plus allowed me to move around quickly and freely." The president's daughter decided to put on a casual skirt she had purchased at Lord & Taylor. She chose a matching wrap top to complete the look.

As it turned out, the speech was televised. Coincidentally, the woman who had designed the skirt Julie Eisenhower was wearing was tuned in. On any other day the designer might have just smiled at having someone of such prominence wear her skirt, and she would have left it at that. But not that day. That day she saw something. She realized that the wrap top and skirt, worn together, had a nice look. It gave her an idea—Why not combine the ensemble into a dress?

The woman was New York socialite Diane von Furstenberg and the dress she created became known as the wrap dress. It arrived in 1973 in a distinct wood-grain print. "The dress was nothing, really—just a few yards of fabric with two sleeves and a wide wrap sash," the designer said. But it took the world by storm. With its wispy elegance, "the wrap" somehow managed to deliver on the promise of the 1970s independent woman unlike any other piece of clothing before it. It had a look that was seductive but not cheap; professional but not boring. The dress and its many prints and patterns spread like wildfire.

Von Furstenberg's business grew by more than 600 percent in that first year. Just a few seasons later, as 1976 drew to a close, von Furstenberg was shipping more than 25,000 units a week and had sold five million dresses in all. Celebrities and other A-list personalities were sporting the look in full force: Bianca Jagger, Gloria Steinem, and, of course, Julie Nixon Eisenhower. *Newsweek* put von Furstenberg on its cover in November of that year—a first for a female fashion designer. Indeed, Diane von Furstenberg, or DVF as she had come to be known, seemed poised to hold a permanent place among fashion's most elite.

Permanent turned out to be a few years. The *Newsweek* cover had caused the wrap to spike in demand all over the country. Her dresses were everywhere. "I remember in Minneapolis, going to a store on one side of the street," von Furstenberg wrote in her autobiography, "then to another store on the other side of the street, and recognizing that both stores had all of these dresses and they were all the same. This can't go on, I remember thinking. It doesn't make sense." Even worse, the dress's success had spurred countless imitations of varying quality. Some industry onlookers suspected trouble ahead. "I think she's peaked," said one fashion editor. "Just how many sun dresses can one collect?"

Not long after that, the bubble burst. In January 1978, in the wake of a debilitating nor'easter, her dresses were marked down in boutiques from coast to coast. Diane von Furstenberg, the Queen of Fashion, was left with $4 million worth of inventory. And just like that, she essentially vanished from the fashion scene.

*

In Part 1 we looked at how randomness drives success. We saw that, contrary to popular belief, most success does not occur as a result of logic and rigorous analysis. Instead, it comes from things we cannot predict and plan for: serendipitous moments, unexpected and spontaneous approaches, unusual combinations, and lucky breaks. Despite all of this, however, and perhaps because of it, we saw that each of us also needs a convincing rationale to fuel our actions—no matter where that rationale comes from.

In Part 2 we will look at how to think rationally about using randomness to drive success in our lives and organizations. This may seem like a strange approach when all our instincts tell us that we can't control randomness. After all, serendipity is what happens on top of the plans we put together. But what I am saying is that randomness should *be* the plan. What gives? This approach only works if we can not only increase the amount of randomness in our lives but also capture it when it presents something amazing. And as you will see very clearly—we can.

We can't escape the role randomness plays in our success or failure, but we can utilize its tremendous and enduring power. We can and must learn to use it as our primary strategic advantage. Gone are the days when a logical, well-analyzed strategy will help you predict success. Instead, unexpected events and insights will increasingly rule our lives. Indeed, it is these types of unexpected moments that can bring someone back from the ash heap of history.

*

After the wrap dress had run its course in 1978, DVF sold her other businesses, including her perfume and jewelry lines. She had fallen in love and followed her paramour to Paris. More than a decade later, in the mid-1990s, she returned to New York alone and ready to start over. But fashion is fickle and her name was "the dustiest you can have." She couldn't get anyone to return her phone calls. When she did manage to connect with fashion's current crop of stars, they treated her like a has-been.

DVF became convinced that her passage back into fashion would ride on the baby-boomers. These women had fallen in love with the wrap dress once—maybe nostalgia for carefree days and those lost decades would turn their heads a second time. The president of Saks Fifth Avenue was game. It seemed so logical, and it made so much sense. But the dress was a flop. The baby-boomers didn't have the bodies they had back in the seventies, and they left the wrap in the fitting rooms.

But then DVF noticed something unexpected. Her daughter Tatiana and her daughter's friends had started wearing *vintage* wrap dresses. Incredibly, they had paid $200 for them at trendy consignment shops. Two hundred dollars for a used dress? It seemed incomprehensible to DVF at first, but she realized quickly what was happening. And it was stunning. The wrap dress of the 1990s wasn't about the baby-boomers—it was about their daughters. The dress had, through some inexplicable transformation, become hot again, and contrary to everyone's prediction, it was hot with twentysomethings. Just as O-Zone couldn't possibly ever predict Gary Brolsma, there was no way that DVF could have guessed that college girls would be pulling her dresses off of back racks in vintage boutiques.

Von Furstenberg saw the opening. She relaunched her own clothing line and arranged distribution through the chic urban retailers that catered to young hipsters and, yet again, the wrap dress became a staple among trendsetters. "Today the wrap dress is simply iconic," said Rebecca Lay of the blog *Styluste*. "If you see one on the street, you either think it's a DVF, or a DVF knockoff." Now, as new and vintage versions of the dress turn up again and again, worn by a new generation of fashionistas, von Furstenberg continues to be celebrated and her world-famous wrap dress is featured in the Metropolitan Museum of Art's fashion collection. Today, she has shops in sixty-five countries, and Kate Middleton, the future queen of England, wears DVF's wrap dress on the covers of magazines. Diane von Furstenberg is once again at the top of the fashion mountain.

*

How can we explain Diane von Furstenberg's strange and winding road to success? There are multiple explanations to choose from. Perhaps it was her famous eye for design? Or maybe she is just a natural trend-spotter who's also extraordinarily tenacious, persistent beyond belief. When she first started her business, after all, she did everything herself, from breaking down boxes in the early morning hours to designing the patterns and prints, taking the orders, handling the invoices, sorting out the shipments in the warehouse, and picking and packing the clothes. So we know she was a hard worker. But we also know that she had good financial backing—she received a $30,000 loan from her father. On top of that, her short-lived marriage to German prince Egon von Furstenberg placed her at center stage in the New York social scene. And DVF had friends in high places within fashion. Diana Vreeland at *Vogue*, for example, was a huge supporter.

All of that is important, but in the end what it really adds up to is a big *so what*. Why? Because all of these explanations miss one crucial point: many people can claim these same advantages and attributes.

Style and a discerning eye for design are not so exceedingly rare—one walk through Nolita in New York City on a Sunday, when designers show off their latest styles, confirms that there is no shortage of design talent. And there are, of course, throngs of tenacious people in New York, Paris, and elsewhere who have both wealth and connections. But only a very few can amass the type of empire that DVF has built.

Just how much did that one dress matter? The year before she created the wrap dress, von Furstenberg had sales of just $1.2 million, even though she had connections at *Vogue*, loans from her father, and a strong work ethic. But the year *after* she introduced the ground-breaking design, her sales broke $14 million. Simply put, it transformed her career. Any credible explanation of her success must, therefore, start with that dress.

There was nothing like it on the market at the time, and that made all the difference. But that being the case, why is it that no one had figured it out earlier? The wrap dress was something special, yes, but it was so simple. *A piece of fabric with two sleeves and a wide elastic sash.* With all the designers, customers, market surveys, focus groups, magazines, and runways in all the fashion centers in all the world—how could they *all* have missed such a major fashion staple? And, perhaps most perplexing, how come von Furstenberg didn't create it even sooner?

"The idea for the wrap dress had not come out of a strategy session or a market analysis," according to von Furstenberg. The fashion industry, more than almost any other, is filled with legions of competitors with narrow advantages. If it had been the result of strategic planning, she very likely would have faced stiff competition from the start. But the wrap dress was not obvious—it was unique. Unique insights are one of a kind; they are random, unexpected, and serendipitous.

Sustainable success, then, requires a sustainable advantage such as uniqueness, whether that has to do with your product or service, business model or distribution system, brand or quality. Randomness delivers that. In the chapters that follow we will look at how to create randomness and take advantage of it when we do. The type of randomness we are interested in comes in three separate varieties, and DVFs rise and fall (and rise) clearly illustrates all three. If we want to understand how to seize opportunities in an unpredictable world we must use all three approaches. Together they make the case for a complete rethinking of the purpose for strategy and how to achieve success.

*

The first type of randomness applies to the specific instant when an unexpected connection or event changes the trajectory of success. It is that serendipitous moment that changes everything. What if Diane von Furstenberg had never seen Julie Nixon Eisenhower's televised speech? Would she have missed the wrap dress altogether? Would her life have been different? It is almost impossible to believe otherwise. Of course, one might argue that maybe—just maybe—our lives have a predetermined destiny and these types of moments do not much matter. If it hadn't been the wrap dress it would have been something else. DVF would have broken through eventually. There is some truth in this belief, as we will see, but it is also true that our destinies are determined by specific, fleeting points in time.

Sometimes success or failure turns on minute, seemingly insignificant moments of unpredictability. These can't be planned or anticipated, because we never know exactly when events will fall into place to spark an insight or change our behavior. Either way they represent a singular moment when our fortunes seem to veer in one direction or another. DVF had many such moments, and one of them was watching the president's daughter on TV.

Could she have engineered such an amazing insight? Of course not—if that were the case she would be introducing a new fashion phenomenon every month. Although DVF may have been sketching designs and reworking patterns and samples for months or years, this specific experience at this particular time—impossible to predict—was the moment when the stars aligned. Everything fell into place. She saw Julie Nixon Eisenhower's skirt and wrap-top and . . . *click*.

This means that one of the ways to increase randomness in our lives is to increase the number of these types of moments. In chapters 7 and 8 we will explore more fully what these click moments are and how we can create them.

The click moment, however, offers an incomplete explanation of Diane von Furstenberg's success. DVF must have had new design ideas all the time, some that she acted on and others she ignored. But how much did she really know about the success potential for any one of those designs? When she created the wrap dress, she had no idea if people would like it. She only knew that *she* liked it. Which meant that von Furstenberg had to take a chance on the wrap dress. She had to spend time at the drawing table detailing and developing her brief moment of insight, and she had to do that at the expense of trying

93

other designs. Then she had to cut it, get material, and try various design combinations over and over until they felt and fit right. Finally, she had to try to sell the piece to distributors and retail stores. Until that moment, and even for a while after that, she had no real clue as to whether this idea of hers was going to take off.

This way of pursuing success says that when you try something new, you are stepping into a world of unpredictability, just as you do when you place a bet. Which brings us to the second method for increasing randomness—making bets.

Not long ago I shared a stage with Ed Catmull, the president of Pixar Animation Studios, discussing how to create amazing experiences. In his case, of course, the experiences involved movies. To date, Pixar has had an unprecedented run of successful movies—twelve in all—from *Toy Story* to *Cars* to *Up*. At one point in the discussion, an audience member asked Catmull if Pixar was playing it too safe—the studio had not lost any of its bets. Catmull surprised the audience by responding that Pixar probably had roughly the same failure rate as every other studio.

"We have had films that failed," he said. "We just didn't release them." Catmull went on to describe what he meant. "*Toy Story 2* was a restart. In *Ratatouille* we kept one line from the original script. The first version of *Up* took place in a floating castle in the sky. The only thing left was the bird and the word 'up.' The next version, there was a house that floated up and landed on a lost Russian dirigible. In the next version the bird laid eggs that conferred long life. You can say that these were failures along the way. The things that don't work right are just things that we tried."

What he is describing is the process of using randomness to your statistical advantage. If Pixar had the ability to predict what will succeed, obviously it would not bother with unworkable ideas. But it does bother because it has to roll the dice many times in order to get it right. In chapters 9 and 10 we will look at these types of bets. We will learn why more money tends not to improve your chances, and what you can do instead to capture randomness and increase your overall odds of success.

There is also a third way to think about randomness. One that acknowledges that success must be a result of dozens, even thousands, of possible forces that change with every action and interaction. Success is a collision of events, desires, and effort that becomes an untraceable and jumbled mix of outcomes. This view says that specific outcomes are a result of interconnectivity as opposed to any individual's detailed game plan. When Diane von Furstenberg launched her wrap dress she could not possibly have factored in all of the outside forces that played a part in how fast the idea spread. Nor was she in a position to foresee how or why her creation would inspire the incredible cadre of imitators that would erode her advantage. Or that the enormous response to her *Newsweek* cover would set in motion a sequence of events that would destroy her success. But she also could not have predicted the combination of forces that caused a new, younger generation to find the wrap dress intriguing more than a decade after its demise. I call these forces complex forces and they can grab hold of us, our ideas, and everyone around us in untold ways that we can neither predict nor control.

This view of randomness holds that a purposeful bet is powerful not because it may succeed, but because it opens you up to unexpected interactions and effects. Our world is interconnected to an unprecedented degree, which means we are more exposed to complex random forces than ever before. We also tend to dramatically overestimate our ability to predict the effects of our actions. In truth, we have no way of knowing how a person, or a hundred thousand people, will act or react when we put something out there.

Complex forces turned "Dragostea din tei" into a success in the United States. The song was released onto the scene with essentially no marketing or promotional efforts. A few years back, with such minimal support, it would have languished. But today, the song was discovered, and through forces completely unknown to the band it starts bouncing around in the endless sea of possibilities. Someone hears it and decides to make a video that he thinks can't possibly interest anyone but his friends. But it becomes the most-watched video in history and the single shoots up the charts. O-Zone could not have planned for this turn of events and the band certainly didn't predict such a

95

turn. And yet, any given idea or project is exposed to these same complex forces from almost the moment it takes shape.

While these complex forces may seem to be entirely out of our control, in chapters 11 and 12 we will look more deeply into their structure and explore ways in which you can harness them.

These three types of random moves together can explain, at least in part, why successful people tend to be personable, hardworking, and somewhat talented. You have an easier time creating click moments if you connect with more people, something that comes naturally to social creatures. You have a simpler time making a successful bet if you try a lot of them, and hardworking people tend to be productive. And you are more likely to get caught up in complex forces if you are out in the world doing stuff, which is easier if you know how to do something well.

That said, most of us do all of these things in an utterly non-random way—we look to meet people who we *know* can help us, we work hard day after day without really taking chances trying anything new, and we use our skill in unsurprising ways. Yet, we *can* push towards incorporating these random moves into our lives.

This book argues that successful people and organizations increasingly invite randomness and take advantage of it when it presents itself. Diane von Furstenberg couldn't (and didn't) foresee the pathway for the rise, fall, and second coming of her famous fashion empire. Her success was far less a result of strategy, planning, and analysis than we would like to believe. Instead it was a result of click moments, purposeful bets, and complex forces. Out of the three random actions described, click moments set the stage for the other two, opening the door for both the bets we place and the complex forces that can arise from those bets. So let's take a look at just what these click moments are and how you can create them. Just consider what happened one warm summer night in Redmond, Washington, when the serendipitous meeting of two men at a party altered the course of what was to become one of the world's most powerful companies.

7

CLICK MOMENTS

On May 22, 1990, Microsoft launched its new operating system, Windows 3.0, to incredible demand. "This is probably the most anticipated product in the history of the world," said a Smith Barney analyst on the day of its release. Within six months, Microsoft had sold two million copies—and a few months later, sales totaled more than nine million. At the time, it was the best-selling software ever.

The release marked a watershed moment that would forever change the company—and the world. Windows 3.0 set the stage for Microsoft to execute one of the most dominant strategies in the history of business. The company went from being one of many successful software makers to *the* global technology titan. A behemoth. In less than a decade it grew to become the largest company in the world, valued at over $500 billion. Windows 3.0 was the chief reason for this success.

This new operating system was an incredible improvement over Microsoft's earlier efforts. Windows 1.0 and 2.0 had been, quite literally, useless. They were catastrophic, bug-riddled disasters—2.0 was never even released widely. But Windows 3.0 was different. It boasted sophisticated graphics, faster programs, and better overall performance. The user interface was so strong that Windows was finally a viable competitor to the Apple Macintosh.

But Microsoft did more than just release an improved operating system—it released a whole suite of business software, later called Microsoft Office. It is hard to overstate just how pervasive these office tools became. Version 3.0 of Windows was the first to be broadly pre-installed on computers. Selling all the Office programs together as part of a "value pack" was the stroke of marketing genius that brought Microsoft software into tens of millions of homes and offices. As the development of the Office suite progressed, the programs began to work better together, so that buying the products separately became relatively rare. The rise of the Windows operating system meant similar success for Word, Excel, and PowerPoint.

In hindsight the basic features of Microsoft's strategy seem deceptively simple: first, create a platform software, one that everyone must run. This was Windows 3.0. Second, create software that runs at its very best on this platform. This was the Office Suite along with many other software applications, such as Money and Outlook. Third, release upgrades of the software. Once Windows 3.0 had been adopted, Microsoft released Windows NT, then Windows 95, then Windows 98, and so on. For each upgrade Microsoft had an opportunity to sell all of its software again and again—and again.

Microsoft went on to dominate the world of technology for well over a decade. People have marveled at the brilliance—and ruthlessness—of Microsoft's strategy, and many have attempted to copy it. The foundation, however, was Windows 3.0. It was the keystone that allowed Microsoft to build a global empire. If its new operating system had failed, it seems clear that some other visually based operating system would have ruled the day in its place. For Microsoft, then, it must have been critical that Windows 3.0 did *not* fail. It was the linchpin of the company's strategy. It *had* to work.

And that's where this story starts to get a little bit weird. If you look closely at how Windows became the centerpiece of Microsoft's growth plan, you'll find that there's something decidedly curious about the company's rise to greatness. If you have eight thousand employees at your disposal, for instance, and you are about to launch the single most important operating system in history, wouldn't you have more than three people working on it? Wouldn't you have your top talent, your very best and smartest programmers, all over it rather than teaming them up with your competitor? And wouldn't you push this breakthrough for all it's worth rather than leaving it to shrivel up and die? As it turns out, after careful deliberation, Microsoft did *all* of those things. In the end, they left what would become the most influential software in history for dead. Windows 3.0 would never have been released had it not been for a chance encounter between two men at a Friday-night party.

*

There is something disconcerting about the notion that a company's fate can hinge on something as fleeting as a single moment in time. Just how much can any one random meeting or event affect the future of an enterprise or an individual's life, anyway? It seems impossible that a large and successful corporation like Microsoft could have reached such remarkable market dominance just because of a single insight or encounter. These types of companies have elaborate strategies, complex processes, tons of people, and are part of a much larger system. No single event, it seems, should be able to make or break an organization of that size.

The vast majority of events or meetings or impressions, of course, have little impact on our lives or on the fates of our organizations, no matter what their size. While I was writing this chapter at a café next to our home, I must have said hi to at least five or six different people who sat down next to me. I can barely recall a single one of them today, and as far as I know none of those moments will have any serious impact on my life. We all have an incredible number of meetings and impressions every day but they almost always keep us on the same trajectory we started out on. They are either reinforcing what we already know or what we are already doing, or they barely register at all. But there are also, clearly, a very few moments that make us see something new, choose a different path, make a decision that changes everything—even if we don't realize it at the time. In fact, if we rewind the history of our lives or of an organization's journey it is inescapable that certain moments, certain meetings, events, impressions and insights, mattered far more than others. I call those moments *click moments*.

*

The idea of a click moment, it must be said, has a somewhat mystical quality to it. It seems like something straight out of a Hollywood movie, such as when Bruce Wayne discovers the Batcave in *Batman Begins* and his past finally catches up with his future, or when Cary Grant locks eyes with his leading lady, and you know they will fall madly in love before the credits roll. That slightly surreal quality is perhaps the reason why we more easily accept the existence of click moments in two specific areas of our lives: romantic love and the moment of idea creation.

Many people accept (and even expect) serendipity in their romantic life. We are on the lookout for, and revel in, romantic chance encounters, such as the one I heard from an acquaintance: "I was sitting next to this guy on a flight to Hawaii when the engine caught fire. We made an emergency landing and we even saw smoke and flames strike out of the engine. The moment we landed we stared into each other's eyes and started kissing. We got married a few years later."

The idea that we can apply logic to figure out how to be successful in our romantic life seems ludicrous. Instead, most people look for opportunities to "get lucky" in love. They attend parties, hang out at coffee shops, go on blind dates, answer online personals, join organizations, pick up hobbies, attend benefits, and go to clubs and bars. What we are often looking for in such scenarios, besides having some genuine fun, is the chance to meet someone and possibly, perhaps, maybe fall in love. We hope that something will click, without having any idea when, where, or with whom.

History is filled with these encounters. Benjamin Franklin met his wife-to-be while she was standing in her father's doorway. Franklin had arrived in Philadelphia that morning and was simply walking down the street, eating a freshly baked bun, when their eyes locked. He claimed it was love at first sight. At the 1972 Munich Olympics, the hostess, Silvia Sommerlath, noticed a man watching her through binoculars from a few feet away. She took the hint and started talking with him. That man turned out to be the crown prince of Sweden, King Carl XVI Gustaf. They were married four years later. When asked by the *Dagens Nyheter*, the leading Swedish newspaper, "What had happened when you two met?" the king answered: "It just went click."

Many of us are likewise prepared to acknowledge the role of serendipity when a new idea strikes. We credit it with inspiring ideas behind successful start-ups, brilliant scientific breakthroughs, and incredible works of art. There are literally thousands of published accounts of these types of moments. For instance, in 1963 the American vascular radiologist Charles Dotter accidentally threaded a catheter through a clogged pelvic artery during a diagnostic procedure. To his great surprise he found that this accident ended up helping his patient. The following year he tried the same technique again, and this time it saved a woman's leg from amputation. A couple of years later another physician, Dr. Andreas Gruentzig, learned of Dotter's breakthrough at a lecture in Frankfurt, Germany. Suddenly he made a connection— Gruentzig realized, out of the blue, that he could take this treatment even further by using inflatable balloons small enough to pass into tiny coronary arteries. Angioplasty surgery was born.

But that is generally about as far as we are prepared to stretch ourselves. Once an idea has moved beyond its genesis, most of us think

101

click moments have pretty much played out. Other approaches take over. The people we hire, the processes we set up, the strategies we develop, and the analyses we run are far more important. We worry more about competition and less about moments of insight or how to set ourselves up to "get lucky." Instead, good fortune now becomes a matter of hard work, smart decisions, and calculated risks. We want to believe that exceptional strategy is the driver of success because that would allow us to understand why everything worked out so well initially—and repeat it in the future. But the truth is that click moments continue influencing events and sometimes entire corporate strategies well after that initial moment of inspiration.

Which brings us back to Microsoft. The fact is that they *did* have a strategy for reaching world domination, and by any measure it was a very good one—it just had *nothing* to do with Windows.

*

In the early 1980s Bill Gates saw that Microsoft was on the verge of being left behind. Its first operating system, MS-DOS, had proved extremely popular, but although it had become the industry standard it was text-based and virtually impossible for most lay people to maneuver. This became a major liability as the world moved toward more visually pleasing operating systems.

In 1982, a company called VisiCorp demo'd VisiOn and it looked beautiful. Microsoft took note. Shortly after, Apple demonstrated the Macintosh, which had cute little icons and buttons to push. Feeling the pressure, Microsoft began developing its own simpler operating system and called it Windows, promising it would be first to market.

Instead it came last. It took three years for Windows 1.0 to be readied for launch and when it finally did take off, it was incredibly buggy—effectively unusable. The *New York Times* remarked that running Windows 1.0 was "akin to pouring molasses in the Arctic." Unfortunately, 2.0 was no better. It was so bug-ridden that after its initial September 1987 release, Microsoft was forced to release several patches immediately just to make it work.

It was roughly at this point that Bill Gates and his number two, Steve Ballmer, realized that Windows had a fatal design flaw, one that made it unlikely *ever* to become a successful operating system. The deal breaker was that Windows was able to access only a scant sliver of the memory it needed to perform its tasks. No matter how much memory a computer actually had available, Windows could only access 640 kilobytes. That led to an incredibly unstable system that would slow to a crawl and inevitably crash. Supplying Windows with greater memory access, however, was no small challenge, and even after years of trying Microsoft was unable to achieve it.

Gates and Ballmer started to devise another strategy. The solution seemed obvious. IBM was the largest technology player on the block back then and it was very interested in developing a new operating system, one without memory limitations. Gates realized that if IBM developed such a system, Microsoft would be toast. IBM was much bigger and far more powerful; it would crush DOS and possibly anything else Microsoft might have come up with. IBM, on the other hand, realized that Microsoft had deep expertise in developing software, expertise that they lacked. A partnership seemed like a perfect match.

The two firms formed an alliance. With Windows on the shelf, Bill Gates and the head of IBM's personal-computing business, Jim Cannavino, were at last fully committed to developing a new operating system: OS/2. It was to be everything that Windows was not. Just six months prior to its release, both companies began promoting it heavily. Gates believed that OS/2 would herald a new future for the organization and he made sure that everybody knew the way forward. It was better to be alive and strong with an industry giant at your side than weak and by yourself.

Simultaneously, Microsoft had developers working on software programs such as Word and Excel, but because OS/2 wasn't ready, they got started by writing the programs for Windows. When OS/2 was completed Microsoft would "port" the code to the new operating system; that is, they would make the changes necessary to ensure that

Word could run on OS/2. This made a lot of sense because it would allow IBM and Microsoft to launch OS/2 with a slate of good applications already running.

In the meantime, Microsoft wound down the Windows 3.0 development project. The budget was cut and the development team was diverted to other projects. Steve Ballmer had pulled every skilled person off the project and placed them with IBM's team, which included more than 250 of Microsoft's people. Ballmer lobbied aggressively to have Windows killed off completely. IBM was Microsoft's life raft: if the company had sensed that Microsoft might keep working on Windows as some sort of hedge, they might have pulled back. That would have been a disaster. In the end, the little "hobby project" called 3.0 continued, but with no budget or timelines, and a skeleton crew of three people. They were pretty much expected to ease the troubled operating system into oblivion.

But they never got the chance.

*

When we think of how large companies become successful, we think of what Bill Gates and Steve Ballmer did. They looked at their strengths and weaknesses; they assessed their opportunities and threats; and then they made a logical call: go for the kill if you can, or team up if you can't.

And in that context, it made perfect sense for Microsoft to partner with IBM. But great strategies are not based on what makes sense. Rather, they are based on what sets you apart and what you can reasonably defend. Those types of insights are almost never the result of a logical calculation. Instead, small, fortuitous observations can tip the balance. Consider how YouTube developed its main strategy. Today it is the single largest site for uploading and watching videos, and it has been since its inception. In retrospect the idea seems dead simple and incredibly obvious, almost unbelievably so. There were any number of people in Silicon Valley beating their heads against the wall because they had not figured it out.

But not even the founders of YouTube were clever enough to figure out what YouTube was all about at first. In fact, their company started out as an online dating site called Tune In, Hook Up. People would post videos of themselves on the site and prospective dates could vote on them. The idea didn't work out, but it laid the technical foundation for another, more potent idea. After two of the founders, Chad Hurley and Steve Chen, were unable to email a video of a dinner party they'd attended, and after the third founder, Jawed Karim, could not find a video of Janet Jackson's Superbowl "wardrobe malfunction," the three made a momentary connection: what if there was a site where you could upload videos and anyone could see them? YouTube launched on February 14, 2005, and took off like a three-stage rocket. Google bought it eighteen months later for $1.65 billion.

When we hear stories like these they surprise us because we tend to believe that a great company must have started with a great idea. We want to think that the minds behind the idea were acting in a carefully calculated and deliberate way. Having a plan in place would mean that we could imitate their approach. But in this case, following YouTube's approach would mean launching a crappy dating site. That seems like a mistake, one that some careful, logical thinking would allow us to avoid. But launching something—even a crappy dating site—is *exactly* what we should do as long as we are open for click moments that can change our trajectory.

Some of our culture's most iconic images were the result of seren-dipitous moments. It seems inconceivable in retrospect, because when things work really well we think they just *had* to be planned. When George Lucas was filming *Star Wars: A New Hope* in Tunisia, he real-ized halfway through the filming that Obi-Wan Kenobi should actu-ally die in his fight with Darth Vader because the Death Star just didn't pose enough of a threat. "As I originally wrote it," Lucas says, "Ben Kenobi and Vader had a swordfight, and Ben hits a switch and the door slams closed and they all run away and Vader is left standing there with egg on his face." Lucas needed Obi-Wan to die since it would illustrate the power of the evil Empire. But with Kenobi's death, another idea followed: his spirit could join the Force and actually guide Luke Skywalker through danger and challenges. When Lucas told Alec Guinness, who played Obi-Wan, that his character would die and become a ghost for the remainder of the movie, Guinness became so outraged he threatened to walk. "I'm not doing this," he warned Lucas. But the director managed to calm the actor down, and today Obi-Wan's death and subsequent "ghost" voice saying *May the Force be with you* has become movie legend.

Click moments can change even the best-laid plans of generals and empires. In 41 BC the Roman Empire edged towards civil war. Following the assassination of Julius Caesar, control of the Empire was split between his adopted son Octavian and his trusted general, Marc Anthony. Both men had larger ambitions. If Anthony could solidify his control of Rome's eastern territories he could use that power to eventually control all of Rome. He summoned the Egyptian queen Cleopatra to what would become modern-day Turkey for help. They both had their reasons for this meeting: Antony needed a benefactor to fund his ambitions; Cleopatra needed the protection of Rome to safeguard her throne. But when the queen came sailing down the river in a gilded barge, dressed in the garb of Venus, Antony was instantly smitten. Antony met Cleopatra on her floating palace for dinner and the two fell madly in love. Soon the general abandoned his military campaign to accompany her to Alexandria. Historians Michel Chauveau and David Lorton remarked that "it is difficult to comprehend the political motives behind Antony's conduct, if indeed there were any." Octavian's retaliation was swift, and Marc Antony fell on his sword while Cleopatra embraced the asp.

YouTube changed paths based on an unexpected connection, Obi-Wan Kenobi became an iconic spirit after a surprising insight, and two of the world's most successful rulers found their plans ruined following a mutual glance during dinner. One moment was enough to change everything. And it was exactly such a moment that changed the future for Microsoft.

*

It became clear pretty quickly that Microsoft and IBM did not see eye to eye on a lot of things. At the time, IBM was big and slow and Microsoft was small and fast. IBM wanted every change in the code documented. Microsoft wanted every line of code changed, documentation be damned. The two companies were soon ensnared in a bureaucratic mess.

Some of the engineers on the Microsoft team had had enough. One of them, Dave Weise, wanted out. Weise, a brilliant computer scientist and physics PhD, had a bit of a subversive streak. While at MIT he had been a member of its infamous blackjack team. He and his roommates ran sophisticated computer simulations that helped them count cards in Atlantic City. Burned out by the red tape at IBM, he needed space to breathe and a tough challenge. The defunct Windows team seemed ideal. But when Ballmer finally approved him to join the team, despite his brilliance even Weise couldn't find a fix for Windows' memory issues.

At about the same time another man, Murray Sargent, showed up on the Microsoft campus. He was a professor of optics at the University of Arizona, a physics PhD, and an all-around hands-on type of guy. In his spare time Sargent had developed a program called an SST debugger. It was an exceptional piece of software and Microsoft bought it when they were unable to hire him (he joined years later, anyway). In 1988, Sargent took a sabbatical at the Max Planck Institute in Germany, but on his way to Europe he took a detour to Redmond to help Microsoft work with his SST debugger.

One Friday night Microsoft was hosting a party during the opening of a new manufacturing plant. "There were at least 500 people there," Sargent recalled. After Sargent arrived he walked around meeting people. That's when he ran into Dave Weise. They knew each other from their time together at Dynamics Systems Research, and the two were old friends. For no particular reason, Sargent decided to give his old friend a hard time.

"Windows . . . is a joke," he started. "You just added 64K to the high memory area, but Windows needs an awful lot more than 64K. It

107

needs a major transfusion." Sargent went on, "What you really should do is get Windows into protected mode and blow away the 640K RAM barrier altogether."

He was having some fun with his friend, and his solution was in the front of his mind because of the SST debugger project. It was completely off the cuff . . . but it could work. By placing Windows into something called "protected mode," significant memory might be freed up. Sargent didn't really expect to be taken seriously, but to his surprise Weise countered with intent in his voice. "You're absolutely right," he said. "Let's go do it."

"Uh, okay," Sargent answered. "How about tomorrow?"

"No, now," Weise said. "Let's go do it right now."

It was Friday, June 3, and the clock had just struck 7 p.m. They left the party, charged up the computer, loaded Murray's debugging software, and started going through the Windows code line by line. Suddenly they faced the first fault in the code identified by the SST debugger. "And Dave just fixed it," said Sargent.

It was a powerful moment. "We knew we were onto something big, at that point," Sargent told me many years later. Microsoft's plan had been all about OS/2. Windows wasn't even part of the equation. But here they were, solving the major sticking points step by step. When they stopped for the evening they both knew that it was possible to put Windows into protected mode and make sure it could run on any machine.

They didn't say a word to Gates, Ballmer, or even the official Windows project manager, Phil Barrett, but they worked feverishly to complete the hacking of the code. Midway through the summer, Sargent was invited for a jog by Ballmer. During their exchange, Sargent didn't give any details about what was going on, but he did get Ballmer thinking about what it would be like to have Windows running in protect mode without any memory constraints. "You know, that's what we wanted to do all along," Ballmer answered. That is, before the IBM partnership.

A few weeks later Microsoft held a Windows planning meeting for which Bill Gates was going to be on hand. Ballmer had finally figured out, on the very night before the meeting, what Dave Weise had been up to, and he interrupted the usual updates and said "Bill . . . I think Dave has something to suggest."

"What do you have?" Gates asked.

"Well, I think basically we should run Windows in protect mode," Weise said. "And by the way . . . I have it running downstairs." Gates listened intently as Weise sketched out the details of his work. Then he fell silent for a few moments before saying "We should do it."

Suddenly, and seemingly out of nowhere, Bill Gates and Steve Ballmer had a protected-mode, graphics-based operating system with a bevy of applications dropped right in their laps. Memory, graphics, speed, and software programs—already written for Windows, no need to port to OS/2—were what people wanted. Windows had them all.

Microsoft employees couldn't believe it. "My jaw was dropping lower and lower as I moved from office to office," wrote Larry Osterman some fifteen years later in a blog post thanking Dave Weise for his contributions to Microsoft. The project had just received the official go-ahead and Larry could scarcely believe his eyes. "They had display drivers that could display 256 bitmap color on the screen. The best OS/2 could do at the time was sixteen colors," Osterman said. There was no comparison between the platforms. "Here was this little skunkworks project in building three that was sitting on what was clearly the most explosive product Microsoft had ever produced."

Fate smiled down on Microsoft that summer and they got very lucky indeed. If it hadn't been for the chance encounter between Weise and Sargent, the world's PCs might be running OS/2 instead of Windows. When domination is so total, it may appear from the outside that it had to have been carefully planned. But the truth is that there are moments when fortunes stand or fall based on chance insights and encounters. Weise and Sargent meeting at a party on the

Redmond campus was one of them. Weise had a major bug to fix and Sargent had debugging software.

Click.

*

I love stories like these. They reveal a remarkable truth about how success happens. But they are also perplexing. How is it possible that such a meeting was left to chance? Why hadn't someone at Microsoft realized the value of putting these two people together earlier? Both Bill Gates and Steve Ballmer, as well as the brilliant hotshot Nathan Myhrvold, knew both men. They knew that Weise had returned to the Windows group, and they knew the power and purpose of Sargent's debugging program. But they couldn't make the connection. Stranger still, Dave Weise and Murray Sargent were old friends, and even *they* didn't put the pieces together until meeting by chance at a party. Sargent makes the point emphatically: "Microsoft had many others that could have made the connection but all of them were busy working on OS/2," he says. Sargent was really the only person left that could have helped Dave. And as it happened, he stopped by Microsoft that summer and went to a party.

With the benefit of hindsight, everything seems obvious. But the reason these people did not connect the dots has to do with how connections and associations happen. The whole reason for bringing in Sargent's software was to improve Microsoft's own debugging program—it had nothing to do with fixing Windows. Our mind tends to keep separate concepts apart. It requires something unusual to spark the connection. The opposite of click moments are planned situations with expected outcomes. On their own, these don't generate the chaos and randomness needed to discover new, unique ideas. They have a harder time shaking the box of concepts, projects, and ideas to form new combinations. As it turns out, click moments have three qualities that distinguish them from our normal approach to making connections and coming up with ideas.

First, they tend to occur when two separate concepts, ideas, or people meet. Weise and Sargent meeting at a party is a textbook case, but so are most other click moments when we scratch the surface a little bit. Wrap top *and* skirt combined, uploading *and* viewing videos, waffle iron *and* running shoes. The list goes on. The key to these connections, however, is that they are not all created equal. Instead, you have a much higher chance of creating a click moment if the two concepts, ideas, or persons are very different from each other, or come to a particular situation with completely different mindsets. I talk a lot about this phenomenon in my previous book and have called the place where these concepts meet the Intersection. These Intersections are fertile for creating click moments.

Second, click moments are impossible to predict. Situations that we think will be amazing tend to disappoint while encounters that we never expected to amount to anything can surprise us. You are more likely to meet someone interesting or hit upon an unusual idea when you *least* expect it. This is something that rings true on the dating scene as much as anywhere else. We tend to have an easier time falling for someone who surprises us. Defining insights are like that as well: they rarely come when we need or expect them. This is not to say that there is nothing at all leading up to such a moment. In fact, much of the time click moments are a series of random insights that come together all at once—latent hunches waiting for something to ignite a connection. But the clarifying moment is a random event that we didn't see coming.

Which brings us to the third characteristic of click moments. They often elicit an emotional response such as happiness, awe, or excitement. David Weise's reaction to Sargent's teasing suggestion was emotional, not purely rational. Emotion is critical because it provides us with an irrationally strong desire to take the idea to the next level, bypassing our need for logical solutions. Emotions fortify our instincts and allow us to avoid the type of overanalysis that can kill a great early-stage idea. Instead of asking whether an idea makes a lot of sense, for instance, we may start to work on a solution right away. Did it matter that Sargent and Weise took off immediately that night to

111

test their idea? We will never know, of course, but it's certainly possible. If they had waited until the next morning, the irrationally strong desire to act might have subsided. It is hard to tell. But we do know that ideas that seem brilliant one day often seem to fade if we get a chance to sleep on them. This uncertainty suggests that one should at the very least process a click moment when it happens so as not to let it slip through one's fingers.

Click moments are a fact of life. They happen without warning and can result from a wide range of experiences, like reading, conversations, observations, sounds, and physical sensations, to name just a few. Philo Farnsworth was plowing a potato field—row after row after row—when it suddenly occurred to him that an electron beam could scan images line by line and—*click*—the television was born. The archduke of Austria-Hungary was assassinated and—*click*—World War One erupted. Velcro, Post-it notes, and Susan Boyle—*click*, *click*, and *click*.

They happen everywhere and influence companies and individuals all the time. In fact, you would be hard-pressed to find successful individuals or companies for whom click moments were not a major reason for their success. It is therefore critical that such moments are part of any formal approach for achieving success. If we wish to increase our chances of reaching greatness we must increase the number of click moments in our life. The following chapter will show you how.

8

HOW TO CREATE CLICK MOMENTS

In the spring of 1983, Howard Schultz, the new director of retail operations and marketing for Starbucks, traveled to Milan, Italy, to attend an international housewares show. On the morning after he arrived, Schultz decided to walk from his hotel to the convention center. Along the way, on a side street he noticed a small espresso bar. He was intrigued. When he went inside, the cashier smiled and gave a nod. Behind the counter another man greeted him cheerfully. Schultz heard a huge hiss of steam escaping the espresso machine. He watched the *barista,* as he later learned the man was called, prepare a shot of espresso for one customer and craft a foamy cappuccino for another, all while engaging in friendly banter with the customers standing around the counter.

Schultz left, but he had walked barely ten feet before noticing another espresso bar only half a block away, this one even more crowded than the first. When he walked inside, he saw the barista greeting customers by name; people were laughing and talking. He found two similar shops just down the block, all packed with customers. He realized these espresso bars were everywhere in Milan.

At the time, Starbucks did not sell coffee by the cup. The Seattle-based retailer carried specialty coffee beans by the pound and sold high-end home brewing equipment. Schultz, in fact, had ventured to the conference to look at kitchen appliances, coffeemakers, and other items for the store. But when the trade show concluded for the day, Schultz returned to the streets to explore more espresso bars. They had piqued his interest. Some were stylish and upscale; others attracted a working-class clientele. Most had just a few chairs, and opera music playing in the background. Schultz was surprised by the sheer number of these establishments. "There were 1,500 alone in the city of Milan, a city the size of Philadelphia," he said. "They were on every street corner, and all were packed."

His biggest revelation, however—the one that made him really stop and take notice—came when he tasted a café latte for the first time. The barista pulled a shot of espresso, steamed a frothy pitcher of milk, poured the two together into a cup, and put a dollop of foam on the top. Schultz was floored by what he tasted. It was, he said, "the perfect drink." He realized that despite his employers' expertise in all things coffee, they had missed something huge. Starbucks had it all wrong. Selling equipment and grinding coffee by the bag wasn't the big opportunity. Coffee was meant to be a communal experience, to be shared with friends, not consumed in private. "It was like an epiphany," he said. "It was so immediate and physical that I was shaking." And that was when he realized: *no one in America knows about this.*

*

114 **Howard Schultz was** probably not the first American to have this insight. But he was the *right* person and the notion struck him at the *right* moment. But as we shall see, there are certain things Schultz did,

and ways that he did them, that increased his chances of having this insight.

At first glance, it may seem like click moments should be easy to manufacture. If you want to increase the number of chance encounters in your life, after all, you only need to meet more people, expose yourself to more ideas, and consequently garner more impressions. If that is true, then it follows that we should attend more parties, travel more, spend more time on social networking sites such as Facebook, go to more conferences, or even move to someplace with a large population, such as New York or Hong Kong.

Although these approaches all have merit, they somehow seem inadequate. Take this guy I met while traveling through Tuscany in northern Italy. He was an American tourist and he had decided to not let a single moment of his vacation go to waste. He had just come from Pisa, and before that he had been to Venice, Siena, Milan, the Amalfi coast, and Sicily, and was about to head to Rome the following day. This was day ten of his vacation. I asked him what he had enjoyed so far or what had stood out in his mind; but he really had no idea. "I'll figure out if I've had fun by the time I come home," he said, "by looking at my photos."

It is possible to travel the world and see nothing that changes your career or your life. You can go to parties and not connect with anyone, and people can live entirely predictable lives even in New York City. Although Diane von Furstenberg saw Julie Nixon Eisenhower on TV and had a powerful insight, most of us could easily spend a hundred hours in front of that same TV and come nowhere near such a click moment. And despite the fact that Murray Sargent and Dave Weise had a game-changing insight at work, most of us can easily spend years at our job and still fail to make that type of connection with colleagues. In other words, if you want to increase your chances of having a click moment, it is not enough to expose yourself to more people or have more impressions. We do that all day. Something else is required.

In this chapter we will examine four ways that individuals and organizations can increase their chances of having moments that will

115

dramatically alter their path to success. The one thing these methods have in common, individually and together, is that each purposefully introduces randomness into our lives, careers, and organizations.

1. Take Your Eyes Off the Ball

One of the most intriguing parts of Howard Schultz's story is how the idea for today's Starbucks actually came to him. His big insight had *nothing* to do with housewares. Yet he had traveled to Italy to attend a housewares convention. He was not there to research the world's best cup of coffee. This brings us to our first approach for increasing click moments. You need to take time, even schedule time, to explore things that are not directly related to your immediate goal. You need to take your eyes off the ball in order to see and connect with the possibilities around you. This is a challenge for most of us, however, because we are wired to stay focused on the task at hand. Consider, for instance, the following exercise: Below are five cards. I want you to pick one and make sure you remember it. Then turn the page.

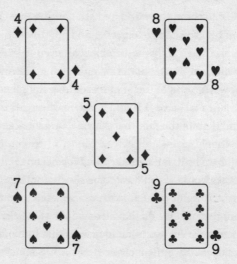

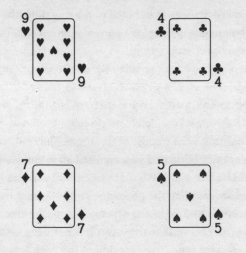

You'll see that I have removed the card you are thinking about. Not bad, considering I wrote the book before you even chose your card. Now, obviously you know there is a trick involved. Do we all think about the same card? That seems very unlikely. The explanation is simple: if you compare both pages you will see that none of the four cards pictured above are the same as the cards on the previous page. I changed *all* the cards.

It is a parlor trick that almost never fails, and there is a reason for that. When you focus on one thing exclusively—in this case, your card—you miss everything else that's going on around you. You become oblivious, in a sense. The name for this phenomenon is inattentional blindness, a frequently studied human phenomenon. The most famous psychological study on this effect is known simply as "Gorillas in our Midst".

You might have heard of it (if you haven't, you can take the test here before reading further: www.theinvisiblegorilla.com). The study is famous because the results are so extreme. The test is a video of two teams playing basketball. Each team consists of three people; one team is dressed in white and the other in black. The players dribble back and forth and throw the ball to their teammates. The subjects of

117

the test are asked to silently count the number of times the white team passes the ball to one another. It seems simple enough, but it takes a certain amount of concentration.

Most people who watch the video are able to count the right number of passes; they usually get close to thirty-four or thirty-five. But the number doesn't matter. What matters is that roughly half the people taking the test completely miss seeing a woman dressed as a gorilla walk through the middle of the room. She is in full view and the players are dribbling and passing the ball around her. Then she stops and beats her chest a few times before walking off camera. When asked about it, half the people in the group have no idea that a gorilla was in the middle of the screen for nine full seconds. Many people refuse to believe that the video has not been switched when they see it a second time. The experiment has been repeated all over the world and the results are always the same. I saw it done in a room with a few hundred people, and half the audience missed it. If we always keep our eyes on the ball—or on our card—we have much less capacity to notice anything else around us. It is, in other words, entirely possibly to miss a connection that is 100 percent in plain sight simply because we are focused on the task at hand. And in real life this intentional bias affects our chances of creating click moments in all kinds of ways.

Take business travel, for instance. The traditional approach is to pack your schedule with meetings. To be efficient and focused. Schultz, for instance, was in Milan to look at brewing equipment. He needed to meet suppliers, listen to panels, and form an opinion about what his competitors were up to. Sure, he may have scheduled some time for fun as well: a few hours to forget about work and enjoy the vibe of Milan. Either way, he would want to make his brief time there count. Even if he had noticed the baristas and the intriguing scene at the coffee bar he would most likely just have moved on to the next item on the agenda; or, even if he was intrigued, he would have had precious little time to satisfy his curiosity. But Schultz made the time. He took his eyes off the ball, if only briefly, and it made all the difference.

This can feel counterintuitive. Usually we are told to keep our eyes *on* the ball, not to remove them—that sounds like a surefire way to fail. We set up goals and targets and we have specific things that need to get done. And then we make sure to *get them done*. Most of us spend our days responding to immediate needs—answering emails, returning phone calls, and going where our emails and texts tell us to go. We are conditioned to focus on the business at hand. There's something satisfying about predictable, steady progress. But this approach makes it difficult to expose ourselves to the unplanned moments that enable us to uncover the ideas and opportunities others have not.

Richard Wiseman, a psychologist from the University of Hertfordshire and author of *The Luck Factor*, spent a decade researching people's perceptions of their luck. He was interested in whether people who considered themselves lucky behaved any differently from people who considered themselves unlucky. (It turns out that roughly 50 percent of us consider ourselves lucky, 14 percent unlucky, and the rest neither one.)

He noticed overarching differences between these three groups and was able to illustrate some of these distinctions in a variety of studies. Wiseman learned that extreme conscientiousness can be a strong deterrent to getting lucky. Conscientiousness is strongly associated with focused achievement. It is the type of behavior that insures execution, but that also allows us to miss the great ideas, projects, improvements or connections that keep popping up around us. Unfortunately, by rigidly pouring all of our effort into one approach we miss out on the unexpected paths to success. In this sense it is quite possible to "try too hard."

Wiseman conducted an experiment illustrating this effect in which he gave subjects a newspaper and asked them to count how many photographs were inside. There were forty three, and most subjects succeeded in finding them within a few minutes. However, most missed the large legend on the second page of the paper that read, "Stop counting—there are 43 photographs in this newspaper." There was also a half-page message that read, "Stop counting, tell the experi-

119

menter you have seen this and win $250.00." The subjects didn't notice this message either.

In another experiment, Wiseman arranged for two people to experience the same chance opportunities—money on the ground and a potential encounter with a valuable business contact. One of the two claimed she was usually unlucky, and the other said "things just always seemed to work out well" for him. The "lucky" guy noticed the money on the ground immediately and pocketed it. He then struck up a conversation with a businessman in the coffee shop (where the businessman had been planted by Wiseman). The "unlucky" woman, focused on the moment, stepped right over the cash, oblivious, and sipped her coffee without saying a word to the same businessman. These people, in a sense, were making their own luck.

The tactical takeaway? We need to allow ourselves to stray off-task some of the time. As ironic as it may sound, it actually pays to schedule time to do something unscripted and unplanned. We need to leave enough room in our day to explore things that are not connected to our immediate goals. We need to free ourselves up to become aware of hidden opportunities and expose ourselves to significant click moments. Leave some flexibility in your schedule. Then, make sure you use the flexibility to explore something unrelated to what you are doing or to follow up on a curious idea you have been considering.

In fact, ask yourself with some frequency, considering my current schedule, is it even *possible* for something unscripted or unplanned to happen? And if a click moment happens, do I have the ability to do anything about it? Murray Sargent and Dave Weise meeting at the party on the Microsoft campus was entirely unplanned. When DVF realized the potential of the wrap dress, it caught her by surprise. You can't manufacture those moments, but if you take your eyes off the ball every once in a while you might discover that they happen more often. One way to take your eyes of the ball is to purposefully look in another direction—at a different field or culture. This is the cornerstone of the next tactic.

2. Use Intersectional Thinking

For Aheda Zanetti, one of the most important click moments of her life, the one that would change her career, came one day in early 2003. A hairdresser by trade, she had quit working after her first child was born. By the time she had child number four, Zanetti was doing tele-marketing and feeling miserable with herself "as mothers sometimes do." So she had gone to watch her niece play a game of netball, the Australian version of basketball, at a local recreational center in Sydney.

Netball entails fourteen players sprinting up and down a court, dribbling and passing a ball while jockeying for position. *How come I didn't play when I was younger?* Zanetti wondered as she settled into the stands. Once the game started, she remembered why. It had to do with the uniforms.

Zanetti is Muslim; she moved with her family from Lebanon to Sydney at age two. The standard uniform for netball—shorts and a T-shirt—was simply not an option for Muslim women who choose to wear more traditional garb. The *jilbab* covers a women's entire body except for her hands, face and feet, for instance, and would have made it extremely difficult to compete in any meaningful way. She knew this because that was exactly what was happening to her niece down on the court that afternoon.

As Zanetti watched, she saw that her niece's outfit was entirely im-practical in a situation like this. She looked uncomfortable to the ex-treme. "That day it was very, very hot and she had to wear all of these flowing garbs. She looked sick. Her face looked, literally, like a ripe tomato." Zanetti stared at the scene unfolding in front of her and be-gan to wonder why things had to be this way. "And that," she told me, "was when I think it really clicked in my head." Zanetti realized all at once that there should be sportswear designed specifically for tradi-tional Muslim women.

That evening, after she put her kids to bed, Zanetti took out her

121

sewing kit. Her first design was made out of the only fabric she had at home—stretched satin. There were pieces hanging everywhere. "It looked like a bridal gown," she recalled. Even though the prototype was impractical, it spurred her imagination and she kept trying. "There were so many changes" she recalled, "I can't even count how many." Two years of experimentation later she had created a sporty *jilbab* that was just right.

But at that point she had another click moment. She realized that netball wasn't the only sport that left Muslim women feeling isolated and sidelined. Australia, after all, has some of the best beaches in the world and life there revolves around surfing. So Zanetti modified her designs yet again and launched the burquini, a head-to-toe two-piece sporty swim suit made from high performance fabric. It turned out that hundreds of thousands of women across the world were waiting for just such a product. When she launched her Web site she was flooded with orders. The market for the burquini was much larger than she ever imagined.

"You know, it's really funny," she told me, "but 30 percent of our customers come from non-Muslim backgrounds. They are Jewish and Hindu and even Western women looking to protect themselves from UV rays."

Today Zanetti has twenty-three employees and her business serves customers all around the world. The burqini is distributed worldwide online and through key retailers in Bahrain, Dubai, France, and the Netherlands, along with a stand-alone store in Sydney's Punchbowl. All because of an unexpected click moment during a game of netball.

The key part of this story is that Zanetti boosted her chances of having an insight by stepping into the intersection of two different cultures. Similarly, each of us has our best chance of creating click moments by searching for inspiration in fields, industries, and cultures that are different from our own—something I call intersectional thinking. In *The Medici Effect* I went into great detail about why these intersections can be so fruitful, but here I will simply say that diversity is the key to unleashing surprising and game-changing insights. In the previous chapter we saw that click moments emerge from a surprising combination of concepts. Well, the chance of being surprised increases dramatically if these concepts are very different from each other. This idea is at the heart of intersectional thinking. If you try to combine a bikini with the idea of a sandy beach, for instance, it is going to be difficult to come up with a random or entirely new concept. The chance of having a genuine click moment is very low because these two ideas have such commonality. But if you combine a bikini with a burka, the situation looks very different. If you can find a connection between unlike ideas, the result is apt to be surprising. That's exactly what Zanetti did. You can do the same—here are some approaches:

Purposefully Explore Fields, Cultures, and Industries Different from Your Own

Marcel Salathé is a soft-spoken biologist from Switzerland with a bit of an entrepreneurial streak. He dropped out of college in the mid-1990s to start a web development firm, but later returned to earn a PhD in biology at the Swiss Federal Institute of Technology (ETH) in Zurich. On top of that, he is a successful artist, having sold almost 800 paintings to date. How did he do it all?

During a vacation in Portugal, Salathé found himself standing in front of a painting of a flower, and suddenly something about that painting struck him. "You look at a painting," Salathé recalled, "and you see the price tag and you're like, 'Why would anyone pay five thousand dollars for a painting of a flower which has been painted seven million times before?'" Then the answer came to him in a rush. "It was one of those instances where something just clicks," he later told me. He realized that when pricing art, the only thing that mattered was the story behind the art. Then something in his science background gave him an idea. "It occurred to me that just painting numbers would be a great way to conceptualize that."

The concept was simple: one thousand paintings of numbers, liter-

123

ally, numbered from 1 to 1,000. Although he had to think through some content issues, such as color and typeface, the main point was that customers would assign meaning and stories to the paintings themselves. Marcel decided that the price of each work would be $1,000 minus the number in the painting: number 1 would cost $999, number 2 would cost $998, and so on.

"The idea of 1,000 paintings is not the greatest idea on the planet," Marcel admitted, but it was distinctive and strangely random. Once Marcel finished designing the pricing mechanism, the Web site debuted in early February of 2006. By May 29, he had sold 106 paintings. Soon after, his site was featured on a popular blog and he sold 119 more paintings overnight. As of 2012 he has sold almost eight hundred of his paintings, each one just a blue number on a 12 x 12 canvas. Marcel made this happen by exploring a discipline very different from the one he spends most of his time engaged in, thereby exposing himself to random combinations of ideas. And he has kept pursuing these types of intersections.

"One of the take away messages from this project is that I'm not afraid of proposing a lot of ideas that perhaps sound wacky. . . . . I'm in the biology department and yet I study Twitter. You can imagine that a lot of my colleagues look at me in a funny way, but . . . I think that it's a great opportunity. I'm just going to go ahead and do it."

Again, the idea is to expose yourself to concepts from fields, industries, and cultures that are different from your own. The more unlike these areas are, the greater the chance that you will expose yourself to a random idea. I have worked with corporations all over the world and we deliberately make them search for ideas in industries, disciplines, and cultures very far afield from what their firm is typically engaged in. The result is always a flurry of unexpected ideas—and some truly astounding click moments, which have then been parlayed into dramatic change for the organization.

Consider another example, Alberto "Beto" Perez from Cali, Colombia. Beto loved to dance, but could not find opportunities to do so following a family tragedy. Instead he ended up working as an aerobics instructor. He didn't love aerobics, but it was good money and he had been teaching it since he was sixteen. "The fitness world [had] become so technical and lacked fun and energy," he later told *Fitness First Magazine*. But one night his two interests intersected. It would, ultimately, change his life.

Beto showed up one night to teach a standard aerobics class when he realized that he had forgotten his usual music. A fitness class without music is like a sporting event without a crowd; Beto could either cancel the class, or use whatever music he could find. He searched his backpack and found a mix tape full of salsa and merengue songs. At first the class tried to do the standard fitness routine, but Beto decided to scrap the idea and improvise the entire exercise by integrating dance routines into it. Suddenly, Beto's passion blended with the exercise: Zumba was born.

Today Zumba is an undeniable fitness phenomenon. The exercise combines dance movements from hip-hop, reggae, merengue, *cumbia*, and salsa with standard fitness squats and lunges. The energy that comes from the program gives even the most modest fitness center a dance club atmosphere. The goal, Beto said, is "to forget that you are working out and feel like you are at a nightclub in South Beach." In 2009, there were Zumba instructors in thirty-five different countries. In 2010, the number ballooned to seventy-five, and today nearly 12 million people across 125 countries regularly exercise using Beto's techniques, making Zumba the world's largest fitness program. Its success took everyone by surprise. "I never thought it would be so big in Scandanavia, the UK," Albert Perlman, the guy who turned Zumba into a business, told our team. All of this was possible because Beto stepped into the intersection of Latin dance and fitness.

Create Diverse Teams

We can increase our chances of finding unique intersections if we surround ourselves with different types of people. When you bring together a diverse mix of people—people with different perspectives and objectives—new conceptual connections and click moments have a better chance of occurring. Tobias Dahl, the lead animator at game developer DICE, put this principle into practice when he created a game called Mirror's Edge.

"Usually animators, designers, and programmers sit in different parts of the building sending specifications to each other," Dahl says, "and I wanted to change that." As the game was being developed, Dahl rearranged the usual creative process to allow animators, designers, and programmers to sit right next to one another and work together in a much more direct, interactive way. After two weeks of gridlock, conflict, and standstill, the group started to hum and "suddenly we were coming up with all kinds of innovative ideas, just by the fact that we were sitting together, but had a different take on whatever we were working on," Tobias says. DICE ended up winning a lot of innovation awards for their game, not because they had a massive R&D budget, but because they changed their way of working. "It was such a simple change and it had such a powerful effect. I was at a loss trying to figure out why we hadn't done this before," Tobias told me as I caught up with him just after his latest game, Battlefield 3, had been released. "Today we don't even think about this as an approach, it's just become our way of working. I actually spend a lot of time on such easy things as where people should sit. We want different people to sit together, and that can take some working out."

While I was visiting the software developer Menlo Innovations in Ann Arbor, Michigan, I found that they had systematized this idea. Programmers there always work in pairs and they switch partners every Monday. It sounds crazy, I know, but their success is legendary. "We get hundreds of visitors every year just to see how the hell we do it," the CEO Richard Sheridan told me while he showed me around.

Creating diverse teams is one of the best ways to encourage click moments. The teams should cut across as many dimensions as possible, including culture, gender, and ethnicity as well as departments and disciplines, age, and level within an organization. All of these separate backgrounds tend to dramatically increase the mix of perspectives required to create surprising click moments. This tactic often is in direct contradiction to what most of us normally do. Usually we try to create teams that we know or think have the skills required to solve a particular problem. But these types of teams are created logically, which means that the ideas, projects, and solutions will generally be similar to those of your competitors' teams, because they will have similar types of teams. In my conversations with IBM executives, for instance, former executives such as Sam Palmisano (formerly CEO), Nick Donofrio (formerly executive VP of innovation and R&D), and Ted Childs (who used to head up Diversity) have repeatedly made the point that the core of their company's success was in its ability to tap into a wide range of diverse perspectives—and they have relentlessly pursued efforts to boost all kinds of diversity throughout the company for that purpose.

Create a Collision-Prone Environment

If you can't create diverse teams, try to create an environment where people from different backgrounds will serendipitously interact with each other. When Steve Jobs designed the Pixar campus, he created this type of effect. "We want to put everybody under one roof," he said in the documentary *The Pixar Story*, "and we want to encourage unplanned collaboration." The effect Jobs was going for was essentially unexpected click moments. He accomplished that, in spades.

If you get a chance to visit Pixar's studio in Oakland, California, the first thing you will see upon entering the building is the atrium—its design is meant to create serendipity. Jonah Lehrer wrote in the *New Yorker* that "the original architectural plan called for three buildings, with separate offices for the computer scientists, the animators, and the Pixar executives. Jobs immediately scrapped it. Instead of three buildings, there was going to be a single vast space, with an airy atrium at its center." But a big space in the center is not enough—you need to actually get people to go there. "Steve Jobs wanted people to meet," Ed Catmull, the president of Pixar, explained to me at the Pixar

127

campus. "He made sure of that by making the atrium the center of the building. And then he made sure everyone had to go there."

So the mailboxes, the meeting rooms, the cafeteria, the coffee bar, and the gift shop are all in the atrium. Lehrer writes that "as he [Jobs] saw it, the main challenge for Pixar was getting its different cultures to work together, forcing the computer geeks and cartoonists to collaborate . . . What Steve realized was that when people run into each other, when they make eye contact, things happen."

Look for opportunities like this in your own environment. Are there times when people can come together for no specific business purpose? Can you make your environment more collision prone? Are there natural opportunities for people to have ad hoc conversations or form teams spontaneously? The bottom line is that you are increasing the chance of having click moments if you bring together people who usually do not have a reason to connect. Perhaps the fastest and easiest way to accomplish this is by organizing social events. That is how Weise met Sargent, after all.

Crash a Conference or a Gathering

Parties and conferences bring a lot of people together, so it seems obvious that these are a likely venue for click moments. But are some conferences or parties better than others for generating unexpected insights and connections? Consider Gina Warren, vice president of global diversity and inclusion at Nike. "I prefer to attend design and innovation conferences," she explained. She told me she only occasionally attends diversity conferences. "I am just not as likely to learn all that many new things by simply staying within the field I know best," she said. "The other conference attendees have pretty much the same experiences, history, and worldview as I do." So she tries to find other sources of inspiration.

Because new ideas and viewpoints spur her imagination, every year she attends conferences, book lectures, and museums that have nothing to do with her field. "I don't want to be an architect, a colorist, or an engineer," she said, "but I am a designer in my field of diversity and inclusion." It is far more interesting and productive for Warren to hunt for intersections in fields like architecture or design, since the click moments she might get there are likely to be far more serendipitous and far more interesting.

When it comes to office parties, invite people from other parts of the company, or even outside the firm, in order to spark similar unexpected connections.

Look for Unlikely Impressions

Various types of media, such as TV, magazines, and online streams such as Twitter or Tumblr can provide a way to get in front of hundreds or thousands of random ideas instantly. Trolling through your Twitter stream or looking on Flickr may help spark an inspiration or solve a problem. But even Twitter can become predictable fast. Once an article is tweeted and retweeted you'll see it all over the Twittersphere—and so will everyone else. Suddenly it's mainstream. We need to work harder and click in unusual places to find connections that are truly random. I once had the CEO of one of the largest media companies in the world ask me what he could do immediately to step into the Intersection. He was on his way to the airport, so I told him to stop by the magazine stand and pick out five magazines he had never read before—the less related they were to his business, the better. I told him to try to connect concepts in that magazine with some of the challenges he was currently facing at work. When we met again a few months later, I discovered that the technique had worked for him and he was repeating the advice to his direct reports. Apparently he had been reading a lot of wedding magazines lately . . .

3. Follow Your Curiosity

The Rubik's Cube burst on to the scene in all of its primary-colors glory in the early 1980s. It was the fad to end all fads. Full-sized cubes, cube key chains, and Rubik's Minis were in every car, bedroom, book bag, and holiday stocking across the land. One of the most successful toys in history, the Cube sold over 350 million units and made its creator one of the richest men in Hungary. More recently, the Rubik's Cube experienced a resurgence of popularity. Competitions have been hosted in Canada, the United States, and other parts of the world. The objective is to solve the cube in as few seconds as possible . . . blindfolded.

What type of mind created this maddening and clever little puzzle? Was he brilliant? Analytical? A mathematical savant? No, not in the usual sense of those terms. In fact, it would be just as fair to say that he had absolutely no idea what he was doing. The Rubik's Cube wasn't the work of careful planning or market research; instead, it was the result of a nagging sense of curiosity that just wouldn't let up.

Erno Rubik was born in Budapest, Hungary, to an engineer father and a poet mother. As a professor of interior design, Rubik became fascinated by the idea of creating a structure that maintained its integrity of shape yet allowed individual objects to move within it. "Space always intrigued me, with its incredibly rich possibilities" Rubik once wrote. "I think the Cube arose from this interest, from this search for expression and for this always more increased acuteness of these thoughts." At age twenty-nine, he filled a small room in his mother's apartment with objects attached to blocks by elastic bands. The blocks were separate from each other, but once assembled they formed a cube. As he twisted them into place the elastic holding them together began to snap. Driven by curiosity, he developed a genuinely simple but brilliant solution to the problem: Rubik connected the cubes by carving tiny notches within the squares and attaching color-coated stickers to identify the individual squares. With his cube completed, he twisted the squares and confirmed that the shape remained intact.

"It was wonderful," he wrote in his unpublished autobiography, "to see how, after only a few turns, the colors became mixed, apparently in random fashion. It was tremendously satisfying to watch this color parade." But now Rubik had a new problem: he had no idea how to solve his puzzle and put the colors back in order. Something inside of him clicked into place. He said it was like staring at a secret code. "But for me, it was a code I myself had invented . . . yet I could not read it. I simply could not accept it."

It takes the current record holder exactly 5.66 seconds to solve the Cube, but it took Erno Rubik, the guy who invented the puzzle, one and a half months to do the same thing. During that time it was curiosity—almost an obsessive curiosity—that allowed him to focus on the secret code until it was cracked. And when he did, he had another realization. This could be an incredible puzzle—an incredible game.

Why is curiosity so good for creating click moments? Because curiosity is the way your intuition tells you that something interesting is going on. You are not sure exactly what that "something interesting" is—*so curiosity propels you to keep digging until you connect the pieces*. These moments are what Steven Johnson, the author of *Where Good Ideas Come From*, calls hunches. If you learn to listen to your curiosity, you will find that you become curious about those things that are different and new. Possibilities and the unknown, not the predictable or obvious, make you curious. That's curiosity in a nutshell—fascination with the new or unexplained. But you have to actually follow it in order for it to bear fruit. Curiosity pursued is one of the things that allow serendipity to happen.

This was certainly true of Howard Schultz. Once he saw one espresso bar, and what was going on inside, he had this nagging feeling that he had stumbled upon something interesting. So he kept looking for clues. The pieces finally came together for him when he tasted his first café latte.

Interestingly, research proves that following curiosity becomes much harder as we get older—not because our opportunities change, but because *we* do. "People in their teens and twenties tend to be more open because they are still discovering who they are," says Todd Kashdan, a psychologist at George Mason University and author of *Curious?* "As we get older we become a lot more crystallized in our thinking. We create rigid rules and eliminate the chances to change all the time."

Although following your curiosity is a key tactic in exposing yourself to randomness, it can sometimes be difficult to execute. We find ourselves so busy that our curiosity is forced to take a backseat. In that case, it can be a great idea to force ourselves to increase the number of click moments on short notice. Intersectional thinking is great for doing that. So is the approach that follows.

4. Reject the Predictable Path

Sometimes a direct approach to increasing randomness is required. While you may think you have a logical plan or course of action, you will open yourself up to more unpredictable click moments if you actually reject the predictable path. The man they called "Conqueror of the World" seemed to know this intuitively.

On the eve of the Battle of Gaugamela, one of the largest and most well-known battles in human history, the odds against Alexander the Great seemed insurmountable. He was facing his archenemy, the Persian king Darius III, and Alexander was wildly outnumbered. Following the Battle of Issus two years earlier—a major defeat for Darius—Alexander occupied the Mediterranean coast as well as Egypt. He then advanced from Syria against the heart of the Persian Empire and crossed both the Euphrates and the Tigris rivers without any opposition. Darius was biding his time and building up a massive army, drawing men from the far reaches of his empire. He gathered about a hundred thousand horse and infantry against forty-seven thousand Macedonian soldiers (including only about seven thousand on horseback).

On the eve of the battle, Alexander's chief military adviser, Parmenion, was under the impression that a nighttime attack should be launched in order to counter the overwhelming advantage in numbers of the Persians. Alexander is said to have dismissed the notion outright, proclaiming that he was no ordinary general and would not act like one.

As it turned out, by rejecting the predictable course of action another set of opportunities now presented themselves. Darius, fearing a twilight attack, kept his army awake and on alert for the whole night, while Alexander's troops were more rested. When the sun rose Alexander attacked. It was a disastrous defeat for the Persians and widely regarded as one of the most iconic underdog stories in history.

Alexander made an unexpected move and rejected the predictable plan. Actively rejecting the predictable insight leaves you nowhere else to go except making unpredictable, random connections. Some of those will click into place and ensure that, whatever solutions you come up with, they will set you apart.

This notion of actively attempting to oppose prediction may be the most difficult of the four tactics we've discussed, because here you are going against the established norm. At times, it may feel incredibly risky, even though the converse—going along with the crowd—is more likely to be a high-risk proposition in terms of finding a path to success.

Ethiopian-Swedish superchef Marcus Samuelsson illustrated this point beautifully one evening when we were talking about how to come up with great ideas. In *The Medici Effect* I wrote about Samuelsson's ability to invent groundbreaking culinary creations by combining cooking techniques, ingredients, and tastes from different cultures. But this approach was a little bit different, and it came into play while he was going through the selection processes to become the guest chef for President Obama's state dinner in honor of the Indian prime minister Mammohan Singh. He told me the story one evening at his new restaurant, Red Rooster, in Harlem:

During the selection process they called me to say I was one of 16 chefs being considered and that they needed sample menus to help them make a final decision. I was on the set filming *Top Chef Masters* that week so it was a pretty intense time with me only able to communicate through a BlackBerry with my team.

I was warned early on that there were some rules I needed to follow. It turns out that every state dinner since their inception in 1874 has served French-American cuisine. This was the clear expectation for the meal. Now, in French-American cuisine the role of meat is important and so the expectation was that there would be a great meat dish involved.

Of course, the other folks in the running were also well-known chefs. How could I stand out when everyone would need to propose something relatively similar? I knew that one approach would be to put together a stunning French-American menu. French cuisine leaves one with a fair number of options to impress, so that wasn't really the issue. The problem was that I was going head-to-head with 15 other excellent chefs. If we all proposed exceptional, but mostly traditional, menus it would be a crapshoot.

So my next option was to reject the most basic guideline: French-American cuisine. Once we started exploring *that*, a number of other ideas clicked into place almost immediately. It now seemed obvious to me that we should have an Indian-American inspired dinner menu. To help me get started I asked my team do some research on the Indian Prime Minister. Well, it turns out that he is vegetarian. Okay—so we're inviting him, he's our guest of honor . . . shouldn't we probably exclude meat from the menu? I was considering a vegetarian dinner, possibly with a fish option. Then I remembered that Michelle Obama has a garden patch in the White House garden. And I was off and running in my own direction.

So we came up with a menu that was a mixture of Indian and American food. We made it fairly simple and we included vegetables from Michelle's garden. Some people would consider this risky, but my thinking is that people are doing the risk calculations all wrong. When you are going up against 15 elite competitors, as I was, adhering to the stated rules and traditions made my chances of winning 1 in 16. I don't like those odds. But if I separate myself from the others—so that I'm not really even competing against them—I'd say my chances are much, much better.

The White House was either going to like my idea or they weren't. What are the chances that they would accept my concept despite the unpredictability in it all? Maybe 50/50. Maybe lower . . . maybe I had a 1 in 4 chance. But that is still a lot better than 1 in 16. They would either accept my separate approach or they wouldn't. If they liked it . . . I had no real competition. I would win."

Samuelsson was selected over the others. He doesn't know for certain what would have happened if he had taken the predictable path—he may still have won—but he feels pretty sure that by rejecting the expected he opened himself up to a number of immediate insights that separated him from his competitors and greatly improved his odds for success.

Creating conditions that are conducive to click moments can dramatically boost our chances of having them. But if click moments were all it took to reach the top, it would be all too easy. Unfortunately, they are not enough. We have to execute our ideas, and in doing so we have to place a bet that our idea is going to work. One such bet took an interesting twist for an Apple executive who heard a knock on his door in the middle of the night at a hotel room in Moscow.

9

PURPOSEFUL BETS

Al Eisenstat woke up abruptly. There was a sharp knock on the door and Eisenstat, Apple's senior vice president of board and legal matters, had been in deep sleep. He got out of bed and went to see who was bothering him at this hour. It was late, and he was tired after spending the evening at the Moscow Ballet. Maybe Eisenstat had reason to be suspicious. This was during the Cold War, and there was no small amount of distrust between the United States and the Soviet Union. Although the Apple II had been introduced to the country two years earlier, quite successfully, it had taken quite a bit of work to get the deals worked out, with all the complicated export restrictions and high-level spy games.

Outside the door stood a young man. He seemed nervous, repeatedly glancing down the hallway as if he was worried about being followed.

He said he was a Russian programmer, and handed Eisenstat a floppy disk. Then the man hurried off into the night, never to be heard from again. When Eisenstat returned to the States and shared the disk with Apple's programmers, they discovered that it contained exceptional handwriting recognition software. It was remarkably accurate and could even adapt to learn each user's handwriting. As it turned out, the Apple team had been desperately looking for just such a program.

The year was 1987 and Apple was just starting on one of its most ambitious projects ever, the Newton. It had the potential to revolutionize the entire computer industry, and the company spared no expense to guarantee success. The amount of money, people, and time that went into this project would supersede anything Apple had ever done before. It was a bet of gigantic proportions. But is it really possible to guarantee success—or even come close to doing so?

*

A click moment represents a sudden opportunity, a turning point that can push us in a new, unpredictable, and random direction. These moments are powerful because they allow us to stumble upon ideas that are not obvious or logical—ideas that may enable us to outwit our competitors. But by themselves these moments don't mean all that much. In order to amount to anything they have to be followed up with some sort of action. Windows 3.0 happened because Murray Sargent and David Weise took the time to test their insight. The wrap dress happened because Diane von Furstenberg designed it and struck distribution deals. The click moment is just the beginning of what has to happen in order to change the world. Someone actually has to make the idea *happen* for it to make a difference.

Such actions, unfortunately, are fraught with risks—small ones and large ones. We don't really know if they will work out or not and so we are exposing ourselves to possible failure. Taking action requires driving some sort of stake in the ground—an initial investment. It's impossible to know if the idea will work out before you invest your time, money, reputation, and energy. You are essentially placing a bet.

Life, in other words, does not just turn on unexpected click moments, it can also be seen as a sequence of bets, some riskier than others. Do you want to ask someone out for dinner? A bet. Should you go for the kiss after dinner? Another bet. Mark Zuckerberg placed a bet when he wrote a computer program that rated girls based on attractiveness, and he made yet another bet when he followed it up with a social networking site called Facebook. Von Furstenberg's pursuit of the wrap dress was also a sequence of bets.

Arguably *everything* we do is one bet after another. You could describe crossing the street as placing a bet that you'll get to the other side, and eating breakfast as a bet that you won't choke on your cereal. But these are not conscious bets—we are not weighing the pros and cons of these decisions, or really reflecting much on them at all. This is not true for the types of bets I'm talking about. Diane von Furstenberg leveraged all of her talent and inspiration to design and manufacture the wrap dress. She was conscious of what she was doing and she was pursuing some sort of reasonably well-defined outcome. Murray Sargent and David Weise intentionally bet on using Windows in protected mode—they tried it and they could have failed. In order to separate the insignificant bets we place all the time from the more elaborate bets we place only occasionally, I have given the latter a name. I call these types of bets, the ones we make with intent in mind, *purposeful bets*.

*

Compared to click moments, which can sometimes conjure up feelings of uncanny connectedness and magic, purposeful bets seem entirely straightforward, even manageable. We may be taking a gamble when we make a bet, but we tend to believe that we can greatly affect our chances of making things go our way. If we just do our research well and take every risk into account, there is no reason to think of our action as a bet; success in those instances is not random—it is earned. We also often think we can significantly lower the risk of losing a bet if we can command more resources. We are far better off starting with

139

a big pile of money than with a small pile or with more time than with less. It is the best way to "load" the dice before we roll.

The fact is that these notions, upon further reflection, don't really hold up. We *want* to believe that deep analysis, if done well, can almost guarantee a sure thing. That is possible in Serena Williams's world, where the rules change slowly (or not at all). If Serena practices her serve she will, over time, get better at it. It is an investment in time and resources that will have an almost guaranteed payout. If she can just work on her serve harder than anyone else, and if she can stay healthy, she has a chance at becoming the best in the world. But in the hyper-adaptive world such logic will place us right alongside everyone else who follows that same prevailing path, and we will be left in the dust by someone who does something entirely different—something even deep analysis could never have uncovered.

But what about the second part of this idea—that more money and resources dramatically increase your odds of success? This notion appears to have quite a bit of merit. It even borders on the obvious. If we just had more money or more people or more time, we could almost guarantee success; and if we fail we often lament the fact that we did not have enough of those things. Seemingly obvious, yes, but it turns out that things are never quite that simple.

*

On August 2, 1993, Apple released the Newton MessagePad. Although the advance hype couldn't match the intensity surrounding their more recent offerings, it was a major event in its own right. Prior to the Newton's debut the *Baltimore Sun* declared that it "could transform the company, reinvigorate the computer industry and—perhaps—launch the 1990s equivalent of the personal computer revolution." Apple's CEO at the time, John Sculley, knew that the company needed another hit. Almost all of the company's revenue came from the Macintosh and Apple II and the enormous profit margins they had enjoyed on those computers were slipping. They needed this to work. Sculley predicted a $3 trillion industry if things went well. His predecessor, Steve Jobs, built Apple by creating the first personal computer made for everyone. Sculley wanted to reinvent the company with a portable one that would sell for the same price.

On paper, the Newton sounded perfect. It would combine in one handheld computer note taking, calendar, and telecommunications. It would be the perfect personal digital assistant, according to Sculley. The first Newton would be a letter-sized slate with a hard drive, an active matrix LCD screen, and infrared ports for high-speed long-distance networking. Today this all sounds very quaint, but back then it was groundbreaking. Getting it right required a lot of innovation.

Consider, for instance, the work that went into the handwriting recognition software. The primary selling point of the Newton—the killer app—was going to be its digital note-taking capability. But Apple's handwriting recognition software simply didn't work. To get around this problem, Apple acquired Arus, a small Oregon-based software company that specialized in handwriting software. Unfortunately, their code couldn't solve the problem either. The disk delivered to Al Eisenstat on that late night in Moscow seemed as though it might contain the unexpected solution. It helped—but it didn't take them all the way. Finally, they simply licensed technology from a Russian firm.

In order to meet these challenges, and many others like it, Apple quickly doubled the size of its Newton team. Then they doubled it again . . . and again, and on and on. The company spared no expense to guarantee success. The amount of money, people, and time invested in this project would supersede anything Apple had done before. By 1993, the company had spent almost seven years on the product, and it was a bonafide breakthrough. It did things that no other handheld device at the time could do. By the time Apple launched its revolutionary device, $500 million had been laid down on this particular bet. How could they possibly lose?

*

In a casino your best move is not to play at all. The house always wins over the long term. In roulette, for instance, you have a slightly larger risk of losing than of winning, so in the long run you will lose while playing that game. The best return on investment you can get in a casino is on the card game baccarat, which has a 99.2 percent payout ratio. If you bet $100 on that game, you should plan to get $99 or so back. Blackjack—if played optimally—has a payout ratio of 98.7 percent. As investments go, these games pretty much suck. Almost everyone is aware of this, though, and so casino gambling is considered to be primarily a recreational activity. Instead of paying $200 for dinner and a movie for two, you could spend some time at the Blackjack table and have just as much fun—or even more if you have a lucky night.

But there is no "house" when placing bets in the real world. Humans are, in other words, generally better off trying to start a new company or investing in the economy than gambling at the casino because the payout ratio is not systematically limited. Even in the midst of financial crisis and recession, we can still find new ways to add value—and so innovations continue to change and improve our world. Technological progress and economic growth have happened at an almost dizzying pace over the past quarter century, at least when viewed globally.

But there is another difference between the real world and a casino that explains why we continue to place bets. In a casino, we have the option, when our winning streak is over, to simply get up from the table and leave. That is why a casino will do anything to keep you playing if you are winning—by comping your hotel room or offering you drinks and swag. They desperately want you to come back for another roll. The casino knows that if you keep playing, they will ultimately get your money. But you don't have to—you can call it quits.

In the real world, however, the game keeps going. Even if you have made a pile of money on an investment, found your dream job, or met the love of your life, you still have to keep taking actions that come with the inherent risk of failure attached. Continuing to invest offers more of an upside than putting the money under your mattress (and even that is risky). To remain viable, over time every job or relationship must change. This is also true for an organization. A company may have had an exceptional year, but the executives still have to deliver results the next year. That explains why Apple placed a bet on the Newton. Yes, they scored huge success with the Apple Macintosh and the Apple II, but so what? Sculley, like executives everywhere else, had no choice but to keep rolling the dice.

*

Unfortunately, he lost badly on this particular bet. Several lists name the Newton as one of the worst corporate mistakes ever. Sales were dismal. Although the Newton was close to being a technological marvel, it was never able to actually *do* the things it was supposed to do particularly well. One of Steve Jobs's first actions when he returned to Apple was to shut the unit down.

But Apple was not the only company going after this market. At the same time Apple was preparing to bring out the Newton, nearly $1 billion was being spent by a variety of organizations trying to crack the mobile-computing market. Backed by the powerful venture capital fund Kleiner Perkins Caufield & Byers, the Go Corporation spent $75 million developing their ill-fated stylus-operated computer. Despite winning numerous industry awards for their Pen Point mobile operating system, the company was out of business by 1994. The company that won the mobile-computing market came out of the blue: Palm Computing. The start-up had twenty-eight people and spent just $3 million developing a handheld device that was so intuitive, at the time, it sent chills up the spines of analysts and reviewers— not to mention users.

Released in 1996, the PalmPilot took the business world by storm. In just one year it did what Apple and Go Corporation had bet the farm attempting to do: it gained control of over half the PDA market. Two years later their market share neared 80 percent. The secret? Palm simplified things. Apple had the resources to develop a three-chipped processor powerful enough to handle a user's unique handwriting. With minimal resources, Palm didn't have that option. Instead, they forced users to write in a way the software understood. It worked. It

143

was easier, sleeker, and cheaper. By 1998, just two years after its release, Palm had sold over 2 million units. In 2001, PalmPilot had become the "symbol of the new economy," with over 13 million units sold. In time, the PalmPilot's dominance eroded, but not its mystique. In 2011, *PC Magazine* named it one of the most influential technology products ever released.

So what really happened here? How did Apple, after having spent $500 million on the Newton, fail miserably, when Palm spent only $3 million to produce one of the most successful technology devices ever? Such an outcome seems to suggest that the amount of money you spend does not much affect your chances of success. How could that be? The answer can be found in how humans deal with risk.

*

December 27, 2011, was one of those fresh, clear days you can only get in Southern California or Arizona in the wintertime. The sun was bright, skies were blue, and the temperature was a bit higher than normal, with almost no wind. It was a perfect day for skydiving, and Michael Unger was a highly experienced jumper. He had logged more than 1,600 jumps and had been a skydiving instructor for two seasons. But something went terribly wrong that day, mere seconds prior to his anticipated landing. Unger came in way too fast and crashed into the ground, which ended his life. Understanding what happened to Unger that day actually helps explain why the Newton was such a failure despite all the money spent on it—and why the PalmPilot was such a monumental success.

When expert skydivers like Michael Unger want to impress onlookers on the ground they often employ a particular maneuver called a "hook turn." The jumper makes a quick 90- or 180-degree turn very close to the ground, maneuvering his parachute in such a way that he dramatically increases his speed and produces a long, elegant—and very fast—glide before touching down. It is a thrilling way to land, and looks very impressive when done right. Someone with Unger's skill can swoop mere inches above the ground at speeds approaching sixty miles an hour before finally settling into a soft landing. This appears to be what Unger was going for that day, aiming to drag his toes across the surface of a pond until he touched down on the opposite bank.

"A lot of jumpers choose to land this way because it's exciting," said Jim Crouch, the safety director for the United States Parachuting Association, "but it's very unforgiving." The moment the jumper goes into the hook turn he starts to drop more quickly. The sharper the turn, the faster the drop. If this is done close to the ground the skydiver can crash at a very high speed. "Accidents occur when parachutists start the maneuver too low and the parachute doesn't have the ability to recover, or fill with air, and float the skydiver to the ground," according to Crouch. Every year people die after using hook turns, and many more get badly injured. Although that may not seem surprising given the maneuver's degree of danger, the deaths are actually quite mysterious.

Before the early nineties, no skydivers died this way. It simply did not happen—ever. It used to be that most deaths in the sport occurred because a parachute failed to open, either because the equipment malfunctioned or the jumper waited too long to release it. "I was actually present and saw people I jumped with get killed right in front of my eyes," Vic Napier, a skydiving expert told me one afternoon. "Every summer, without fail, people lost track of altitude or had an equipment failure." But that was not Unger's problem. His chute opened just fine. In fact, nowadays a parachute will open every time you jump—recent technology basically guarantees it.

In the early nineties a device called the Cypres became part of the standard-issue gear for skydivers. The Cypres opens the parachute automatically if the jumper is just a few seconds from impact, and it is extremely effective in preventing what are called no-pull or low-pull fatalities. In 1991, before the Cypres was widely adopted, there were fourteen no-pull or low-pull deaths. In 1998, after use of the Cypres had become widespread, twelve Cypres saves were recorded, and there were no low-pull fatalities. Everyone wore Cypres devices, and they saved many skydivers from injury or death. The safety technology had worked exactly as intended and made skydiving much safer. Or had it?

145

Strangely, just as the Cypres safety technology eliminated no-pull or low-pull deaths, a sudden and dramatic rise in an entirely new type of fatality occurred. Where were these deaths coming from? From the kinds of maneuvers that led to Unger's death. Swooping and hook turns increased markedly and, despite the Cypres, the total number of deaths in skydiving remained constant during the nineties. In fact, in a widely circulated paper, Vic Napier was able to show that the same number of lives saved by the Cypres device were lost in risky landing attempts. The improvements in equipment safety, it turns out, did *not* lead to a decreased number of fatalities. How come?

*

There is a concept in psychology called risk homeostasis. It refers to the idea that humans have a degree of risk that they find acceptable and strive to live their lives at that level. So if risk decreases in one area of life—such as the appearance of an automatic chute-release system for skydivers—we tend to adjust our behavior to increase risks elsewhere . . . just as skydivers became more likely to attempt swoop landings.

In his 2001 book *Target Risk* Gerald J. S. Wilde hypothesized that we each have our own level of acceptable risk and that our actions tend to drive us toward that particular level. We experience this effect frequently. Imagine that you are driving a car at a good clip under these conditions: the road is curvy and the lanes are narrow, the asphalt is slick with rain, and it's dark outside. What would you do? If you're like just about everyone else, you'd slow down. It's a no-brainer. Now imagine that the road straightens out, the lanes widen, night turns to day, and the rain stops. Would you speed right back up? Yes, of course. But these actions—so obvious when presented this way—only make the risk of an accident roughly the same in both sets of road conditions. You slow down when the environment is riskier in order to maintain a certain level of risk, and you speed up when the environment is safe, for the exact same reason. You compensate for risky conditions by driving more safely, and compensate for safe conditions by driving in a riskier manner.

This is exactly what is going on with skydiving accidents. Skydiving veteran Bill Booth put it this way: "The safer skydiving gear becomes, the more chances skydivers will take." The Cypres device made the sport safer, lowering the risk of fatalities dramatically, but as a result participants elevated their risky behavior, driving up the total risk—right back to where it was in the first place.

The counterintuitive nature of risk homeostasis throws us for a loop in a variety of settings. In a Munich study of taxicab safety, for example, half the cabs were fitted with an antilock braking system (ABS), while the other half maintained conventional braking systems. Despite the fact that one group was better prepared, crash rates for both groups were exactly the same. Wilde concluded that drivers of the ABS-equipped cabs increased their risk taking, assuming the equipment would compensate for their behavior, while drivers of the non-ABS cabs took greater precautions, also in order to compensate. Other examples show that sex workers in Nevada, who tend to have far more partners than most people, also tend to have lower STD rates than others because they test themselves far more often and consistently require their customers to use condoms. On the other hand, risk homeostasis also has been cited to explain why condom distribution programs in some regions of the world have failed to stem the tide of HIV prevalence. When people think they're safer because they're using condoms, some of the time they respond by actually engaging in even riskier sex, thus neutralizing the safety benefits. Football players are still suffering from concussions and other injuries despite the fact that their protective gear has improved markedly during recent years. As explained in the *Wall Street Journal,* "While these helmets reduced the chances of death on the field, they also created a sense of invulnerability that encouraged players to collide more forcefully and more often."

Risk homeostasis also affects how we think about placing purposeful bets. Having more money to spend on a bet is the equivalent of driving on a straight road with wide lanes on a sunny day. Having all that money makes the road feel safer, so you speed up: you hire better

147

talent, invest in newer technology, make a few more strategic acquisitions. I mean, if you had $500 million to develop a new product, wouldn't you behave differently than if you only had $3 million?

*

This, then, explains what happened to the Newton and the PalmPilot. Apple increased its chances of success by having $500 million in the bag, but by spending that money they drove the risk of the project back up to a level they were comfortable with. They added complicated enhancements and tricky features that made the project a risky proposition. Lucky for Palm Computing, their risk equation needed to be much different. They did not have nearly enough money to do the type of fancy stuff Apple was attempting, so they focused their bet and behaved in a less risky way. In fact, The PalmPilot was Jeff Hawkins's second attempt at creating a useful handheld device. His first product was something called the Zoomer. It cost $4 million to develop and was a complete failure. "It was the slowest computer ever made by man," said Hawkins about the poorly designed PDA. "It was too big and too expensive. We executed badly." Fortunately, Donna Dubinsky, his partner at Palm Computing, had reserved enough capital to try again, this time creating the Pilot. At Apple, they only really gave the Newton one big shot. Even though they did launch different versions of the device, all of them were variations of the same flawed concept. In the end it is quite likely that the chances of success were the same for both the Newton and the PalmPilot, no matter how much money each company invested. It was the fact that Palm computing was able to take a second shot that made the difference.

This idea, that almost no amount of planning or dedicated resources will greatly affect our chances of success, is extraordinarily counterintuitive, but it is the best way to understand how the size of a particular bet seems not to be correlated with its level of success. Examples are everywhere. In 1999, for instance, the CEO of Andersen Consulting (now Accenture), George Shaheen, left his $5 million-per-year job to head up one of the hottest Internet start-ups of its time,

Webvan. The plan behind Webvan, which aimed to revolutionize grocery shopping in cities around the United States, was incredibly ambitious. In a span of about eighteen to twenty-four months they were to open fourteen fully automated warehouses in order to fulfill grocery orders in twenty-six separate markets. All told, the bet amounted to one billion dollars. The company failed within eighteen months.

Only months later, however, a start-up appeared with what seemed like a similar business model. This one, however, was based out of New York and catered to its surrounding area. Like Webvan, it needed to build a new warehouse with specialized technology, but unlike Webvan it did so in just one region. FreshDirect initially raised $34 million and with that money was able to create a business with hundreds of millions in revenue and enough stability to survive the recession of 2008–2009. Today it is expanding into a number of other cities. The risk of failure was probably similar for both companies, but one firm spent everything it had on one big bet and the other one didn't. The latter was able to remain flexible enough to adapt as new opportunities and challenges changed their game.

The conclusion here—that we can't affect our chances of success—is supported by research in other fields, such as science. Dean Keith Simonton, a professor of psychology at the University of California–Davis, is one of the world's leading experts on creativity and has studied scientists across decades in order to get handle on their hit rate; that is, how often they end up writing excellent, groundbreaking papers.

What he has found drives home the point of thinking about the pathway to success as placing one bet after another. However strange it may sound, the chance of writing a groundbreaking paper (one with a lot of citations from other researchers) is directly correlated to the number of papers that a scientist has written. Those scientists who published the most had the best chance of writing something truly successful. The reason this sounds strange is because we tend to believe that the number of groundbreaking papers a scientist publishes should be correlated with how *smart* or *experienced* the scientist is. But there is little evidence of this.

149

When scientists structure their research and then translate their findings into published papers, we can safely assume that, generally speaking, they are trying to be as successful as possible. They are certainly not planning to write mediocre papers. But, on aggregate, no matter how much they try, they still have no ability to predict which type of research will have a significant impact. Their chance of success remains the same across all the papers they publish. It's as if they roll the dice again and again. Simonton calls this principle the *equal-odds rule* and he has studied its effect for decades. It has some fascinating implications that have turned out to be true.

For instance, the equal-odds rule implies that scientists who publish the most high-quality papers should also publish the most low-quality papers. They do. It also implies that there should be no real trend in when they write groundbreaking papers during their career. If experience mattered, for instance, we should expect research papers to get better over time. They don't. Instead, scientists have the best chance of writing groundbreaking papers when they publish a lot, no matter *when* that happens in their career. Simonton has found the same relationship in other disciplines, such as musical composition, as well. Whether we talk about corporations, start-ups, scientists, or artists, our chances of success while placing a purposeful bet remain more or less the same for each bet.

*

Success cannot be guaranteed by hefty resource investments and market research. Nor can we disregard our tendencies to adjust our risk-taking behavior to suit a certain comfort level. In other words, it is not possible to turn a purposeful bet into a sure thing. If we take a step back we can see that this conclusion makes intuitive sense. Pretend for a moment that you can actually guarantee success by putting enough money behind an idea. Let's say that investing $10 million in a project, instead of investing $10,000, yielded a guaranteed profit. The obvious result would be that venture capitalists everywhere would allocate $10 million for every idea they came across, in order to ensure that those projects would succeed.

This isn't how it works, of course, which is why placing a purposeful bet is a random endeavor. The implications of the equal-odds rule and of risk homeostasis are surprising and wide-ranging. If examined carefully, for example, they actually suggest that there is a particular way one can place a string of purposeful bets that should increase the overall chances of success. We will see what the tactics are for doing just that in the chapter that follows.

10

HOW TO PLACE PURPOSEFUL BETS

The church bells rang in the Spanish village of Guernica, signaling an incoming airplane. Like almost every other day, the market in the center of the Basque town was bustling with women and children. At 4:35 p.m. a low-flying German bomber appeared on the horizon, heading straight toward the town. Minutes later it dropped six heavy bombs.

Five minutes later another bomber followed, but this time the intensity of the bombing increased. Soon even more planes arrived. Over the next three hours at least forty German and Italian bombers dropped more than a hundred thousand pounds of explosives on the town. "They kept going back and forth, sometimes in a long line, sometimes in a loose formation," an eyewitness noted. "It was as if they were practicing new moves." Some of the civilians took cover in churches and bomb shelters. Others tried to flee, only to be gunned down by the fighter planes' machine guns.

The April 26, 1937 bombing was an exercise to test a new type of warfare: blitzkrieg. The results were devastating. Seventy percent of the town was leveled and more than 1,000 people were killed. By the first of May, news of the Guernica bombing reached Paris and more than a million people rushed into the streets in protest. The Spaniard Pablo Picasso saw a black-and-white photo of the aftermath in the newspaper and was outraged. But he was also inspired. He hurried through the crowded streets back to his apartment, where he started sketching. We don't know exactly when Picasso outlined the bull—the centerpiece of the new work—but it must have come early in his revisions and sketches.

He might not have known it at that moment, but that bull would become a focal point in one of the world's best-known works of art, called simply *Guernica*. The painting displays the horrors of war with an intensity greater than perhaps any other in history. Naked and stark, *Guernica*, more than twenty-six feet wide and eleven feet tall, depicts the darkest depth to which humanity can descend. It has become an iconic reminder of the tragedies of war and the suffering of innocent people in wartime.

Originally commissioned by the Spanish republican government, *Guernica* was put on display at the 1937 World's Fair in Paris and then went on to occupy prominent venues in the United States and around the world. As it circulated, it became the most widely discussed and celebrated painting of its kind, evoking vigorous debate about its political and cultural relevance as well as its aesthetic value. The implications of the painting reverberated throughout the world. It was said that while Picasso was living in German-occupied Paris a Gestapo officer entered his apartment and saw a reproduction of the famous painting. The officer pointed at it and asked, "Did you do this?"

"No," Picasso replied. "You did."

*

Most people view Picasso's revolutionary interpretation of the attack on Guernica as, among other things, a testament to his brilliance. Picasso's impact on the world of art has been unrivaled. He is widely considered to be the most influential artist of the modern era. We tend to believe that randomness is far removed when someone like Picasso comes along, and it is downright insulting to suggest that a masterpiece like *Guernica* is the result of mere luck.

But just like the Apple Newton and the PalmPilot, *Guernica* was a bet, regardless of its creator's genius. Picasso could not simply *decide* that he was going to create a masterpiece. He had to roll the dice with each painting he made. His path to success was not just to employ his great technical skill, which he could have used to copy other excellent styles and techniques while still drowning in a sea of other artists. No, in order to become the best in the world he needed to try something new, with little understanding of just how well this new concept was going to fare. His ability to improve the chance of success for any individual piece of art was limited.

This counterintuitive notion has major implications for how we think about achieving greatness. In this chapter we will look at five major tactics we can employ in order to lace together a successful string of purposeful bets. These tactics all derive directly from the implications of the equal-odds rule and the effects of risk homeostasis.

1. Place Many Bets

If you only have a certain chance to succeed when you place a purposeful bet, it follows that the more bets you place, the greater the chance for you to succeed. The more times you try, the better off you are. Picasso's impact on the world of art suggests that he must have rolled the dice far more often than we might initially guess. Indeed, he did.

Pablo Picasso created more than fifty thousand works of art in his career. Some estimates put the number beyond a hundred thousand. That translates into roughly two to four pieces *per day*. He is by far the most prolific artist who ever lived. In 1980, one thousand of his works were put on exhibit at the Museum of Modern Art in New York City. During four months over a million visitors attended the exhibition, which displaced MoMA's permanent collection. "I don't think there is any other artist whose work could sustain such an exhibition," said William Rubin, MoMA's then-curator of painting and sculpture.

When one reads praise like that, it is easy to forget that Picasso is also the person who produced more crappy artwork than probably any other renowned artist in history. Many of his canvases collected dust in basements around the world, and with good reason. They sucked. Picasso could not predict with any certainty which of his pieces would become celebrated and which would be recycled. He was, in essence, placing a bet that a percentage of his work would take hold—in accordance with the equal-odds rule. Consequently Picasso's output gave him an incredible edge in becoming successful. And he's not alone.

The Virgin Group has launched over four hundred companies, Google has created hundreds of products, Albert Einstein wrote hundreds of papers, Thomas Edison had 1,093 patents to his name and carried out tens of thousands of experiments. Apple, as we know of it today, has a failure rate of some 90 percent when creating new ideas.

Consider the game maker Rovio, creator of one of the best-selling games of all time: Angry Birds. Chances are you or someone in your household has played this game—it has scored over 700 million downloads since its release in 2009. If you've played it, you know why. The game is colorful, fun, and highly addictive. It is very easy to play but quite hard to master, with new rules and tougher challenges at each level.

Rovio, a company that appeared to come out of nowhere, was valued at $1 billion a little over a year after the game's launch. As a result, people tend to believe it was a so-called overnight success. They also tend to believe that there was an incredibly powerful strategy behind the success of the game. At a glance, that might seem to be the case. Take Rovio's marketing strategy. Instead of launching the game to a broad audience, only to watch it fade into obscurity, Rovio's makers concentrated its efforts on specific countries in Europe. They figured out that it might not be all that difficult to top the bestselling app chart in Greece or the Czech Republic, with only two hundred to three hundred downloads needed to hit the number one spots. So they went after those markets first. With those early successes in their pockets, they pursued a marketing partnership with a firm that had a solid working relationship with Apple. Soon Angry Birds was featured on the front page of iTunes. With that, everything changed. In the UK it went from the number 600 spot to number one in the UK app store—overnight.

Just how smart must someone be to both create a game this good and to market it with such flawless execution? Rovio must be packed with brainiacs who have the uncanny ability to understand not only what people want in a game but also how to market it. Right? Well . . . they *are* very smart people. But if being smart was enough, they should have pumped out a whole string of successful games. That has clearly not been the case. Rovio had been producing games for eight years before they created Angry Birds, and the performance of all their earlier attempts paled by comparison. In fact, Angry Bird was the company's *fifty-second* game. You would have a good shot at a major success, too, if you tried that many times!

We see this relationship between the number of bets placed and resulting success even with people we would not in a million years consider grouping with Picasso. Take Bethenny Frankel. Frankel was cast in the original *The Real Housewives of New York*, a reality-TV show launched in March 2008 by the Bravo Network. Her work on the show allowed her to publicize a product called the Skinnygirl Margarita, an alcoholic beverage designed for women who are counting calories. Frankel and her partners eventually sold Skinnygirl for an estimated $64 million (although the real number has been highly disputed). Lucky girl, some people said. And, yes, there is no doubt that Frankel has been very lucky. But here is the thing: she gave herself *many chances* to get lucky. Look at her career to date.

First she started a party-planning company called In Any Event. It didn't really work out. Then she started a pashmina import business, specifically targeting actresses. It went okay, but she couldn't grow it. She followed that up with an unsuccessful health food store called Blanches. That experience prompted her to launch Bethenny Bakes, a health-conscious bakery based in Manhattan. While running Bethenny Bakes she applied for a spot on Donald Trump's hit show *The Apprentice* but was not selected. Soon after that, she landed a part on Martha Stewart's ill-fated *The Apprentice: Martha Stewart*. She went on to launch a custom-meals business for celebrities and wrote a column for *Health Magazine*. That led to an endorsement deal with Pepperidge Farm. When she finally joined the cast of Bravo's new reality show, *The Real Housewives of New York*, Frankel's idea for Skinnygirl was already in the works, and her constant plugging of the brand on the show gave it unexpected notoriety. Skinnygirl took off like a rocket. And *then* she sold the brand for $64 million.

When you think about it this way, Frankel's success starts to make a lot of sense. Yes, she got lucky, but she also rolled the dice over and over again. So did Picasso, the folks at Rovio, and Thomas Edison. They all rolled the dice many times and they all found their way to success. It is not surprising, then, that remarkably successful people and organizations use this strategy to harness randomness. Taking many bites of the apple compensates for our inability to predict success. This holds true for any individual or organization that wishes to become great, even if it may not appear to be the case from the outside.

Placing many bets is an effective way to harness randomness, but it has a major, obvious limitation. How on earth are you supposed to place many bets if the investment required for each bet is so high it ties up all your available funds? If this is the case you only get to place one bet, and if it doesn't work out, you're done. This is what happened to the Newton project: one bet and out. Fortunately for Apple, it had enough resources to keep going with other bets. But unless there is another piece to this puzzle, placing many bets could, by all accounts, be a completely ruinous strategy. How do you avoid such a fate?

2. Minimize the Size of the Bets

If you drive east on the autostrada A4 in northern Italy towards Slovenia, you'll pass a small town called Palmanova, widely considered to be the perfectly designed Renaissance city. Unlike Rome, which resembles a tangled mess of spaghetti, Palmanova is shaped like a flawlessly symmetrical nine-sided star.

The star originates in a hexagonal piazza, which is outlined by the city's main administrative buildings. Six streets radiate from the piazza, crafting perfectly proportioned quadrants. Three of the streets lead to the city's gates, while the others lead to what once were powerful defense partitions. Four concrete veins mimic the outer wall and concisely intersect the six main roads, providing increased defenses and creating successively larger quadrants. Each successive ring is larger in exact proportion to its predecessor. You can get a perfect view of Palmanova on Google Earth or Google Maps, where it becomes clear that the city's design extends beyond its wall into the very landscape of the hill it sits upon.

In the early sixteenth century the Venetian empire began an aggressive fortification campaign after attacks by the League of Cambria left their frontier vulnerable to invasion. Founded in 1593, Palmanova was to protect the eastern front against a looming Turkish attack. The unique design has a purpose: it is almost impenetrable from the outside. The intricate road system allows defensive reinforcements to effectively navigate the city, while during peacetime each quadrant is easily accessible. Structurally, the city was planned without a glitch.

Palmanova was meant to be self-sufficient, with artisans, businessmen, and farmers living in meticulously planned harmony. And yet in 1622, almost thirty years after its completion, the streets were empty. The empire had spared no expense in funding a city that looked abso-

159

lutely ideal on paper but was, in reality, not especially livable. The remote nature of the city, and the perceived danger of invasion, rendered it a place where no one wanted to settle. Planners were so desperate for tenants that criminals from nearby regions were pardoned and given building materials if they agreed to make the move. "Yet even the prisoners did not move voluntarily," wrote art historian Wolfgang Braunfels. But there was no way to reverse course at that stage—there weren't enough resources for another bet.

Purposeful bets that are colossal in size can have a big upside, but only if you get them exactly right the first time. And that's not likely. Since the probability of success doesn't correlate with the amount of resources you have invested in an idea or project, it usually makes sense to drive down the size of the bet. The failure of Palmanova highlights the need to place many bets but also shows that you can only do so if each one is small enough.

Because we can make far more of them, small purposeful bets maximize our chances of having something random and unpredictable happen. The idea of small bets has received significant support in recent business literature. Peter Sims's excellent book *Little Bets*, for instance, defines a small bet as "a low-risk action taken to discover, develop, and test an idea." One example Sims gives concerns the rockstar-level comedian Chris Rock. When Rock puts together an hourlong routine for HBO, he prepares by spending months hitting up small comedy clubs around the country, trying joke after joke after joke. Most of them fall flat and audiences wonder just what happened to the comedic genius they have all seen on TV. He's still there, of course, it's just that he is minimizing the costs of his bets by trying a few at a time, and for a limited audience. That allows him to place tons of purposeful bets—and to later double down on those that pay off, with audiences rolling on the floor.

Smaller bets not only allow you more opportunities to get lucky—they allow for more iterations within any given idea because you get more shots at getting the project right. This is what Palm Computing did when they tried the Zoomer, failed, and then tried again with the

PalmPilot. The more iterations you can get through, the higher the chance of success. Take someone like Jimmy Wales. He founded Wikipedia, the world's largest online free encyclopedia. It is a stunning achievement, particularly considering that it is continuously created through the voluntary efforts of thousands of people around the world who freely submit and edit entry after entry. People initially had great reservations about the process. "We should be more academic than Britannica," argued one early contributor, "because, as it's from the Internet, no one will trust us unless it's very serious." This was a common sentiment, and everyone who expressed it turned out to be wrong. Maybe Jimmy Wales is a genius who intuitively understood better than anyone else the altruistic and collaborative nature of people on the Web. Or maybe not—let's take a look at the whole story.

There were, in fact, seven earlier efforts at creating online encyclopedias through some sort of collaboration-driven approach. Jimmy Wales was behind one called Nupedia, which used a completely different process for creating entries than the one Wikipedia eventually adopted. To bolster the site's credibility, an advisory board of credentialed academics and experienced professionals developed an intensive editing and acceptance process. After eighteen months and a few hundred thousand dollars, Nupedia had only amassed twenty articles despite a mailing list of more than two thousand interested contributors. It clearly wasn't working. Wales needed to roll the dice again, but with another approach. The fact that his bet was small allowed him to do just that.

This time he got his inspiration from a new movement within software development described as "agile." Unlike traditional software development, where the solution is "planned, designed, and detailed before the project begins," agile development relies on small teams that produce incremental but workable software. Agile programmers advocate going live with the earliest possible version of new software and letting many people work simultaneously to rapidly refine it. This sparked an intersectional idea: why not let *anyone* contribute to the encyclopedia? This was vastly different from Nupedia's model and the advisory board promptly rejected it. Wales decided to launch Wikipedia as a separate

161

project in January 2001, and in just two weeks more than six hundred articles had been produced. Today it is one of the most popular Web sites in the world. Nupedia turned out its lights in 2003.

Obviously, if Jimmy Wales could have created Wikipedia from the start, perhaps he would have; but that's not the way it works. By minimizing his bets he was able to harness the random nature of success. What is really remarkable about this story is that Wales's approach for Nupedia is the way most of us would have tried to make such a project come to life. We would have looked at how encyclopedias have been done in the past, understood the need to establish credibility, and so on. In other words, if we had tried to launch Nupedia we would probably have done it the exact same way Jimmy Wales did it! This is an insight that most people miss and it is critical in helping us understand just what drives success—and notions of brilliance. If you try something new and it works, you will quickly find yourself called an expert on it. Indeed, the reason we call Wales a genius today is because after his first bet fell through, he tried again. And *that* worked.

3. Take the Smallest Executable Step

In my firm we have developed a way to think about these minimized bets. We call it taking the smallest executable step. What step can you take that actually tests the validity of some aspect of your project? Design this smallest executable step as a test, and then get going. The point is not that this step is part of a larger, detailed action plan. There is no larger plan at this stage—you can safely assume that you are already making all kinds of mistaken assumptions about your project. Unfortunately you don't know which ones are wrong, and there is no way for you to figure it out unless you create a small bet—and then test it.

This smallest executable step usually requires thinking very creatively about existing resources. In our engagements with some of the largest corporations in the world, we help teams develop potentially breakthrough ideas and then force these teams to start testing those ideas with *no extra budget or time*. These teams are still often expected to deliver real revenue to the corporation over the next four to six months. It seems impossible at first, but soon they realize that if they are ever to have a chance at finding a breakthrough idea within that time frame, they need room to do at least two or three tests. So they quickly ratchet down their immediate goals, stop analyzing, and start executing. It also forces them to find help wherever they can. Can you rely on partners or volunteers (including other employees) to get started? Do it. Can you rethink the scale of your project to test something within the next four weeks? Do that.

Consider what Howard Schultz did after his entirely unpredictable and random moment of clarity in Milan. Once he returned to Seattle, he tried to convince his colleagues that they should open a coffee shop like the one he had seen in Italy. But it was a risky move. Instead of opening an entirely new shop, he managed to convince them to try a small espresso bar in their existing store, which sold coffeemaking equipment and beans. Schultz's espresso bar soon had lines going out the door. It was the smallest executable step for him and it proved a critical point—that there was a market for this type of coffee vendor.

One can see this pattern emerging in the start-up community. Eric Ries might be the most well-known proponent for this approach and in his book, *The Lean Start-Up*, he illustrates over and over again the power of running small experiments in order to learn what works and what doesn't. "If you cannot fail, you cannot learn," he says. Indeed, there has been a tremendous rise in angel investors funding start-ups, crowding out more established venture capitalists, or VCs. The chief difference between angel investors and traditional VCs is that angels invest significantly less money in each idea, and they tend to do it earlier. Some investment or incubator firms, such as Y Combinator, have turned this practice into an explicit strategy: they give start-ups $5,000 per founder plus an additional $5,000 for good measure (it has now evolved into a somewhat more complicated setup, involving, among others, a Russian billionaire). The start-up, then, has to survive on that sum for an entire summer. These are incredibly small bets compared

163

to traditional early-stage investments, which tend to range from half a million to a couple of million dollars. As risk homeostasis would predict, however, this has not negatively affected Y Combinator's success rate. In fact, it has become one of the hottest investment funds in Silicon Valley.

Of course, sometimes the smallest executable step is impossible to make all that "small." There is a big difference between a software developer and a biotech start-up. Y Combinator's numbers are small because it just doesn't take all that much money to build a Web site or an app. That is not true for a biotech start-up, though. Still, your best chance to have enough resources to try again when the first attempt fails is to shoot for the smallest executable step.

Not long ago I was discussing these concepts over dinner with the CEO of a large global conglomerate. He told me about a dilemma he was facing. "I gave an executive three million dollars last year to create something groundbreaking. She is an outstanding executive, but what happened? Nothing horrible, but nothing terribly exciting, either," he said. "How should I think about that?" he asked me.

"If nothing comes out of it, would you be willing to give her another three million?" I asked him.

"Of course not," he said.

"Well, that is a problem, right there," I answered.

It was very likely that under those circumstances the research executive would shoot for a version of what was already working in order to protect herself from failure; in other words, nothing "terribly exciting." It also seemed clear that the executive had placed the money mostly on one major bet—that's how she got the budget approved to begin with. Both actions would drive her away from the random and towards the logical. "Next time, if there is one" I said, "split your budget into six parts of five hundred thousand dollars and guarantee her all six parts no matter what the result—as long as she uses them on six separate bets." I added, "Tell her to take each chunk of five hundred thousand and try to get something to happen with a quarter of that sum. That is all the resources she needs to take the smallest executable step."

4. Calculate Affordable Loss, Not ROI

Using small bets and small executable steps appears to be a very manageable tactic, but there are also some problems associated with it. Most notably, it does not tell you exactly *which* small bets to focus on. You certainly can't pursue every single click moment in your life—if you did, you'd soon be overwhelmed. The most logical approach in guiding our thinking in this regard is to calculate the return on investment, or ROI, for an idea and see how it stacks up to other projects you are considering. Which project can provide the greatest return for the smallest investment? The fact that it is the most logical approach, however, should at this point make us suspicious since logic is not a good guide in an uncertain world.

In 2005 Rupert Murdoch's News Corporation bought MySpace for $580 million. At the time, based on the estimated ROI of the deal, it seemed like the global media conglomerate had managed a steal. "The News Corp.'s purchase of MySpace is looking like that rarest of rarities in the media world, a much-ballyhooed acquisition where it turns out that the buyer underpaid," Marc Gunther wrote in *Fortune*.

It must have seemed like a safe statement at the time. MySpace's growth exploded after the deal. Measured in page views, MySpace was the second most popular site on the Internet: behind Yahoo!, but ahead of MSN, AOL, and Google. It had 66 million members with about 250,000 new ones signing up daily. But by 2011 MySpace was in free fall. It lost its foothold and News Corporation unloaded it for $35 million after Facebook had pounded it into a bloody pulp.

All this really tells us is that calculating a reliable future return is a tricky thing to do. And it is becoming increasingly difficult in our hyperadaptive world. Yet, over the past couple of decades, return on investment has become a divining rod for individuals and organizations. Many decision makers ask for an ROI analysis as a prerequisite for almost any action. It indicates that you've done the basic legwork to establish what an idea might be worth. And logically the metric does make quite a bit of sense. If you are going to spend a certain amount of money, you want to be sure that it is put to good use. If we still lived in a world of rules that change slowly and with well-entrenched main players, that principle of predictable returns would make sense. But it does not hold up in a world where the nature of the game changes randomly, unpredictably, and very quickly. In this world, ROI loses all value as a tool for prediction.

This stands in stark contrast to the demands often made by managers who hold ideas to a very high ROI expectation at a very early stage in development. I have frequently seen it happen when the details of a project are so slim they amount to nothing but some Post-it notes and a few pieces of paper, yet questions such as whether it can justify an investment are already being bandied about. Can it add $50 million in revenue or not? Unless the idea can clear such a hurdle, it will get dropped. But just how much can one possibly know with certainty so early in the life of an idea? Yahoo did not think Google was worth $1 million even *nine months* after the company had launched. And News Corporation thought MySpace was worth $600 million a *few years* after it had launched. Both calculations were dramatically off base.

There are several other drawbacks to using ROI as decision-making tool. First, it makes it difficult to place a small bet. Let's say that you run an ROI analysis that shows a significant return. Such an analysis can seduce an organization into going out with a large bet right away—to shoot for a Palmanova—on the basis of unreliable data. Second, the logical nature of an ROI analysis means that others may arrive at similar conclusions, which makes it difficult to stand out. And finally, let's say that the ROI analysis is inconclusive. So instead of placing a small bet, you have to go looking for more data. You need to run some more surveys, create more strategy maps, and so on, in order to actually achieve certainty. But certainty is impossible. So all you get, for the most part, is delays.

So if an ROI analysis is fraught with problems in an uncertain world, what type of numbers should you run instead? There is another calculation that is far more useful in placing purposeful bets, and it can be done quickly. Instead of measuring the acceptable return on investment, focus on calculating the affordable loss. The term comes from a paper called "What Makes Entrepreneurs Entrepreneurial," published by Professor Saras Saravathy of Darden School of Business. The calculation allows you to determine if you (as an individual or organization) are in jeopardy if your project fails. Ideally, you should be able to continue operating without much hardship. Put another way, is the potential loss from pursuing a failed idea affordable? If it doesn't work at first, can you do it a few more times? Affordable loss is generally a much simpler number to generate, and the process should help you think through how to execute your idea. If the organization or department or career is in jeopardy if there is only one chance of getting it right, then it is not affordable and you have most likely not thought creatively about how to minimize the size of the bet.

Rovio figured it could spend forty thousand dollars to develop and test Angry Birds. It was enough to see if the game had legs but not enough to ruin the company's fortunes if the project failed. No ROI analysis could have predicted the stunning success the game garnered, and, conversely, if they had needed to clear such a daunting hurdle they would likely have hesitated in placing the bet initially. The least amount of resources, money, or reputation you are willing to put at risk in pursuing a new idea, then, is what will fund your smallest executable step. In turn, the more tightly you can define this smallest executable step, the smaller your loss will be if the test leads you to reconsider the idea.

When Amazon launched the Kindle reader, the device had an incredibly uncertain future. But it has turned out to be a huge success. "I think we have gotten pretty lucky recently," Jeff Bezos said in regard to the Kindle at a shareholder meeting in 2011. A more interesting piece of the story, however, is how Amazon appraised the bet as they were developing the product. It was never a break-the-company proposition. "If you invent frequently and are willing to fail, then you never get to that point where you really need to bet the whole company," Bezos said. "Go back in time to when we started working on Kindle, almost seven years ago. . . . There you just have to place a bet. If you

167

place enough of those bets, and if you place them early enough, none of them are ever betting the company."

What Bezos is saying, essentially, is that he could afford several of these bets even if they didn't work out. Instead, he is basing his company's approach to success on the inherent randomness involved in any enterprise: "One of the nice things now is that we have enough scale that we can do quite large experiments without it having significant impact on our short-term financials." In other words, Amazon's purposeful bets have increased in size but are still utterly affordable.

But there are still risks with using affordable loss as your only criteria. A large company, for instance, might find that it can afford to test an incredible number of ideas. But not all organizations have the ability to deal with so many distractions from their core business. Companies that are distracted can get killed simply because they lose sight of what really matters at any given time. Is there another way to evaluate the potential of a purposeful bet?

5. Use Passion as Fuel

In February 2005, the married couple Jon Payson and Naomi Josepher opened the doors to their new storefront business The Chocolate Room, just in time for Valentine's Day. They had moved from the Upper East Side of Manhattan to Park Slope in Brooklyn, eager to participate in the Fifth Avenue renaissance that was taking place there. The couple noticed that there were no chocolate cafés in Park Slope, and they figured there might be an opportunity in the market—maybe they could open one?

Neither Jon nor Naomi had any deep experience making chocolate, but they had a lot of experience eating it. And the more the couple researched chocolate, the more passionate they became. Over time they became obsessed with the idea of making the best chocolate cake in New York City. They couldn't shake the desire. "It really started with us eating our way through every chocolate cake served in New York. We started with dessert places in the village, moved on to the restaurants on the Upper West Side, tried out cafes on the Lower East," Naomi said. They were trying to find the chocolate cake that trumped all others, "but it was difficult. We couldn't find one that tasted the way we wanted it to."

So they decided to create that cake themselves. They conducted culinary experiments to get it just right, but the taste they were seeking continued to elude them. The chocolate was too bitter, or it was too sweet. Or the cake was too dry. What's the difference between two or three layers of chocolate? How important is the tint of the icing? The sugar ratio? It took them almost a year to isolate the texture and the not-too-sweet flavor. "It had to slide right off the fork and bring indescribable pleasure," Payson said.

Jon and Naomi's experience exemplifies the approach to harnessing randomness that we have talked about in this chapter: many bets, each of them small and affordable. But what can sustain such an approach? Being wrong, again and again, is incredibly taxing. Even if we know that it "is not failure, it is learning" those words can seem trite and clichéd when it has been a while since something good happened. It is easy to say that we should place bet after bet, but when we don't have the luxury of knowing if we are right, we can start to lose faith in what we are doing. Over time our willingness to place many bets may dissipate, and eventually we give up. Picasso, Hawkins, Frankel, and the folks at Rovio and many others must have felt this way time and again. They had no idea how many times they would have to be wrong in order to get it right. This is why they, and others like them, need a strong motivator for getting through it all. I call that motivation *passion*, and it leads to our fifth tactic: use passion as fuel to get past inevitable failures.

It is often said that passion is the key to success. But what does that statement really mean? For starters, there has been a tremendous amount of research done—much of it by leading Harvard Business School professor Teresa Amabile—supporting the notion that passion is critically important in driving creativity. If you are driven by an intrinsic motivation such as passion, you have a better chance of producing creative work than if you are driven by external factors.

But passion also solves another piece of the success puzzle. It has to do with how we think about making success happen—about the actual execution of ideas and projects. In a world where finding success requires more and more bets, you need the wherewithal to sustain yourself through the inevitable failures. Passion is what sustains us. In fact, the passion one has for an idea might give us the *best* measure of its potential—it gives us a sense of how much a person or team is willing to go through in order to become successful. And we see it in every story where success has been unpredictable. Howard Schultz was passionate about creating the perfect environment for drinking exceptional coffee. Diane von Furstenberg lived and breathed fashion; Dave Weise was driven by the idea that he could fix Windows, and Picasso had a passionate reaction to the tragedy at Guernica.

In the case of Jon and Naomi, passion is what sustained them through many months of fruitless (albeit tasty) efforts. It is what provided them with the drive to try so many different chocolate-cake iterations until they found what they were looking for. "We really wanted to get this right," Naomi says, "particularly Jon—he was almost obsessed. It kept us going." Someone with less strong emotions around the matter would have settled much, much earlier. Instead, Jon and Naomi found their passion to be, unarguably, one of the primary ingredients of their success.

For them it worked out well. They did finally figure out the to-die-for recipe. I know this because my wife was their very first customer. She came home one day claiming that I'd "go crazy for this cake," which was saying something because she knows I'm not the world's biggest chocolate fan. With that cake as a flagship item Jon and Naomi launched The Chocolate Room, where they sold all things chocolate.

The reaction was instantaneous. Word of their incredible three-layered chocolate cake spread across the five boroughs. Late-night crowds started lining up outside their café. After an *Oprah Magazine* editor visited the place she described the cake as a "ménage à trois of opulent, buttery filling, rich but not overpowering frosting, and perfectly moist cake [that] turns most Chocolate Room customers into basket cases—and addicts." The lines outside their café grew, and a few years later they opened a second Chocolate Room in Brooklyn, a few blocks away from their original shop.

The idea that passion is such an incredibly strong criteria for success frequently appears to be lost on organizations hoping to achieve greatness. Passion is a topic to which we are hesitant to grant a lot of credence. In part it might be that we feel more comfortable using traditional metrics, such as ROI, in our selection process and passion has no part in that process. But that is a mistake—one that decreases the chances of something unexpected happening because without it, people place fewer purposeful bets.

It is critical, then, for organizations to screen an idea's criteria based on the passion of the people involved. That is the best way to understand if they will have the wherewithal to keep placing many bets. Because the success of virtually every aspect of an organization, or even the world at large, is becoming increasingly random, it follows that it has become more important than ever to find and fuel the passion that drives you and your team.

Just as passion can launch a business built on chocolate, so too can it change entire industries. Consider John Boyd. A fighter pilot by training, he wrote the monograph "Aerial Attack Study," which became the fundamental tactics manual for air forces around the world. Boyd had a passion for dogfighting he had fighter pilot blood coursing through his veins—but he didn't just want to fly airplanes, he wanted to design better ones. He also knew that if he wanted to change the industry a second time, he needed to speak their language. Which is why he found himself staring at a thermodynamics textbook in 1962.

In its simplest sense, thermodynamics is the study of energy. Boyd realized that the most effective fighter plane didn't need fancy instruments or complex radar technology; it simply needed to manage energy efficiently. All the technology in the world wouldn't help if a plane couldn't quickly decelerate, accelerate, turn, and bank to outmaneuver its enemy. This meant a lightweight and agile plane, something that the air force simply wasn't interested in developing.

171

After graduation Boyd relocated to Elgin Air Force Base where eventually he settled in as a maintenance worker, one of the lowest jobs on the air-force career pyramid. He spent every night and every free moment scribbling equations that would prove his theory. Sometimes he would spend weeks on an equation, only to learn he had made a mistake in the first line. When he learned that the base's computer could do thousands of equations per minute, Boyd tried to get bay time, but the base commanding officer rejected his request. "Once the air force understands what I'm doing," he brazenly told the commanding officer, "they're going to tell me to spend all of my time developing these theories of mine."

Unfazed and undeterred, Boyd met Thomas Christie, a young air force mathematician who helped him gain access to the computer bay. Thereafter, Boyd spent hours at the lab every day, perfecting his formula. By the early sixties, he'd perfected it. After obtaining flight specifications for both American and Soviet aircraft, Boyd realized that the planes the United States was developing were worthless. He briefed the higher-ups with this information, including the head of Tactical Air Command. His evidence was irrefutable. Soon after, Boyd was transferred to the Pentagon, where he used his theory of energy to help develop what many consider to be one of the best modern fighter planes: the F-16. With a tenacity fueled by passion, Boyd relentlessly pursued ideas that upended how fighter pilots use strategy and revolutionized fighter jets.

Making many small, purposeful bets, fueled by passion and calibrated by affordable loss, is the second out of three ways to channel the randomness in this world; and we have already explored click moments. But there is a third way that holds even deeper lessons about what we must do in order to capture the randomness around us. This third way suggests that the true power of placing a purposeful bet lies not simply in learning if the bet might work in our favor, but in the unexpected, complex forces that follow placing it. As the following chapter will show, these forces have been responsible for the toppling of dictators, the rise of eBay, and the suspense of *Jaws*.

11

COMPLEX FORCES

When Faida Hamdi met Mohamed Bouazizi one morning at the marketplace in the small Tunisian town of Sidi Bouzid, they set in motion a series of events that would ultimately lead to the capture and killing of the Libyan dictator Muammar Gaddafi. The year was 2010. The date was December 17. They met at ten a.m. and they started arguing almost right away.

There was nothing in Faida Hamdi's past to indicate that she would ignite a swift and sweeping revolution. Likewise, there was not a thing in Mohamed Bouazizi's history to suggest that he would do the same. But these two people crossed paths that morning, and their fateful meeting provides some important clues about what really drives most types of success in the world.

Although the exact nature of the events that transpired are still in dispute, they appear to have played out something like this: Hamdi, a forty-five-year old municipal inspections officer, was inspecting fruit vendors' stands during the morning hours. A police officer's daughter known for her strong personality and spotless professional record, Hamdi's job was to inspect buildings, investigate noise complaints, and fine vendors who did not have a license to sell their goods. That morning she found just such a vendor in Mohamed Bouazizi.

Bouazizi was twenty-six years old, quite poor but also happy, according to his family. The previous night Bouazizi had borrowed $200 to buy vegetables and fruit that he planned to sell the next morning. His typical profit each day from his fruit cart was about ten dollars, and much of that went to pay for his sister's schooling and support for his widowed mother. Bouazizi started out at eight o'clock that morning, as usual, pushing his wooden cart from the supermarket where he bought his produce to the local marketplace, or souk, two kilometers away. Everything went well until about ten o'clock, when two municipal officers came along and proceeded to harass Bouazizi. One of the officers was Hamdi.

Bouazizi was no stranger to this treatment. According to his family, the police and other government workers had been targeting him for years. On this occasion they wanted to confiscate his fruit, cart, and scale ostensibly because he did not have a license. The scale was worth about a hundred dollars and Bouazizi had absolutely no intention of giving it up.

This actually appears to have been a classic shakedown, with Bouazizi expected to pay his "fine"—really just a code word for "bribe"—in order to continue selling fruit. But on that particular day he decided to fight back. Although witness accounts vary, it seems clear that although some sort of fight broke out, Bouazizi was unable to get his scale back. Hamdi and her colleagues pushed over the cart and swore at him. And then Hamdi did something that could not have possibly meant all that much at the time. She slapped him. And that one action—along with his response to it—ignited a chain of actions that would in a matter of months topple some of the most powerful regimes in the Middle East.

*

Sometimes events play out in a straightforward way, exactly according to plan. There is a simple cause-and-effect transaction: we act, and our actions bring the result we expect. Put a piece of bread in the toaster and press down. Two minutes later the toaster pops up and you have a nice warm breakfast. You are sitting in your car, idling at an intersection and waiting for the traffic light to turn green. It does turn green. You put your foot down on the gas and—predictably—the car starts to move forward again. This much is obvious. Unfortunately this predictability has convinced many people that the world behaves, more or less, like a machine; a complicated machine, perhaps, but a machine nonetheless. If we study this machine carefully we should be able to pull back the curtain that covers its mechanics and effect change in a far more thoughtful manner.

But that's not how most of the world works at all. We can never really be sure that pushing this button or pulling that lever will have the result we are looking for. We may, for instance, think it is obvious that we can increase sales if we increase sales commissions, but any number of other events can disrupt such an outcome. If we give higher commissions, salespeople may fight harder with one another for a sale and actually turn customers off. Or in the same scenario, if we increase our commissions, our competitors might do the same, which means that nothing really has changed. Or maybe it induces them to raise commissions even higher, and so now we are actually behind. In fact, it is possible that commissions will have *no* impact on sales because our services are becoming obsolete; all we are doing is increasing our expenses. Unlike brake pedals, people do not always respond the way you expect them to.

Creating click moments is one way for us to escape a predictable view of the world, and so is placing purposeful bets. Click moments allow us to find opportunities we may never have considered using a logical approach. When we make purposeful bets we view the world less like a machine working according to the laws of cause and effect and more like a game of chance. You can try a new approach or idea— and it may work or it may not. It is impossible to know with any certainty because we're rolling the dice anew every time and exposing ourselves to the effects of randomness.

Over the next two chapters we will look at a third way of harnessing randomness. Any action we take is likely to create a number of unintended consequences, ripple effects, and other unexpected outcomes that can have huge effects on our end results. The fact is that far more forces are at play in the world than we can ever keep track of or account for, and these forces interact with one another in myriad random ways that multiply their effect. I call these forces of randomness that allow for events and actions to change, build, and propagate in unexpected ways *complex forces*.

*

Complexity is inherent in the interconnected web of relationships that make up the world in which we live and work. Its dynamic nature is what makes complexity so valuable and interesting. Form a new connection and your options and opportunities change. Any action we take in response to a click moment, for example, will open up a wide range of new ideas, possibilities, and connections. And any move we make to place a purposeful bet will set us in motion. As we move ahead to explore one bet after another, we come into contact with a different set of options, opportunities, and inflection points. For our purposes, I've pared down the science of complexity to simply state that complex forces come in three different varieties. Let's explore them in turn.

The first such complex force involves **unintended consequences**. These occur when a person or organization takes an action expecting some sort of result, but the actual result is completely different than the one they expected, and sometimes even its direct opposite. Stiffer penalties intended to decrease incidents of drunken driving in the 1980s, for example, caused a short-term increase in hit-and-run accidents. In 2011 Alabama passed a controversial law meant to curb illegal immigration and bolster the state's economy. In 2012, the University of Alabama estimated that the law would eliminate upwards of 140,000 jobs, costing the state nearly $11 billion annually.

And when Barbara Streisand tried to have aerial photos of her Malibu home removed from the Internet, her actions only served to exponentially increase the circulation of the photos online. The result was dubbed The Streisand Effect.

Unintended consequences sometimes occur through a series of interrelated steps that can be impossible to foresee. Complexity researcher Michael J. Mauboussin illustrates this principle in a short post on *Harvard Business Review*'s online forum by telling the story of how park rangers tried to improve conditions at Yellowstone National Park:

> In the late 1800s rangers brought in the U.S. cavalry to try to improve the game population by hand-feeding elk. The elk population swelled, and the elk started eating aspen trees, and aspen trees were what the beavers were using to build their dams, and the beaver dams caught the runoff in the spring, which allowed trout to spawn. More elk equaled less trout.

We often consider unintended consequences as something undesirable, but this is just our natural resistance to randomness. Instead they can provide an amazing opportunity for us to avoid our predictable, instinctive reactions. Consider one of the greatest movies of all time, Steven Spielberg's *Jaws*. The film heralded the birth of the summer blockbuster. When it was released in 1975 it became one of the highest-grossing movies of all time, and it still holds the number 7 spot on the list. There are several brilliant aspects to the movie, but perhaps the most surprising is how Spielberg chose to introduce his protagonist: the shark. The first visual of the shark is a two-second shot of a fin. You don't actually get a decent look of the shark until an hour and twenty-one minutes into the movie, at which time Chief Brody (Roy Scheider) utters the famous line, "You're gonna need a bigger boat." Even then, it is again a two-second shot of the head—but it is incredibly effective. Throughout much of the rest of the film the shark is represented through barrels it's tethered to in the water; that and the ominous da-dum "shark theme" in the soundtrack. The fact that you don't actually *see* the shark for most of the movie accounts for a good deal of what makes the film so scary and suspenseful.

Great direction, yes—and yet Spielberg never intended for it to happen that way. He very much wanted to show the shark in the opening scene, with the girl skinny-dipping at twilight, and then plenty more times after that. And why not? The movie, after all, was called *Jaws*. The movie's mechanical shark represented untold hours (and dollars) in cutting-edge special effects and photo wizardry. But despite all their efforts, the special-effects team simply could not bring the shark to full operation. It either sank or looked far too unrealistic or the timing didn't fit the action. The movie should have been an utter disaster.

But it wasn't. Spielberg said, "The shark not working was a godsend. It made me become more like Alfred Hitchcock. . . . When I didn't have control of my shark it made me kind of rewrite the whole script without the shark. Therefore, in many people's opinions the film was more effective than the way the script actually offered up the shark." Spielberg was forced to develop a solution, not because he planned it a certain way but because he had to try something different. The shark not working had an unintended consequence—it made *Jaws* a much better, more suspenseful movie.

What all of this suggests is that we should pay great attention to unexpected consequences. They indicate that we may have been fortunate enough to encounter something random, something we never would have figured on given even extensive analysis—something that might ultimately set us apart.

This is what happened that December morning in Tunisia. If an inspections officer slaps a merchant, the merchant is expected to back down. But what actually happened was completely unexpected. In the eyes of Mohamed Bouazizi, being slapped by a woman was the ultimate insult. He reacted instantly. Yes, he had been humiliated in front of his peers before and, it appears, more or less suffered through it. But to be slapped in public by a female municipal worker made him furious. He took off in a run for the government office in the center of town. He wanted his scale back and he demanded to be let in. But the doors did not open. Bouazizi then ran to a gas station, bought a can of gasoline, and doused himself with it. And then he stood in front of the government building, in the middle of a busy street, and lit a match. A few seconds later he caught fire and stood like a human torch among the passing cars.

*

The second type of complex force is what might be called a **cascade**. A cascade is an action that has consequences that spread far beyond anything predicted or expected, like the rings on the surface of water. The initial action can be very, very small, but its effects seem to take on a life of their own and propagate throughout society. These types of cascades are becoming far more common today with the increasing connectedness of people across countries and across fields. Social media sites such as Facebook and Twitter provide an infrastructure for viral trends to take off at an instant. The young artist Justin Bieber rose to fame shortly after his mother uploaded videos of him to YouTube. Her son had just won second place in a talent competition in Ontario, Canada, and she wanted her family and friends to see the videos of his singing at the event. The videos spread far beyond what anyone could have foreseen and eventually found their way to producer Scooter Braun, who ultimately managed to turn Bieber into a superstar.

Increasingly, these types of cascades will impact corporate successes and failures because of the speed at which people are becoming connected. In 2011, McDonalds sponsored a Twitter campaign around the hashtag #McDStories. McDonalds hoped the campaign would draw the attention of online "foodies" and allow people to meet the farmers that supply McDonalds with fresh produce. But just a couple of minutes after the campaign started, something unexpected happened. The tweets being published were of a decidedly mixed nature. Some tweets read like this:

```
"When u make something w/pride, people can
taste it."
```

But other tweets read like this:

179

"I haven't been to McDonalds in years, because
I'd rather eat my own diarrhea."

Maybe that would have been okay if it had ended there. But the negative Twitter comments ignited a cascade that spread throughout the Internet in a blink of an eye. In just a few minutes, negative tweets flooded Twitter. "Within an hour, we saw that it wasn't going as planned," said McDonalds' social media director Rick Wion. The entire campaign was shelved a few hours later. McDonalds had no way of knowing that their well-intentioned marketing campaign would backfire. There was no reason to think it would, but reality proved the best strategic analysis wrong.

To most international analysts, Tunisia was one of the least likely Arab countries to experience a revolution. It was not only relatively stable but also seemingly peaceful. Although its people were poor, with over 50 percent unemployment, political protests were uncommon. This, of course, could have been because its leader, Zine al-Abidine Ben Ali, tended to jail anyone who spoke out against him. "The legal opposition parties are mostly prevented from publicly criticizing the ruling regime or its policies," wrote the *Economist Intelligence Unit*. "This has stopped them from building a support base among the population." In fact, the country had no real tradition of organized protests or of large-scale violence. Much of the police force in Tunisia at the time didn't even carry guns.

But Bouazizi's desperate act sparked something. It incited his friends, peers, acquaintances, and many others around him to demonstrate for an end to the system's corruption and injustice. The country was ready for this type of action; and by this time, the president was well hated by almost everybody. While some dictators spread their wealth around to ensure loyalty from key groups in society, President Ben Ali's family pretty much kept all the money, and they had a lot of it, for themselves.

The demonstrations spread and were followed by more self-immolations. Within ten days President Ben Ali was forced to act. He promised to create new jobs. He even went to visit Bouazizi in the hospital in an attempt to show that his attention was focused on the people. But Bouazizi, the unlikely hero, died just a few days later, with the blame laid squarely at Ben Ali's feet.

Now things really started to heat up. The demonstrations intensified. President Ben Ali responded by instructing police to fire upon demonstrators. Snipers were killing citizens. Previously, even appalling human-rights abuses went largely unnoticed due to the state's grip on local media. But not in 2011. With roughly 20 percent of Tunisians on Facebook, videos and images of the killings appeared immediately. They were also tweeted, re-tweeted, blogged about, and reported on. The groundswell of demands for the president's removal rose like a tidal wave. On January 14, less than a month after the fateful day at the souk, with the Tunisian capital locked at a standstill by demonstrators, Ben Ali stepped down.

It was a remarkable event—and completely unforeseen. And yet the events of that spring did not stop there. On January 17, only three days after the fall of Tunisia's dictator, a man set himself afire in the streets of Cairo in protest against Hosni Mubarak's dictatorial regime. Only seven days later the Egyptian capital had turned into a war zone, with fights breaking out between protestors and the military, and a few days after that, the military sensed a change in the wind and refused to fire on protestors. By February 11, Egypt's Mubarak had resigned. Around the world people were stunned and wondering what could possibly happen next.

The answer came days later as the tsunami of transformation moved on to Libya. Muammar Gaddafi refused to go down without a fight and responded to the uprising with a murderous crackdown. Demonstrations continued and support for the revolution grew. Roughly one month later the United Nations passed a security resolution clearing the way for military action intended to protect the citizens of Libya. Air bombings ensued. On October 20, 2011, Gaddafi was dragged out of his drainpipe hideout and violently killed by an angry mob of rebels in his hometown of Sirte. The dictator's final moments were captured on a grainy cell-phone video, a grisly sign of the cascade that was seen around the world.

The Arab Spring wave of change, which blew through not only Tunisia, Egypt, and Libya but also other Arab countries including Algeria, Jordan, Syria, and Yemen, was ignited by a slap on the face but composed of much more than a single resulting event of self-immolation. History undoubtedly will make this sequence of events appear preordained. The conditions for such a dramatic revolution were all set in place: unemployment, civil rights violations, corruption, and inequality, to name just a few. It was a tinderbox in the making, waiting for the right catalyst to spark it into flames. It will all seem quite obvious in retrospect, and yet *no one saw it coming*. This will also be true for many events that can change your own life or that of your organization.

Just as it was impossible to predict that Bouazizi would light himself on fire after the slap, so too was it impossible to know that his death would topple a dictator who was so solidly in control of the nation just a few weeks earlier. Complex forces took hold of the situation and allowed it to cascade in unforeseen ways.

*

There is a third type of complex force, which I call a **self-reinforcing loop**, and I think it's the most interesting of them all. Self-reinforcing loops are situations where past success continually reinforces future success. The initial success can sometimes be very, very small—just enough for other people to notice it—but this small initial win makes it more likely to become increasingly successful. If one is truly fortunate, such a loop will allow a person or an organization to not only reach greatness, but also make it difficult for others to emulate this particular pathway.

I mentioned this type of force in Chapter 4 while talking about the dynamics surrounding Stephen King's success. The fact that King attempted to recreate his success as an anonymous writer makes for a fascinating study in self-reinforcing loops. In one version of his career he achieved success with *Carrie*, which dramatically increased his chances of success in the future. In the other version he struggled as the author Richard Bachman because there had been no initial success significant enough to ignite such a loop, at least by the time his experiment was revealed.

In the corporate world, exhibit A of this phenomenon in action is eBay. The online auction and shopping website is, by a wide margin, the most successful company of its kind. The site exceeded established auction houses Sotheby's and Christie's in terms of sales within a few years of its launch. In 2011, the number of active users on eBay was reportedly close to 95 million. So what underlies eBay's success? It clearly is a well-managed and well-operated company, but it wasn't eBay's customer service that originally set it apart from every other player in the space.

In the case of eBay, the value of the service depends upon the number of people who are using it. eBay is a two-sided market, meaning that it needs to attract buyers and sellers. More buyers on the site serves to attract more sellers, and more sellers attracts more buyers, creating a virtuous cycle. It didn't take long before a small lead gave eBay an insurmountable advantage.

This type of complex force has been studied deeply by sociologists, economists, and marketers around the world, who have given it many names, including the tipping point, critical mass, cumulative advantage, virtuous circles, and increasing returns. In a famous paper from 1968, the sociologist Robert Merton christened it the "Matthew Effect," citing a passage from the Gospel of Matthew in the New Testament: "For unto everyone that hath shall be given, and he shall have abundance. But from him that hath not shall be taken away even that which he hath." Those who have will get more and those who don't will lose.

There is a reason why self-reinforcing loops have garnered so much attention. Their mere existence suggests that even a small initial advantage can lead to huge success and fortune. It can, in other words, make success possible for virtually anyone, no matter what resources he or she initially possesses. According to research by Brian Arthur, the Santa Fe Institute economist credited with identifying and explaining this particular aspect of complexity (which he called "in-creating returns") in the mid-1990s, success at eBay most likely has little to do with the quality of the service itself. Instead, its success is due to the tendency under certain circumstances for a product or service that is already ahead to get further ahead. eBay had a number of competitors during the late nineties, including Onsale, Yahoo! Auctions, and Amazon Auctions. None of them made it. By the end of 1999, a few years after eBay had launched, the company had more than $10 million a day in gross sales, which was twenty times more than its closest competitor.

Arthur suggests that if you could actually rerun history there might be different winners each time in these types of situations, depending on who had a small initial advantage. This notion has been examined in research conducted by the sociologist Duncan Watts and two of his colleagues at Columbia University. As part of one study, Watts asked fourteen thousand people to listen to a number of different songs. They could rate the songs they liked and download the songs they thought were good. The participants were divided, without their knowing, into two groups. The first group had access only to the name of the songs and artists before they were able to listen and download. But the second group, referred to as the "social influence" group, was also able to see the number of times songs had been downloaded by other participants in their sections.

Watts and his team found that the songs that earned an early lead in terms of votes and downloads picked up steam quickly—and never slowed down. When participants could see what others were downloading, momentum carried songs that had gained early popularity. They divided the second group into eight additional groups—sort of like rerunning history eight times—and found the same thing again and again. There was no real way of predicting which songs would end up as number one, instead, the initial advantage was all that mattered. Of course, some songs were genuinely better songs, and these never came last. And some truly awful songs never made it to number one. But that was pretty much it for predictability.

This type of self-reinforcing loop, then, explains much of the success of Stephen King and the *Twilight Saga*. It explains Facebook and the Windows' platform continued dominance. But it also explains less flashy business success stories. Early advantages can often be parlayed into sustained advantages in virtually any industry. Once a company gets a lead, it may achieve an economy of scale that allows it to further pull away from its competitors. Consider Dell, for instance. Once Dell started getting a bit of volume through its ordering system, it was able to purchase supplies at far lower prices than its competitors. These lower costs meant that Dell could then lower prices to its customers. Lower prices meant more customers, which in turn allowed Dell to buy components at an even greater discount. And so on.

These complex forces—unintended consequences, cascades, and self-reinforcing loops—raise an important question: Can we, if we think about it hard enough, identify a way to trigger them on purpose? The question is not trivial. If we can figure out how to do it on a repeatable, regular basis we would have a far better chance of making our organizations and ourselves successful, with far fewer resources. We can finally leave randomness behind and use logic. We could dominate entire industries, launch sweeping revolutions, crank out summer blockbusters and launch fast-growing start-ups. Is this even possible?

*

There was a time, not so long ago, when scientists earnestly believed that, given enough inputs, they could understand and possibly manage nature itself, as if it were a machine. By solving a few equations, for instance, oceanographers had demonstrated their ability to accurately predict the tide level, and it was believed that the same process could be applied to other natural phenomena, including the weather.

In 1961, American mathematician and meteorologist Edward Lorenz inadvertently proved that such hopes were completely unrealistic. Lorenz, who later became a preeminent pioneer of chaos theory, was leading a forecasting project to predict weather patterns, based on a variety of atmospheric measurements. One day he decided to run a forecast twice. He used the same numbers, the same data, and the same inputs. But when he ran the second forecast, his jaw hit the floor. Although the numbers had been the same, the results came out wildly different the second time. It would be like using your calculator to figure out the product of 10 x 10. The first time you run the calculation you get 100. The second time you get 9,405,789. How is that even possible?

Confused, Lorenz tried to figure out what had gone wrong. He soon realized that he had made a mistake. It turned out that he had inadvertently used the printed inputs the second time around and those rounded up; so, 0.506127 became 0.506. Okay—so the numbers were not exactly the same, but Lorenz was still puzzled. How could a miniscule variation lead to such a drastic difference in output? Well, the computer ran the equations in multiple iterations and steps. A tiny variation early on in the process led to a slightly larger variation in the next step. This in turn led to an even greater variation in the following step. More than a million interactions later, the end result looked entirely different. One small variation became drastically magnified. This, he realized, represented how the world at large worked.

In chaos theory this cumulative impact is known as the butterfly effect, a phrase coined by Lorenz. The idea is that when a butterfly in India flaps its wings, the atmospheric pressure in the area is changed and, compounded over millions of interactions across the globe, can cause rain in Brazil. The butterfly effect exemplifies the complex way in which actions can have unintended consequences, cascades, and cycles that are excruciatingly difficult to predict.

Yet, even with so much complexity in the world, our ability to predict events such as changes in the weather does continue to improve. Today we have massive computing power and a multitude of forecasting techniques that ensure greater accuracy. For example, two-day forecasts are as accurate today as one-day forecasts were in 1988; and seven-day forecasts are now as accurate as the five-day predictions once were. These advances indicate that we are mastering the complex forces in our world, and might lead us to conclude that our predictive abilities continue to improve in aggregate. Do these advances suggest that we can look forward to a future in which we can indeed trigger cascades or self-reinforcing loops in human affairs?

Unfortunately, it appears not. The average lifespan of a company on the S&P 500 was about seventy-five years in 1937. Today it is fifteen years. If we had a better understanding of how to predict success we should see the exact opposite trend. But time and again we see that sure bets are not so sure anymore. MySpace seemed like a sure bet. So did Nokia. But they were not. Today one unexpected piece of bad publicity can place an entire company in jeopardy. Congress took the CIA to task for failing to foresee the political unrest in 2011. Intelligence agencies spent $125 million on forecasting software and computer modeling with the explicit purpose of better predicting what would happen in the Middle East three years prior to the Arab Spring, and yet their work showed they had no clue about what was going on. Why is our ability to predict complex natural events, such as the weather, improving, while our ability to predict other types of events dropping off?

*

Weather is produced by a physical system. A region's weather is created by the climate system, made up of atmosphere, biosphere, cryosphere, hydrosphere, and land surface. Rain is a function of several variables including humidity, air pressure, and cloud cover. Although it is true that even tiny variations in the initial conditions of a system can yield vastly different results, we have become much better at understanding these tiny variables. Not only that, but we have far more technical and computing resources available to calculate the impact of tiny differences in numbers. We may not yet be able to calculate the precise effects of a butterfly flapping its wings, but we do have a better understanding of what it means if ocean temperatures rise another one or two degrees.

But human beings and their corresponding social systems are different. We are not the same as cloud formations, dust particles, or humidity indexes. Humans have the ability to anticipate. We have

187

memories. And we adapt. This ability to adapt and use our minds to stay one step ahead of everyone else makes us unlike so many other systems. A dust particle does not know what another dust particle is doing and will not make a choice, rational or otherwise, in response to it. But people do react to one another and make choices, and those choices can vary each time. We are influenced by our friends and colleagues, by our enemies, and even by those we don't know at all. The wild complexity of the human mind and the interactions between people make it almost impossible to understand what is required to initiate or harness the complex forces swirling around our world. We could take the exact same actions under seemingly similar conditions, but still get completely separate outcomes.

Consider the video-format war that took place in the late seventies and early eighties between Sony and Matsushita. At the time, two rival videocassette formats, Betamax and VHS, each tried to become the winner in a brutal battle to corner the video market. Matsushita's VHS ultimately won out over Sony's Betamax, and there has been a lot of discussion as to what they did right. One explanation is that the Betamax technology was better than VHS, and, counter-intuitively, that was its downfall. Better technology made Betamax tapes harder to produce and limited the number of potential manufacturing partners able to meet the necessary specifications. When they did find partners, many were reluctant to agree to Sony's restrictive licensing agreements. Meanwhile, VHS was a simpler technology, easier to make, and was licensed to nearly anyone who would produce it. More manufacturing partners led to competition and lower prices, and only true technology fans noticed the inferior quality.

That set the stage for, possibly, the most important differentiator of all. In an industry like video rentals there are crushing network effects. If a video store can avoid having to carry two versions of each videotape, it will do so. And if customers sense that video stores carry one format over another, they are much more likely to buy the type of machine that matches that format. Any edge, even a small one, can quickly kick off a self-reinforcing loop and grow into an insurmountable lead. VHS had such an edge—and it wasn't all that small.

Sony was very much against allowing adult-entertainment producers to use Betamax, so they did not license any of them to do so. If porn had been a small portion of all video purchases and rentals, it might not have mattered much. But they were, in fact, a huge part of the early video industry. According to the *Washington Post*, in 1980 the home-video market was worth $1 billion. *Half* of that billion came from porn—and that half was all on VHS. "I think early on, adult was a cash cow for VHS," Dan Miller, the managing editor of adult trade publication *xBiz*, told me. "It played a huge role in making it the dominant format of the time." Despite a two-year head start by Sony, by 1980 VHS's market share had reached 70 percent. At that point it was game over. Sony never recovered, and in 1988 they officially shut down the Betamax line. Killed off by *Debbie Does Dallas*.

Live and learn. If they were ever faced with a similar situation, they wouldn't make the same mistake again, right? Well, by 2006 Sony found itself in the middle of another format war. This one was against Toshiba, and the prize was the future of the high-definition disc market, billed as the successor to the DVD. Toshiba had HD DVD as their format and Sony had Blu-ray. Remarkably, Sony was sticking to its guns on porn. According to the *Wall Street Journal*, a leading adult-entertainment company accused Sony of pressuring disc manufactures to not accept their business, and they concluded that "the adult-entertainment industry's preference could give one camp an edge over the other."

The *WSJ* wasn't alone in its assessment. "The situation is playing like a repeat of what happened with rival videocassette formats in the 1980s," wrote *Investor's Business Daily*. "A wild card could tip the scales in HD DVD's favor" they continued, naming porn as that wild card. *Macworld* concluded that "the pornography industry will likely play a big role in determining which of the two blue-laser DVD formats . . . will be the winner in the battle to replace DVDs for high-definition content." Sony had taken itself out of the game again.

Analysts and journalists saw the way this movie would play out. "Is a sequel in the works?" wrote *Business Week*.

The answer to that question was *no*. There was no sequel. Blu-ray went on to decisively win this one. On the face of it, it looked like Sony was repeating its past mistakes, but in fact it wasn't. Why? Because it was no longer playing the same game. In 1980 the world viewed adult content on video, but by 2006 the Internet had become the dominant medium for porn consumption. No one cared about Blu-ray or HD DVD for skin flicks. Author Michael Raynor, in his book *The Strategy Paradox*, showed that there were tons of lessons Sony had "learned" from its war against VHS, but that when it tried to use those lessons to succeed in later product launches, it just didn't matter. The world, their competitors, and the company itself had changed.

If you look at Tunisia's history you will find that there have been several attempts at revolution there in recent years, but none of them made it. A director at the African Development Bank described to me the various efforts at challenging the status quo: "We had the same demonstrations, tension between the population and the police in 1978 and in 1984 with the bread strike, and the late 1990s and 2000 with the phosphate region," he explained. But Ben Ali was not toppled. Instead it was a face-slap that got everything started—but that might never happen again.

Just as you cannot engineer a revolution in the Middle East with only a well-directed slap on the face or jump-start the next eBay by selling Pez dispensers, you cannot plan for the exact click moments that will make all the difference for your career or your organization. But that does *not* mean that we cannot harness these types of complex forces. Even if you can't purposefully ignite specific complex forces around your project, you can—and must—take advantage of those forces once they start acting. The following chapter will show you how.

12

HOW TO HARNESS COMPLEX FORCES

There are at least two sure signs that you are about to suffer a stroke. First, one side of your body becomes numb. This was exactly what Ecuador's Jamil Mahuad, one of the most successful mayors in Latin America, noticed first. He had just delivered a keynote address at a conference in Barcelona and was sitting in a panel in front of hundreds of audience members and press from around the world. "I had lost the feeling in my left arm," he told me, "and then my entire side went limp. That was when I realized I was having a stroke, so I turned to the people next to me and said that they needed to call an ambulance."

The second sign of a stroke is that you lose consciousness, but, re-markably, that did not happen to Mahuad. "I was aware of the entire episode, and the logic part of my brain was not affected by the stroke," he said. "I could processes what was happening to me."

Jamil Mahuad's stroke occurred as millions of Ecuadorians tuned in to the morning news, and it was reported live. It was a tense moment. The doctors attending to Mahuad began arguing about how to proceed and two divergent opinions emerged. One held that they needed to do surgery immediately; the other that Mahuad should be induced into a coma for three days. Neither side had an entirely conclusive argument, but the latter won out. The people of Ecuador waited in shock as the man heralded as their country's best hope for a bright future lay unconscious half a world away. Mahuad, as the mayor of Quito, Ecuador's capital, had overhauled the public transportation system, delivered a long-term water supply system, and secured $500 million in international aid. Many had assumed he would someday win the presidency, but now they weren't even certain he would make it through the night.

The choice the doctors made saved Mahuad's life. He was incredibly lucky and was able to launch a presidential campaign a year later with a clean bill of health. He sailed to victory in 1998 and the reason was simple: Jamil Mahuad seemed like the ideal person to turn his troubled Latin American country around. "Since taking office," wrote the *Economist*, "Ecuador's new president has won a standing ovation from investors [and] praise from the IMF." Mahuad planned to reform the country, as he had done in the capital, and he set himself up perfectly to do so. He had one of the most accomplished cabinets in the country's history. He had expert advisers from the world's most prestigious institutions, and he had the perfect plan. What could possibly go wrong?

A tremendous amount, it turns out. Ecuador is a country funded primarily by oil revenues. Oil regularly tops $100 a barrel today, but as Mahuad took office it plummeted below $9 a barrel, instantly crippling the country's cash flow. At the same time the country suffered from the worst El Niño event in five hundred years. The ensuing storms and flooding left more than twenty thousand people homeless along the western coast, with $2 billion in damaged infrastructure. To make matters still worse, El Niño had decimated the country's fisheries and destroyed the ports, which meant that the country's banana crop could

not be shipped. Because fishing and bananas constituted a major portion of the country's non-oil revenue, the economy was truly decimated.

Things were also grim elsewhere in the world. The East Asian
Financial Crisis in 1997 turned the economies of South Korea,
Indonesia, and Thailand from success stories into cautionary tales.
Banks and international agencies tightened credit, and small develop-
ing countries like Ecuador felt the pressure. "They thought, if this is
happening in South Korea, what about Brazil?" Mahuad remembered.
"And if it happens in Brazil, imagine what would happen to Ecuador."

As if things weren't bad enough, on the eve of the election Mahuad
received word from his advisers that Ecuador's neighbor and longstand-
ing enemy, Peru, was possibly hours away from carrying out an invasion. Given the dire economic circumstances, Ecuador clearly could not
afford a war. Whatever plan he had put in place had to be scrapped. "I
am a good planner, which means having a goal and charting towards
that goal," Mahuad said. But even so, he realized that "we have to be
open to serendipity." He needed to catch a lucky break somehow . . . he
needed to find an opening. As we shall see, that is exactly what he got.
The question was: What was he going to do with it?

Success in a complex, unpredictable world involves not only creating click moments and placing purposeful bets, but also harnessing
the random forces that affect our lives, organizations, and, sometimes,
even entire nations. In this chapter we will look at five different tactics
that accomplish this. While I can't presume to tell you how to manufacture complex forces, these tactics will help you attract these forces
and take advantage of them when they are moving in your direction.

1. Create Large Hooks

In order to harness complex forces you must first to create something
for these forces to latch on to. You must actually *do* something, even if
you are not sure where it will lead. This tactic is based on the idea that
the most important part of a purposeful bet is the fact that you took

action. Once you start executing, whether or not the bet actually works in your favor, you are exposed to complex forces that can pave the way for future success. Even if you do not have a crystal-clear goal in mind, it is still better to do something—and to tell people about it. The complex forces of the world will now have a concept to work with, and you will have exposed yourself to the possibility of positive unanticipated consequences, cascades, and self-reinforcing loops.

One can see how this has played out over the past twenty years in a small town called Jukkasjärvi, located next to the mighty Kalix River in northern Sweden. Situated 125 miles north of the Arctic Circle, Jukkasjärvi has never been anyone's idea of a tourist hot spot. During the summer, days there are very long and bright, but during the winters they are bitterly cold and dark. In fact, in early December the sun drops below the horizon and does not reemerge until late January. Visitors would come to see the midnight sun in the summertime, perhaps, but for most of the year the town was vacant except for a few hearty souls in search of the northern lights. Then something happened to change that. By the early 1990s, thousands of visitors were pouring through the town each year—and that number grew into the tens of thousands in no time.

The curious success of Jukkasjärvi's tourism industry can be attributed, ultimately, to Yngve Bergqvist and an absurd idea that he refused to ignore. Bergqvist, a hardworking entrepreneur in the old northern tradition, decided to build a hotel . . . made entirely out of ice. On the face of it, the notion of an ice hotel is ludicrous. The idea that tourists would travel to the northernmost part of Sweden to sleep on a slab of ice in a building where everything from tables to drinking glasses were made out of ice must have seemed insane. It should never have been tried and it certainly shouldn't have worked. But the Ice Hotel has worked—exceedingly well. Within just a few months of opening, the venue became one of *Newsweek*'s top ten hottest hotels in the world. Today it is one of Sweden's most visited tourist attractions and has even spawned imitation ice hotels in cold climates around the world, including several in Canada and one in Romania.

When I talk about the Ice Hotel and its astounding success I usually get one of two reactions. Some people are amazed by Bergqvist's vision; where others saw snow, he saw a building so unique people from all over the world would travel to behold its splendor. Where others saw ice, he saw an economic development opportunity. The second reaction tends to be one of awe. "I could never manage to do anything like that," they say. It seems such a radical idea, one reserved for the most extreme, most creative, and most iconoclastic individuals.

Perhaps these reactions make sense—but they fail to take into account that you don't have to start with a bold vision or extreme sensibilities to bring something like this to life. Both of these reactions assume that Bergqvist had a detailed plan for how the Ice Hotel should come about when he started his journey. But that is simply not true.

"It took me a while to figure this idea out," Bergqvist told me one day over Skype. But he knew it would involve snow. "If you are born in Norrland [northern Sweden], your mom sends you out at age three with a shovel. You shovel snow until lunch; she brings you in, feeds you and then out you go into the snow again and you shovel until the afternoon."

Bergqvist wanted to get something started in the area, but he wasn't sure exactly what. "I wanted to get something off the ground," he says. So he arranged to fly in some artists from Japan. They created an exhibit of ice sculptures—bears, eagles, and a reindeer. "That exhibit stood there until March and it got some great attention," he said, including some local press. There was much more interest than he expected, which encouraged Bergqvist to think bigger. The following year he got some buddies together to make an entire building out of snow—just to see if they could. "We came up with the idea of making large wooden forms, like cake forms, and stuffing them with snow. Once we had that idea we had to try it out immediately. I like that way of working—you don't just talk about it, you try it. No matter if it doesn't work."

This large igloo—which is what it was, essentially—caught a lucky break. "The Swedish king happened to be visiting Kiruna, which is

195

nearby, and we decided to see if we could get him to come by. And he actually did," Bergqvist said. Before long, their "igloo" was all over the news. That got even more people involved and the following winter they were able to build a snow building large enough to host a small expo. The expo featured a number of unlikely objects made out of ice and snow. It had an ice bar, which was relatively new at the time, for instance, and a movie screen made out of snow.

That's about when the idea clicked into place for Bergqvist. During the expo, some adventurer types asked if they could stay inside the building overnight. "They were looking for some type of extreme experience," Bergqvist recalls. And they were willing to pay for it. They slept on ice slabs in super-warm sleeping bags, and they loved it. All at once Bergqvist realized that he had a business model. Maybe he could make an entire building out of ice beds, just like a hotel?

The next winter Bergqvist figured out how to cut ice out of the river in large quantities and used it to make the building. Pretty soon it was full speed ahead. People were writing about the Ice Hotel in tourist brochures and including photographs of the spectacular views. All at once they were legit. Even Absolut vodka, which had passed on the project previously, saw the photographs and contacted Bergqvist, looking for a partnership opportunity.

Twenty-two years later, the Ice Hotel is an elaborately sculptured ice castle with sixty guest suites that are designed anew and rebuilt every winter by a team of sculptors, painters, architects, set designers, and artists from all over the world. The artistry is astounding—and apparently dazzling enough to entice more than thirty thousand guests each season to make the trek up to Swedish Lapland to see it.

Bergqvist didn't even know where he was headed during his first attempts. He got things off the ground—barely—by arranging an ice exhibit. Most people reading this sentence could manage that right now. It requires neither a stunning vision nor an extreme personality. His story underscored the first approach for harnessing complex forces: in order to have a chance to trigger these types of forces, you must create something for them to latch on to. You must actually *do* something. Once Bergqvist did that, his project was caught up in a swirl of complex forces that turned the small Scandinavian hamlet into a global phenomenon.

That said, Bergqvist was scoping out opportunities to spread the word about the project and to make it easy for others to join it as volunteers, employees, or partners. From a complex forces standpoint that makes perfect sense. More interactions equals more people engaged in the idea, which makes it all the more likely that the swirl of interest will allow the project to take off. And once complex forces start to kick in, growth can happen fast.

What would have happened if Bergqvist *had* somehow started with the Ice Hotel in mind rather than "just anything that had to do with snow"? He might still be working on his business plan, recruiting volunteers, supporters, and investors. He would need money, market research, a team of experts, and some proof that the idea could succeed—assuming anyone would even take him seriously. Now, market research and financial backing are fine, but because the world is so unpredictable, they are no guarantee of success. In order for an idea like the Ice Hotel to take off, complex forces need to grab hold of it. In fact, complex forces provide the single strongest argument that you cannot simply wait to figure out every detail and specific before taking a step forward. Do something, anything. Get started.

Although action can expose your idea or project to the positive effects of randomness, it is not the only way to attract complex forces. If we want to get on the winning side of unexpected consequences, we should also take a closer look at surprises. Consider, for instance, one surprise that was critical in creating one of the most profitable companies in the world.

2. Take a Closer Look at Surprises

"It's the fastest takeoff of a new drug that I've ever seen," Michael Podgurski told *Time Magazine*. The director of pharmacy at the

4,000-outlet Rite Aid drugstore chain thought he'd seen it all. Within the first twelve weeks of Viagra's release, however, sales reached $411 million. Over four million prescriptions were filled in its first six months and sales exceeded one billion dollars in its first year. Podgurski was astounded.

By 2002, the drug would propel its patent holder, Pfizer, to the fifth most profitable corporation in America. Viagra's cultural impact on the world was even greater. Writing for the *New York Times*, Jack Hitt declared that the drug had sparked a "second sexual revolution." But this revolution was entirely accidental.

In 1986, Pfizer, a relatively small American pharmaceutical company, began to speculate that blocking an enzyme called PDE 5 would relieve angina, a form of chest pain. Angina occurs when arteries in the heart get clogged, preventing blood and oxygen from entering. The consequences can be serious, even deadly, and can ultimately lead to heart attacks. The research team at Pfizer thought they had figured out a way to relieve the pain associated with angina and lessen its effects.

The enzyme PDE 5 works by degrading a compound in the body that causes smooth muscles to relax. The scientists at Pfizer's research center in Sandwich, England, believed that if PDE 5 could be blocked, the heart's arteries would dilate and blood would flow freely to the chest. After testing hundreds of compounds, they isolated one chemical, sildenafil citrate, that relaxed the arteries in rabbits, dogs, and rats, causing artery dilation. They were onto something.

In 1991, the company began testing its drug on healthy human volunteers. A year later it launched its first multiple-dose study, with volunteers given three doses of tablets a day. "The drug did okay for their chest pain," Dr. Vera Stecher, senior global medical director at Pfizer, told my team one afternoon at the company's New York headquarters. But it wasn't as good as some of the angina drugs that were already on the market. What they found next was odd. Some of the men taking the "just okay" drug kept asking for more of it.

During follow-up interviews it became clear that the drug had a curious side effect. Eight out of the seventeen men taking multiple high doses of the drug said they kept getting sustained erections after taking the pill. Well, that was a big surprise.

The idea that a pill could cause an erection was unheard-of. "At that time it was felt that most erectile dysfunction was eighty-five percent psychogenic and fifteen percent physiologic," Dr. Strecher said. But, she added, "we now know it's exactly the opposite." Researchers began scouring the data, looking for a connection. They knew that blocking PDE 5 from forming allowed smooth muscle cells to relax and increased blood flow. What they didn't know was the biochemistry of erections.

Soon they found the link they were looking for. Dr. Jacob Rajfer and Dr. Louis Ignarro, both of UCLA Medical School, had figured out that nitric oxide regulates blood vessels. Dr. Ignarro would go on to win the Nobel Prize in Medicine for his work. The Pfizer team had set out to find the cure for angina, but with the research from UCLA they had stumbled upon a very different treatment. In men with erectile dysfunction, nitric acid would flood the penis, only to be blocked by the PDE 5. The PDE 5 inhibitor in Viagra, as the drug came to be marketed, removed this roadblock.

In the case of Viagra, researchers at Pfizer found something surprising and unexpected—something that did not fit within the scope of their research. It would have been very easy to call it an amusing distraction and move on. In fact, that is exactly what most of us do in similar situations. If we are looking for something specific, we set aside anomalies and remain focused. But Pfizer recognized an opportunity nestled in the surprise and ran with it.

And therein lies the beauty of complex forces. The big opportunity is almost never what you would guess, because your best guess is based on the prevailing logic. Surprises are likely to harbor unexpected opportunities—the type that are a far cry from obvious. So much so that anyone who is not a party to the surprise would be hard-pressed to come up with anything like it.

This is what happened to Yngve Bergqvist. "We had nothing, really," he said of his project's early days, "no business model, no real *idea* that could keep going on its own." But when the group of backpackers appeared, eager to pay to sleep on ice beds, Bergqvist did not dismiss them as oddballs, as many would have. Instead, he saw an opportunity.

We are apt to overlook or ignore results and outcomes that don't conform with our expectations or focused needs. We tend to deem surprises on the periphery to be outliers or anomalies—interesting but not relevant—and we move on. But surprises and outliers actually matter a great deal. They may be indicative of something bigger, something that has not yet been explored but that can set you apart. Viagra became a blockbuster drug because, at the time, there was nothing else like it. Likewise the Ice Hotel. These surprises were sticky enough to attract attention in the networked world—and that can be a very powerful thing.

Sometimes a surprise can reveal that we have an unexpected opportunity, one that may not last very long. If that is the case, we must move quickly because windows of opportunity can soon close. We must, in other words, look for an opening—and step through when we find one. This is exactly what Jamil Mahuad realized in the early days of his presidency.

3. Look for an Opening

Negotiating a peace accord with Peru wasn't at the top of Mahuad's agenda when he was running for office. He campaigned on a plan of economic liberalization and good governance. But on his third day in office in 1998, Mahuad received a surprising phone call. It was an invitation to celebrate the election of Paraguay's president Raul Cubas. Alberto Fujimori, the president of Peru, would also be attending the event. Mahuad saw at once that this was an opening.

Mahuad hadn't spoken to Fujimori yet, but the latter had spent his previous term attempting to negotiate a treaty to end a border dispute that had simmered between the two nations for more than a century. His attempts failed and in 1995 Fujimori had personally commanded Peru's war against Ecuador.

The conflict centered on a disagreement over a 78-kilometer strip of borderland between Ecuador and Peru. In 1941 war broke out, and a successful Peruvian offensive pushed Ecuador's boundary back. Despite eventually losing the war, most Ecuadorians believed the land was rightfully theirs, and in 1981 and 1995 war engulfed the countries again. This time Ecuador was successful in retaking sections of the land, most notably a small area called Tiwintza that held cultural significance for both countries. But the brief war cost $900 million, a fortune for a country in need of so many other things.

Mahuad realized that the inauguration might be an unexpected opportunity to end the costly conflict, and he began to assemble a team of experienced negotiators. "I thought we had a small possibility to succeed with this," he told me. "Maybe ninety-five percent of the people in Ecuador and Peru thought it was impossible."

When talking with Fujimori at the event it became clear that the Peruvian president had three primary goals for his presidency: eliminate hyperinflation, dismember the Shining Path guerrilla insurgency within Peru, and solve the border issue with Ecuador. Suddenly it clicked. Despite their centuries-old conflict and offensive posturing, both men had similar goals: to live in prosperity and peace. And now they were talking, forming a bond.

It had taken a random phone call, freak weather, a financial crisis, and a collapse in oil prices to create an important opening for peace. "I don't like the phrase 'window of opportunity,'" Mahuad said. "These very well-repeated phrases can lose their meaning over time. But in this case that is exactly what it was."

Because it is impossible to fully control the events that occur around us, we must use complex forces to our advantage. The constant reshuffling of actions, desires, and consequences causes windows of opportunity to open and close unexpectedly. These windows provide a pathway to breakthrough success. They may not be open for long, however, so we need to be prepared to make a quick decision before complex forces cause conditions to shift once again. "Possibilities can be disguised. They can be blurred, and the most important thing— they flicker," Mahuad explained. "Both Fujimori and I are today both convinced that three months later we would not have been able to get it done, since he was starting a reelection campaign."

Over the next ten weeks the leaders drew up an innovative peace agreement that stands today. The disputed land would become an international conservation park, void of military or economic activity. The sovereignty of Tiwintza was returned to Peru, but the property itself is under control of the Ecuadorian government.

Mahuad saw an opportunity and he seized it. He himself acknowledges that the culmination of extreme and random events played an important part. "There are very specific points in time, and in our lives, when we see an opportunity and we have to act," Mahuad said. "What we do in those moments really changes the direction of our life."

It was Democratic Senator Tom Daschle who described Barack Obama's chance to run for president as a window of opportunity that could close at any time. Obama's opening was completely unexpected, and if he wanted to go for it, he needed to act fast. Likewise, complex forces had created an opening for President Mahuad to negotiate a peace treaty with Peru, and by doing so he averted a devastating military and economic crisis. A year later, however, these same forces precipitated a debt renegotiating disaster. This time Mahuad was unable to find an opening. Some eighteen months after becoming president he was ousted in a military coup—an outcome most onlookers would have considered inconceivable only two years earlier.

4. Spot Momentum and Intensity

The holy grail of complex forces is when success feeds on itself in a self-reinforcing loop or cascade. Although we can't rationally figure out exactly how to trigger such forces, we can be prepared to harness them when they occur—assuming we are able to spot them in the first place. But how do we know if an opportunity has true promise? We need a way to identify when complex forces are at play, in order to narrow the range of prospects upon which to focus. Surprise is one signal, but we also need to be able to spot momentum or intensity as it builds. That intensity can help us determine if an idea is about to be swept up by forces exponentially greater than any we could amass on our own.

The Spanish fashion house Zara, with more than sixteen hundred stores around the world, is a company that makes some of its most important business decisions based on where it sees momentum. This is what has allowed the company to achieve such remarkable success through the first decade of the new millennium. Zara's parent company, Inditex, has a market capitalization of $54 billion and Zara accounts for nearly 60 percent of its revenues and even more of its shareholder value. In 2011 alone the company saw profits increase by 32 percent to nearly $2.3 billion.

One explanation for this success centers on the way Zara decides what to stock and sell in its stores. The company doesn't use elaborate forecasting techniques to predict trends six months ahead, like many of its competitors. It doesn't worry about managing overstock and liquidating items that fail to sell; and it barely advertises. Yet Zara produces garments continuously and brings them to market all over the world in seven to twenty days. This is unheard-of elsewhere in the fashion industry. Daniel Piette, fashion director at Louis Vuitton, described Zara as "the most innovative and devastating retailer in the world."

Zara has built its business empire around speed and agility. In addition to selling clothes, Zara also designs and manufactures them. The control it maintains over its merchandise and supply chain gives it a huge advantage in terms of response time. The linchpin is that it uses its retail stores as a direct line to consumers. Store managers in cities around the world are trained to engage with local customers. They provide designers in Spain with a stream of intelligence twice weekly. Designers then factor customer feedback into their work and create new lines year-round. But the winds in fashion change direction fast, so Zara produces and ships frequently and in small quantities. Using real-time feedback from store managers allows designers to refine items or create entirely new designs based on what customers in each city say they want next.

Skinny jeans are in demand? Fifteen thousand units coming right up. Oh—women want skinny jeans with a torn pocket and reverse seams? Done and done. Zara's buyers are trained to look for anomalies. If sweater dresses aren't moving but leg warmers are selling out—stop the machines. Small merchandise runs lower risk and keeps demand for popular items high. To make the best design decisions, Zara looks for intensity in sales. Its customers literally tell them what items and trends have the greatest momentum.

I've cast aspersions on forecasting algorithms previously in this book, but the type of real-time intelligence and fast response that Zara's brings to its business is different. It does not presume that it can predict success. In fact, the entire model is based on the idea that it can't know what will be popular. Instead, it tries to spot early signs of demand—that is what allows Zara to move quickly when it sees a fashion idea taking off.

Unfortunately, few people or organizations have access to data this current. Instead, we have to look for proxies—traces of evidence that something is poised to take off. Chris Yeh, a well-known angel investor in Silicon Valley, says that using intensity as a metric is key to understanding whether complex forces are at play for a particular product or service.

"I would rather invest in a company with a hundred rabid evangelists than somebody who has a hundred thousand registered members that never actually go and use the product," he told me. Yeh pays attention to customer intensity to gauge momentum because enthusiasts are the ones most likely to spark a cascade or self-reinforcing loop. They share their opinions and spread the word, generating genuine buzz. Someone, somewhere may react to that intensity by posting a review or sending a tweet that kicks off a series of complex forces.

The question is, of course, what exactly *is* intensity? In Zara's case that might be easy to pinpoint because it is reflected in the company's data. A rapid rise in sales, customers demanding a particular item, people returning to buy more, and so forth. But in many other cases momentum can be more difficult to isolate.

Yeh looks for chatter—people in his network and beyond who can't stop talking or tweeting about a company, product, or service. Another sign is volunteerism—people spending time on something without explicit compensation. I was recently involved with a strategy team within a global conglomerate that had an idea but very little money to test it. The smallest executable step in this case turned out to be a prototype, but they needed engineers to get the prototype off the ground. The idea itself, however, was so cool that within days they had half a dozen company engineers volunteering their time to get the prototype in order. This internal momentum helped the organization gauge the product's potential. Once they witnesses the enthusiasm, they funded the project in a bigger way.

Or consider Diane von Furstenberg's plan to reintroduce the wrap dress to baby boomers twenty years after her first successful run. Boomers were not interested. Instead, DVF was surprised to see women in their twenties snapping up vintage wrap dresses for $200 each. It would have been easy to ignore such a signal as isolated and irrelevant. Instead, she not only paid attention to the surprise, but also took note of the intensity with which these young women wanted her dress. It indicated that the product had great potential—which leads us to the fifth tactic: double down when you have discovered complex forces working in your favor.

5. Double Down

If we find something that works, particularly something that seems to be swept up by complex forces, we need to double down. In this context, doubling down means that you invest time, money, reputation, or other resources into the project with the expectation that it will not only continue to be successful but in fact go big. You are, in other words, *finally* making some sort of prediction. If things have gone according to plan, you may have identified the opportunity in the first place by taking advantage of randomness, which boosts the chances of it being special in some way. If you now see evidence that this idea is being lifted by exponential forces, such as a cascade or self-reinforcing loop, you must take advantage of it. These types of opportunities are rare and we can only truly harness them if we double down when we see them taking off.

Sony's defeat by VHS during the format wars, described in the previous chapter, has often been called one of the company's greatest mistakes and one of the worst business blunders in history. But does that summary accurately reflect the outcome of those wars? The answer is no—and the reason provides a great lesson about the need to double down when you have a winning hand.

When Sony realized which direction things were heading with its competitor, VHS, it needed to find another market for its Betamax technology. So in 1981 Sony introduced the Betacam, a field camera for professional videographers. High quality had been a hurdle in the standards war because it made the tapes more expensive to produce, but now their quality emerged as a strength. Sony focused on this new opportunity and were quick to see a rapid increase in sales to broadcasting professionals. This market also had a self-reinforcing loop in the form of network effects—studios preferred to work with one dominant format instead of many. They chose Betacam. The early lead was just as important here as it had been with the consumer videotape, and suddenly Sony was leading a new market. "Betacam," wrote Horace Newcomb, an expert on the history of television, "became the standard professional field camera for location video work."

Competitors like Panasonic, Bosch, and RCA tried to compete, Newcomb wrote, "but all proved costly losers to Sony." With the best product and a near monopoly, Sony was able to charge premium prices. Depending on the model, the video cameras were priced between $10,000 and $70,000. Local television stations could expect to spend well over $1 million equipping their facilities with Betacam equipment. "In just one year," wrote Carl Howe on the popular economics blog "Seeking Alpha," "Sony logged nearly a billion dollars in profit from its professional video technologies for the broadcast industry."

Compare that to the VHS market. In 2000, the year the market peaked, fifty-five million VHS devices were sold worldwide. During that year, the three major manufactures split about $330 million in profit. In just one year, Sony made three times more than the top three VHS manufacturers *combined*. In other words, it is fair to say that Sony came out of the standards war not as a loser but as a Godzilla-stomping champion. When they found something that worked, they doubled down on it.

We see this type of opportunistic, entrepreneurial approach working in a variety of settings and industries. For example, there is no doubt that the *Lord of the Rings* film trilogy, shot largely in New Zealand, supercharged that country's tourism industry by showcasing the nation's otherworldly beauty. What is more intriguing, perhaps, is how the movies also jump-started New Zealand's film business.

The New Zealand Film Commission has long been the driving force behind the nation's film efforts. Established by the Parliament of New Zealand in 1978, the commission's goals are to encourage the making, promotion of, and distribution of motion pictures in New Zealand. But the commission did not exactly have a lot to work with. Located in Wellington—6,700 miles from Hollywood—New Zealand's movie nexus boasted just three films released between 1940 and 1970. Compare that to Fox, a Hollywood studio that released forty-five films in 1925 alone.

All of that changed with the massive success of the *LOTR* trilogy. The movies cost over $310 million and filming spanned 438 days, but the trilogy transformed the local economy. After *The Lord of the Rings*, investment in the film industry in New Zealand went from $16 million in 1999 to $308 million one year later. The government knew a good thing when they saw it. They doubled down on *Lord of the Rings-*

related tourism and on film efforts in general. The country rebranded its airline "the official airline of Middle Earth" (in a reference to director Peter Jackson's movies) and leveraged this new opportunity to the hilt. Before long, tourism surged and New Zealand became a regional capital of film and other creative endeavors.

The blockbuster success of *The Lord of the Rings* is one thing—it's not the first movie to succeed. But the cascade of positive effects on New Zealand and its economy has been a one-of-a-kind game-changer for the local film business and the nation. Due to the efforts of one pioneering director and an enterprising government, New Zealand went from producing just four films in 1998 to creating a vibrant industry nearing $3 billion in 2010. In fact, it is more or less impossible for any region to predict just what industry is going to drive its economic development. There have been lots of efforts that assumed this was possible—in areas such as biotech and film, for instance. Instead, the focus of local development organizations should be to encourage as many people to grow different types of businesses or projects as possible and then double down on those that start to take off. This is what happened in both New Zealand and Jukkasjärvi.

If, as in the case of *The Lord of the Rings*, your idea or project has been swept up in a swirl of complex forces, doubling down is a necessity. You may have gotten lucky, but you need to take advantage of that luck. But that is not always so straightforward a move. In a conversation I had with entrepreneur and venture capitalist Randy Haykin, he told me that the most difficult thing about doubling down is that it requires "killing your darlings." For a venture capitalist, at least, he said that for every company you double down on, you have decided to end your involvement in five other projects. "That is very difficult and I think the issue is we have a very hard time making that choice," he said. "And so we spend eighty percent of our time on start-ups that don't really go anywhere. Experienced VCs, I think, have an easier time making the choice."

Occasionally, however, complex forces can be so strong that all you need to do is get out of the way. For instance, when Andrew Conru, a

Stanford PhD with a conservative Indiana upbringing, started the Web site FriendFinder, his goal was to help introverts link up with others who shared similar hobbies—you know, golf and fishing enthusiasts. "When I first started, I thought I could help people," he said. "I was going to give more options to people who weren't social and didn't get out much." It worked in ways he had never envisioned.

Just days after the site went live, people starting uploading pictures of themselves. Without clothes on. Engaged in sex. It seemed that most of these people—and there were a lot of them—were interested in playing more than just golf. Conru immediately deleted the pictures. The pictures came back. He deleted them again. But they kept reappearing. He had stumbled into a reinforcing loop that was starting up over and over again. Finally Conru gave up and switched gears.

Conru renamed the site Adult FriendFinder. It was the only site of its kind at the time and it gained momentum quickly, becoming one of the highest-trafficked sites on the Web. Two years later Conru sold his company to Penthouse Media Group for $500 million.

Over and over we have seen the impact of doubling down once you've found a good thing: when Rovio saw that that Angry Birds was gaining momentum, it went into overdrive to support it. Rovio developed derivative games, such as Angry Birds Rio and Angry Birds Seasons and a large array of related products and merchandise featuring the iconic characters. All told, Rovio ships two million T-shirts, plush toys, and backpacks a month. Bill Gates, realizing that Windows 3.0 was beginning to take hold through a mélange of complex forces, also doubled down. As did Starbucks. Howard Schultz had his difficulties with the coffee-shop concept initially, but once he figured out what worked he doubled down and never looked back. Same with hedge fund manager John Paulson, *Twilight* author Stephenie Meyer, and fashion queen Diane von Furstenberg. They all doubled down because they wanted to take something that they found had potential and harness it to something greater.

By harnessing complex forces we can take a click moment or a purposeful bet and make it into something significant. Although it is not possible to trigger these moments on command, we can certainly put ourselves in the running. We can spot the hints of complexity by homing in on the surprising outcomes or insights in our lives and organizations instead of simply brushing them off, as we are accustomed to doing. Then, every once in a while, we will find that some of these surprises accumulate momentum or elicit great enthusiasm from our customers, colleagues, or partners. We may even see the idea taking off, all on its own, spreading and building in surprising ways. This is the moment to double down. We try to boost randomness in our lives in order to create moments like these. We have to take advantage of them when they happen.

EPILOGUE

As I am putting the final touches on this book I find myself thinking about what made my first book, *The Medici Effect*, successful. Despite knowing the critical role serendipity played, and even after having now written a book on the idea, my mind still searches for patterns. It is the rock-paper-scissor paradox in full force: even if we *know* success is entirely random, we *still* search for some sort of strategy to guide us.

When that happens I take some time to think about the people in this book and to remind myself how they set themselves apart. I think of how Windows was saved, how the burquini sprang to life, how Angry Birds took over the world, and how *Jaws* became a masterpiece. And, sometimes, I think about a man I met here in New York City named Roy Preston.

After making a steady living selling children's books up and down the East Coast, Roy Preston and his business partner opened a storefront in Greenwich Village in early 2008. Nestled between Washington Square Park and New York University, the neighborhood's quirky ethos and heavy foot traffic made it a perfect place for an independent bookstore. Their excitement didn't last long. One month later, in April, the city closed the park's Fifth Avenue entrance for renovations, halting all foot traffic while the economy simultaneously took a nosedive. The combination drove the store to the brink.

The duo began to experiment. They transformed the store into a souvenir shop, but with the decline in tourism, that quickly proved a failure. Next they tried a comic-book store, but that didn't work either. It had been two and a half years since the store opened and it soon felt like a curse rather than an opportunity. Funds dried up, and Preston had a choice: keep his apartment or keep his comic-book store. He chose the store, and moved into the crowded stockroom. "It was just an awful, awful experience," he would later say.

Figuring he had about three weeks before he lost his store, Preston stocked three T-shirts from one of his favorite movies, *The Big Lebowski*, and his business partner drew a life-size portrait of the movie's main character, Jeffrey Lebowski, or "The Dude," for the window. "I figured I'm going to get thrown out," Preston said. "I might as well have some fun." To his surprise, the shirts sold almost immediately. Preston was still living in the back room of the store, but for once items were selling, so he got more of them.

One weekend morning, disheveled and barely awake, Preston put on his robe and opened the store for business. As he did every morning, he placed the drawing of Jeffrey Lebowski outside the door. Right at that moment, two reporters from *Time Out* magazine happened to walk by. When they looked across the street, they saw a guy who *looked* like Jeffrey Lebowski standing next to a life-size picture *of* Jeffrey Lebowski. They immediately asked him what he was doing. "I didn't want to tell them that I had lost my apartment and I was sleeping in the back of my store," Preston said, "so I just lied to them. I said, 'This is a Lebowski shop.'"

Suddenly he had a Lebowski shop. He started expanding his inventory to include movie memorabilia such as a "kit" that included a fake severed big toe and an oriental-rug mouse pad that "really ties your desk together." Then an unknown Northwestern University film student pushed him over the edge. Adam Bertocci had written *Two*

Gentlemen of Lebowski, a "Shakespearean" adaption of the film. Preston found that individuals from as far as Switzerland came to New York specifically for the play's run. At that moment everything clicked for him. He realized that if people were willing to travel across the world for a play based on a cult movie, he could run a store that sold only that movie's related merchandise.

The Little Lebowski Shop now boasts action figures, thirty different T-shirts, posters, books, and anything Lebowski-related. People from all over the world come to see his store. In what must be the most surprising fact of all, Preston estimates that 90 percent of his customers are foreigners. He has even had New Yorkers tell him they heard about his shop in London.

Perhaps one day, in an effort to guide others to do the same, someone will tell the story of just *how* Roy Preston became successful. Whoever does it might then say something like this: 1) If possible, leverage a built-in audience for your product or service. *The Big Lebowski* has fans all over the world and Preston was brilliant to take advantage of that. 2) Set a laser-like focus on your audience and your brand. Preston made his entire store about Lebowski, and you should do the same. 3) Go for clever marketing. Instead of spending a lot of money on ads, for instance, try to get stories about your firm placed in media that hits your core target group. Preston's customers are international, so shooting for coverage in *Time Out* was perfect.

It's a neat story. But you know what really happened. If we can learn anything from Preston, it is that success happens in unexpected, serendipitous ways. Whatever plan he originally had in place was destroyed within a month of his opening the store. Instead, click moments, purposeful bets, and complex forces all played their part in bringing him back from the brink and guiding him toward success. There are three key lessons for the rest of us.

*

The first lesson is that the world is unpredictable and changing at a record pace, and that unless the rules of the game are locked in, such as in tennis or chess, these rapid changes will make success ever more random. It might seem like a blessing that we can look at the formula someone else has used to become successful—but the very existence of that formula will quickly invalidate it. As soon as we see something that seems to work, something we can set a benchmark against, we often try to use that specific framework to our advantage. It all seems very logical—but it wasn't logic that set Nike or *Lost* or DVF or the iPod or Picasso or Windows 3.0 or even Sony's Betacam apart. That is the lesson we need to take to heart. It is never about someone's specific strategy, because when you delve into it, you realize that the specific strategy came from an unexpected meeting, a surprising deal, a serendipitous insight, or a lucky turn of events.

The second lesson is that we are truly reluctant to actively court randomness in our lives. We have created a society in which we are taught the great virtues of planning and predictability. Increasingly, the world will not let us, yet increasingly, success comes unexpectedly. How do we reconcile these two facts—that we hate randomness, and yet need it to succeed? Create a focused plan to court randomness. The tactics outlined in the second half of this book do that, but perhaps the most important strategy of all is to use passion as a guide. Passion is what allows us to keep going, to keep placing bets, to keep exploring avenues even after some of them have not worked out. Passion drove every successful person mentioned in this book.

The third lesson is that we cannot control all of the complex events around us, but we can recognize when something is moving in our direction and when events unfold to our benefit. We need to double down on those moments. They are rare, and they do not appear every day. We have a strong desire to control complex forces, but they are not easily manipulated. Instead, we are better off trying to create something for complex forces to hook on to, identify when one of our projects has been caught up in one, and then go for the gold. This is true for spectacular ideas such as the Ice Hotel or Viagra, but also for much smaller ones, such as the Lebowski Store in the Village.

The world has never behaved in a predictable fashion, and that has never been truer than it is today. But this means that any one of us has the opportunity to change the world in the most unexpected of ways. An opportunity can present itself in the blink of an eye. It can happen when you least expect it. It can happen in an instant, when the various pathways of our lives come together in surprising ways and connect.

Click.

ACKNOWLEDGMENTS

When I started this project my expectation was that it would be easier to write this book than my last one. Well, it wasn't. The complexity of the ideas in this book could have made it into a tangled mess if I didn't have help in pulling it all together. I did have help from a great many people, and I want to acknowledge them here.

First off, I had a great team supporting me throughout the writing process. Jacqueline Murphy was the editor for my first book, *The Medici Effect*, and we extended that collaboration to this one as she not only helped me pull the text together but also expanded the ideas, and challenged the logic of my argument. Eric Gardner has been my tireless research assistant through most of this project. He tracked down fascinating examples, interviewed people around the world and handled my various whims gracefully. There were at least thirty detailed case studies or so that never even made it into the book but he was undeterred and kept going with enthusiastic write-up after write-up. Early on in the project I also had the help of two research interns, Kendra Hefti and Jon Laxmi, who got me going in some fascinating directions.

My agent, Kim Witherspoon, lived up to her legendary reputation every step of the way, for which I am incredibly thankful. Her sure hand guided me to the great team at Portfolio, who were the best supporters of this book from day one. Many thanks to Adrian Zackheim, who saw the potential for this book and injected constant enthusiasm in every meeting we had. Many, many thanks also to my editors, Courtney Young and Emily Angell, along with copy editor Ted Gilley.

Many people were interviewed for the book during the research phase and I am extremely grateful for the time they gave me during the process. You were all game for the many phone calls, e-mails, and meetings, and for that I am very thankful.

The ideas in this book evolved from the numerous conversations I have had with various thought leaders and friends around the world. Kristian Ribberström, who joined my firm a couple of years ago and is one of my very best friends, has been a constant sounding board throughout this process. Special mention must also go to Matt Mason, Mark Tracy, and Martin Johansson. They were incredibly willing to share their time and perspectives on the concepts as they evolved. Others that helped shape my thinking include Chris Yeh, Marcus Samuelsson, Randy Haykin, Peter Sims, Nick Donofrio, David Krieger, my cousin Christian Johansson, and of course my sister Sandra Ljung, whose hesitancy to agree with her brother pushed these ideas even further. Other people who helped out in this regard include Pamela Carlton, Chantal Yang, Corbin Younger, Markus Wråke, and Tom Gates. They all read the manuscript and provided great feedback.

Professor Teresa Amabile, who was critical in inspiring me to write my first book, probably had no idea what it would start—I certainly didn't. She has been a constant sounding board and has provided me with invaluable advice through the years. Ove Ribberström also deserves a special mention as he helped me track down facts in the Olof Palme assassination case.

My parents deserve my constant and ongoing thanks. I feel incredibly lucky to have their support in the various endeavors I have gotten myself into and this book was no exception.

The people at the Medici Group have had incredible patience with my comings and goings throughout the entire writing process. Not only that, but everyone played a role in developing the ideas of the book through casual conversations in the office, and also in thinking through aspects such as book covers and titles. Some have already been mentioned but everyone on the team deserves thanks. Their support meant a lot to me. A special shout-out goes to Lily Tang, Erin Lee, and Jesal Trivedi for their constant input. I also want to give special mention to Andria Younger, who helped me build a career as a thought leader.

Early on as I was testing ideas for the book, and later, as I was pulling the text together, I received great input and help from all kinds of members from my class at Harvard Business School, for which I am very thankful.

Finally, I want to thank my family. My wife, Sweet Joy, has been an undying supporter, sounding board, and inspiration to me in life. This has been particularly true during the writing of this book. Writing for me comes slowly, incrementally, and with no small amount of pain. Sweet has not only helped me through all of that but also helped me evolve and hone these ideas. I consider myself incredibly lucky. I am also eternally grateful for our young daughters, Amara and Serena, as they constantly find ways to brighten my day. They keep proving a basic tenet of this book: Every minute, every hour there is another surprise around the corner. They create them all with smile on their face.

NOTES

INTRODUCTION

1. The program came out of nowhere and delivered 18.7 million viewers to the struggling network. For more information on the development and impact of Lost, see James Stewart, *Disney War.* (New York , Simon & Schuster, 2005) and Variety's rating's recap after the premier, "ABC, Eye have quite some night." *Variety*, September 23, 2004.
2. "Good news," she said. "You can meet him." These quotes are from Damon Lindelof's Keynote at the 2011 New York Television Festival. Tim McCoy of *The Wrap*, recapped the speech, "Damon Lindelof's History of 'Lost' (A Show He Longed to Quit)." *The Wrap*, September 23, 2011.

CHAPTER 1

8. Spread like an epidemic through Europe. Eugene Tomiuc, *Radio Free Europe* covered the spread of the song, "O-Zone Breathes Fresh Air into European Pop Music Scene." *Radio Free Europe*, May 6, 2004.
8. At one point there were *five* different versions of the song. O-Zone's original version topped the charts during the week of June, 20 2004. Covers of the song that charted included "Le Poulailler" by Le, "Ma cé ki? Massimo" by Massimo Gargia, Dragostea Din Tei, Haiducci, and "Argent Argent" by Cauet. "France Top 40." http://top40-charts.com/chart.php?cid=11&date=2004-06-20.

9. The song still climbed the charts without any visible promotional efforts. O-Zone reached number 14 on the Hot Dance Airplay charts.

9. "They all had a good laugh, and I thought nothing of it." This quote is from an interview Gary gave to Newsgrounds, "Interview with Gary Brolsma." NewGrounds.net, Nov. 19, 2011. http://theinterviewer.new grounds.com/news/post/652185.

9. The video is believed to be the most watched in the history of the Internet. Many videos claim the title of most watched in Internet history. Most experts conclude it is either Gary or the Star Wars Kid. Mark Sweeney. "YouTube Promotional Blitz Launches New Version of Trivial Pursuit." *The Guardian*, September 8, 2010.

10. The bottle was shaped like something you'd find on an episode of M*A*S*H. This quote is from a profile by David Major. "Absolute Roux." *New Jersey Life*, http://www.crillonimporters.com/News/roux-media/roux-njlife -absol1.html.

10. One hundred thousand cases sold in 1980 to some 10 million in 2007. Data is available from Absolut, "Absolut Vodka Sales." http://www.absolut .com/content/about/pdf/en/ABSOLUT_VODKA_Sales_2008.pdf. Last modified 2008.

11. You can't think of any strategy or any formulas to create a song like "Dragostea din tei." Author interview with Dan Balan, July 2011.

12. Represented a turning point for the shoe company. For a detailed story of Bowerman's insight read Michelle Norris, "Found: The Waffle Iron That Inspired Nike." National Public Radio, March 3, 2011.

13. Estrada was one. For a complete profile of the disgraced president visit BBC News, "Profile: Joseph Estrada." http://news.bbc.co.uk/2/hi/asia -pacific/1063976.stm.

13. "He is not just a gambling lord." Quote is from BBC's coverage of the event. Emma Batha, "A Tale of Betrayal and Revenge." BBC News, January 19, 2001. http://news.bbc.co.uk/2/hi/asia-pacific/1057819.stm.

14. Who the Heck Is This Guy. William Bunch, "Who the Heck Is This Guy?: 10 Things You Might Want to Know about Tonight's Star, Barack Obama." *Philadelphia Daily News*, July 27, 2004.

14. "Important voices in American politics," as written by Jeremy Dauber, "A Star Is Born." *Christian Science Monitor*, July 29, 2004.

14. "He should never count on that window staying open." As told to Kate Zernike and Jeff Zeleny, "The Long Run: Obama in Senate; Star Power, Minor Role." *New York Times*, March 9, 2008. The quote is found near the end of the article.

CHAPTER 2

20. She had committed 57 unforced errors. For a complete recap of Serena's first major victory see "Serena's Super Saturday." *Sports Illustrated*, September 12, 1999.

20. The public rise of one of the most formidable tennis players of all time. On her 30 birthday, *Sports Illustrated* debated whether Serena was already the best tennis player of all time. "Taking Stock of Serena Williams on Her 30th Birthday." *Sports Illustrated*, September 26, 2011.

21. When Serena was a toddler. Serena's early travels are covered briefly in her autobiography as well as in a number of online biographies including "Serena Williams," Biography.com. http://www.biography.com/articles/Serena-Williams-9532901.

22. In his book *Outliers*. For a fuller explanation of the 10,000 hour rule see Malcolm Gladwell, *Outliers* (New York: Little, Brown, 2008).

22. "I just remember playing, all the time." As quoted in her autobiography, Serena Williams, *On the Line*, chapter 1.

23. "I just practiced so hard." As told to Frank Fitzpatrick after the win. "Serena Williams Breaks Through, Captures Open." *Philadelphia Inquirer*, September 12, 1999.

23. Gladwell writes. Gladwell, *Outliers*.

23. In his 2008 book. Geoff Colvin, *Talent Is Overrated: What Really Separates World-class Performers from Everybody Else* (New York: Penguin, 2008).

23. "Nothing except practice, practice, practice." This quote was found in the epilogue of David Shenk's *The Genius in All of Us: Why Everything You've Been Told about Genetics, Talent, and IQ Is Wrong* (New York: Doubleday, 2010).

24. Venus was ranked number one among girls. *Sports Illustrated* detailed all of the Williams sisters early accomplishments; includes quotes from Macci, "Timeline: Venus and Serena Williams." *Sports Illustrated* online.

26. No other substantive changes have been made in the rules of tennis. Each year the ITF releases an updated rulebook. Rules have remained exceptionally consistent. International Tennis Federation, "Rules of Tennis 2011." http://www.itftennis.com/shared/medialibrary/pdf/original/IO_54584_original.PDF.

26. There are just four main styles of singles tennis. The authors break down the physical mechanics of tennis in Paul Roetert and Mark Kovacs,*Tennis Anatomy* (Champaign, IL: Human Kinetics, 2010), p. 3–6.

27. According to Mikhail Botvinnik. Botvinnik is considered one of the

most influential chess players of all time. He outlines his vision of chess in *Botvinnik: 100 Selected Games* (New York: Dover, 1960), p. 11.

28. "Susan dominated the New York Open chess competition." The Polgars have been increasingly profiled over the years. The most in-depth study is Carin Flora, "The Grandmaster Experiment," *Psychology Today*, July 1, 2005.

28. "I was brought up in an ambience where it was believed that there is no such thing as talent." Interview with Susan Polgar, February 16, 2011.

28. Their education by and large. This quote is from Serena Allot, "Queen Takes All." *The Telegraph*, January 16, 2002.

30. According to Jason Strout, a trainer at Manhattan's famous Church Street Boxing Gym. Author interview with Jason Strout, August 2011.

31. Society imposes a somewhat fixed idea. For a thorough description of classical music see "Classical," *The Oxford Concise Dictionary of Music*, ed. Michael Kennedy (Oxford, UK: 2007).

CHAPTER 3

34. Right now, information saves lives. This quote can be found in an article published immediately after the tsunami. Mitch Wagner, "Sri Lankan Chronicles Tsunami Aftermath Using Text-messaging and Blogs." *Information Week*, December 30, 2004.

34. Proven to be a very effective and fast way of getting information online. Ibid.

34. At first the screen looked like an aquarium. A simple Google search reveals hundreds of stories about Nokia's ruggedness. This one is from YouTube. "Nokia 3720 Classic Toughness Test." http://www.youtube.com/all_comments?v=pxeSBChfBCg&page=1.

35. "Has unrivalled prowess in logistics." Quote is from "Nokia's Turnaround: The Giant in the Palm of Your Hand." *Economist*, February 5, 2005.

35. "Dominance in the global cell-phone market seems unassailable." Mark Scott, "Nokia: Wired for Profits." *Business Week*, August 2, 2007.

35. "If you judge a brand on influence or reach." Originally written by Bruce Upbin. "The Next Billion." *Forbes*, November 12, 2007.

36. It was referred to as the Burning Platform Memo. The "Burning Platform Memo" was leaked to the Internet and quickly flooded nearly every business Web site. You can find a recap by Doug Aamoth, "Nokia: 'We're Not Even Fighting with the Right Weapons.'" *Time*, February 9, 2011.

38. Steve Starr had worked at Disney for twenty-six years. For more information on the plight of traditional animators refer to Claudia Eller

and Richard Verrier, "Animation Drawing New Respect in Hollywood." *Los Angeles Times*, February 12, 2002, A1.

40. Negotiated the pair down to $750,000. The full story on Excite passing up Google was reported by Seth Weintraub, "Excite Passed Up Buying Google for $750,000 in 1999." *CNN Money*, September 29, 2010. http://tech.fortune.cnn.com/2010/09/29/excite-passed-up-buying-google-for-750000-in-1999.

40. Next up was Yahoo. In 1998 it was all but certain to many experts that Yahoo would control search for the next decade. This article expands on the reasoning. Randal Stross, "How Yahoo Won the Search Wars." *Fortune*, March 2, 1998, p. 148–154.

40. "I don't know what they're really worth." Originally quoted in "How Yahoo Blew It." *Wired*, February 2007. http://www.wired.com/wired/archive/15.02/yahoo_pr.html.

41. No correlation between the papers expected to become game-changers and the number of citations those papers ultimately. Dean Keith Simonton, *Creativity in Science: Chance, Logic, Genius, and the Zeitgeist* (Cambridge: Cambridge University Press, 2004).

41. The riveting account of Tetlock's. Philip Tetlock wrote an entire book on failed predictions of experts. *Expert Political Judgment: How Good Is It? How Can We Know?* (Princeton : Princeton University Press, 2005).

42. We would have heard as much from the experts. Nearly every technology site and expert doubted the viability of the iPhone. This is simply a partial list. Michael Kanellos, "The Apple iPhone Flop." *CNet*, December 7, 2006. Matthew Lynn, "Apple iPhone Will Fail in a Late, Defensive Move." *Bloomberg*, January 14, 2007. Charles Golvin, "Apple's iPhone Changes the Stakes, Not the Game." *Forrester Research*, January 11, 2007.

43. Today there are nearly seventeen thousand Starbucks stores around the world. This official document details Starbucks' rapid expansion. "Company Timeline." http://www.starbucks.com/assets/aboutustimelinefinal72811.pdf .

43. In September 2011. *Consumer Reports* is considered by many to be the definitive watchdog publication. Here it reviews premium coffee and Starbucks finishes surprisingly low. "Best Coffee." *Consumer Reports*, September 2011, p. 40–42.

44. There are currently roughly eighty-seven thousand variations. Deborah Arthurs, "As Starbucks Reveal They've Got 87,000 Combinations of Coffee, We Spot a Galaxy of Stars Clutching Their Cups of Iced Brew." *The Daily Mail*, July 10, 2009.

44. "Translated to higher in-store sales and more bottles sold." Original

quote can be found at Wendy Kaufman, "Innovation Helps Starbucks to Turn Around Sales." National Public Radio, August 2, 2011. http://www.npr.org/templates/story/story.php?storyId=128923338.

44. Despite its best efforts. Burger King is famous for introducing a variety of different products. Two examples can be found below: Jeff Reeves, "Burger King Fries Hit Your Grocery Store Freezer." *Investor Place*, June 9, 2010, and Daniel Bukszpan, "15 Major Fast Food Failures." *CNBC*, October 18, 2010. Unfortunately, Burger Kings continues to lose market share: Joseph DiStefano, "McDonald's Crushing Wendy's, Burger King, All Others." Philly.com. April 19, 2011.

44. Apple's willingness to *decrease* the number of products. For a complete breakdown of Apple's project strategy see Peter Burrows, Ronald Grover, and Heather Green, "Steve Jobs' Magic Kingdom." *Business Week*, February 6, 2006, and Walter Isaacson, *Steve Jobs* (New York: Simon & Schuster, 2011).

44. This generates loyalty. Quote can be found at Jennifer Reese, "Starbucks: Inside the Coffee Cult." *Fortune Magazine*, December 9, 1996.

44. In *Wrestling with Starbucks*. Kim Fellner, *Wrestling with Starbucks: Conscience, Capital, Cappuccino* (New Brunswick, NJ: Rutgers University Press, 2008), 56.

45. And we need a computer information system. Howard Schultz, *Pour Your Heart Into It* (New York: Hyperion, 1997), p. 142.

CHAPTER 4

47. As soon as I had a free moment." Originally told to "Interview: *Twilight* Author Stephenie Meyer." *A Motley Vision*, October 26, 2005. http://www.motleyvision.org/2005/interview-twilight-author-stephenie-meyer/.

48. Writers House eventually signed. Meyer has been incredibly open about the origins of her book. On her Web site you can find the entire quote and story: "The Story Behind *Twilight*." StephenieMeyer.com. Last modified Oct 5, 2005. http://www.stepheniemeyer.com/twilight.html.

48. Of those weeks, 136 found her in the number one spot. Les Grossman's profile of Meyer includes a complete account of the story, "It's Twilight in America: The Vampire Saga." *Time*, November 23, 2009.

49. "Have a pillowy quality distinctly reminiscent of Internet fan fiction." Ibid.

49. "I don't think I'm a writer." Original source is Stephenie Meyer, "The Story Behind *Twilight*."

49. Yet the *Twilight Saga* has sold. Sales data is from press release. "Little, Brown to Publish Official 'Twilight' Guide." *Publishers Weekly*. http://www.publishersweekly.com/pw/by-topic/childrens/childrens-book-news/article/44733-little-brown-to-publish-official-twilight-guide.html.

50. In 1996, the median income. 1996 US income data is referenced from John McNeil, "Changes in Median Household Income: 1969 to 1996", *U.S. Department of Commerce*. http://www.census.gov/prod/3/98pubs/p23-196.pdf. New lawyers' salary information can be found at "How Much Do Law Firms Pay New Associates? A 16-Year Retrospective." *National Association for Law Placement*, October 2011. http://www.nalp.org/new_associate_sal_oct2011.

50. That's an increase of 60 percent. LSAT testing data is collected by LSAC. In 1999–2000, 107,153 took the test. That number increased to 171,514 in 2009–2010, a change of just over 60 percent. LSAC, "LSATs Administered." http://www.lsac.org/lsacresources/Data/lsats-administered.asp.

51. From 2007 to 2010. The legal industry is facing a period of disequilibrium. The American Bar Association keeps track of law school graduation numbers; graduation rates continue to climb. "Enrollment and Degrees Awarded." http://www.americanbar.org/content/dam/aba/administrative/legal_education_and_admissions_to_the_bar/stats_1.authcheckdam.pdf. For more information on the lack of supply, see Annie Lowrey, "A Case of Supply v. Demand." *Salon*, Oct 27, 2010.

51. Just 68 percent of 2010 graduates. National Association for Law Placement. "Class of 2010." http://www.nalp.org/classof2010.

51. "Legal services are almost like Miami condos." The quote originally appears in Jennifer Lee, "Unemployed and Struggling Lawyers Seek Solace." *The New York Times*, June 16, 2009. http://cityroom.blogs.nytimes.com/2009/06/16/unemployed-and-struggling-lawyers-seek-solace/.

51. Lawyers teaming up with software companies. John Markoff, "Armies of Expensive Lawyers, Replaced by Cheaper Software." *The New York Times*, March 4, 2011. http://www.nytimes.com/2011/03/05/science/05legal.htm.

54. "I am going to wait for the next big thing." This story was recounted by Richard Rumelt on page 14 of his book *Good Strategy, Bad Strategy: The Difference and Why It Matters* (New York: Random House, 2011).

56. "Thoughtful individuals who don't want to harm anyone." This quote is from an interview at Changing Hands Bookstore. "BookStories Interview with Stephenie Meyer." Last modified August 2006. http://chbookstore.qwestoffice.net/fa2006-08.html.

56. It epitomizes the sexual tension and confusion felt by teenage girls. Les Grossman, "Stephenie Meyer: A New J. K. Rowling?" *Time Magazine*, April 24, 2008.

57. "Of course, I was far too invested in my characters." Changing Hands Bookstore, "BookStories Interview with Stephenie Meyer."

57. "Didn't want to find out just how many rules I was breaking." "10 Questions for Stephenie Meyer." *Time Magazine*, August 21, 2008.

58. In a letter to his clients . . . Paulson's full words were covered by Neil Hume, "Dear Paulson Investor." *Financial Times*, April 21, 2010.

60. The chart Pellegrini produced. Paulson's trade is now perhaps the most famous trade in recent memory. The entire story is told by Gregory Zuckerman, *The Greatest Trade Ever* (New York: Random House, 2009).

60. Jesse Livermore, who made $100 million by shorting during the Great Depression. Ibid.

62. His book *Thinner*. This quote was referenced in Stephen Spignesi, *The Essential Stephen King* (Franklin Lakes, NJ: New Page Books, 2003), p. 158.

63. The moment it became known that Richard Bachman was Stephen King. Precise sales data is unknown. When released on its own, the book sold 280,000 units as referenced by Chuck Klosterman, *Eating the Dinosaur* (New York: Scribner, 2010), p. 114. King was outed in April 1985. By Nov. of that year sales reached nearly 3.1 million. Michael Collings, *Scaring Us to Death: The Impact of Stephen King on Popular Culture* (Mercer Island, WA: Starmont House, 1997), p. 50.

63. How it can be very easy to mistake randomness for skill. Taleb has written two influential books on risk: *Fooled by Randomness: The Hidden Role of Chance in Life and in the Markets* (New York: Random House, 2004) and *The Black Swan: The Impact of the Highly Improbable* (New York: Random House, 2010).

CHAPTER 5

65. The Swedish prime minister Olof Palme was declared dead on arrival at the hospital. The full account of that night is available in the official report: Swedish Audit Commission Report, "Brottsutredningen efter mordet på statsminister Olof Palme." http://www.regeringen.se/content/1/c4/12/44/6a2655da.pdf.

66. Another plot involved . . . An exhaustive breakdown of the different conspiracy theories can be found in Kris Hollington, *Wolves, Jackals, and Foxes: The Assassins Who Changed History* (New York: Thomas Dunne Books, 2007), p. 288.

69. Both were succeeded by a man named Johnson. Discover Games, "Kennedy–Lincoln Similarities." http://www.discovergames.com/sense less3.html.

70. In *The Perfect Thing.* This book provides a great account of how the iPod was developed. Quotes from Steve Jobs and Jeff Rubin can be found in chapter seven, "Shuffle," in Stephen Levy, *The Perfect Thing: How the iPod Shuffles Commerce, Culture, and Coolness* (New York: Simon & Schuster, 2006).

70. According to Mueller. Richard Mueller, University of California at Berkeley. "The Illusion of Randomness." http://muller.lbl.gov/teaching/physics10/old physics 10/chapters (old)/4-Randomness.htm.

71. In a series of interesting experiments. The researchers conducted a total of six experiments, which can be found in Jennifer Whitson and Adam Galinksy, "Lacking Control Increases Illusory Pattern Perception," *Science* 322, no. 5898 (2008): 115–117.

72. Harvard University biologist Kevin Foster and Hanna Kokko, "The Evolution of Superstitious and Superstition-like Behaviour." *Proceedings of the Royal Society B* 276 (2008): 31–37.

72. Believing that the familiar rustle. Michael Shermer, "Patternicity: Finding Meaningful Patterns in Meaningless Noise." *Scientific American*, November 25, 2008.

73. The song "Brain Damage" begins. For a complete recap, see The Straight Dope, "Does the Music in Pink Floyd's Dark Side of the Moon Coincide with the Action of The Wizard of Oz?" http://www.straightdope.com/columns/read/1773/does-the-music-in-pink-floyds-em-dark-side-of-the-moon-em-coincide-with-the-action-of-em-the-wizard-of-oz-em.

73. "When asked about the linkages. Nearly everyone involved with the album has denied the connections. Both Nick Mason and Producer Alan Parsons denied it to MTV in "The Pink Floyd/Wizard of Oz Connection." MTV News, May 30, 1997. http://www.mtv.com/news/articles/1433194/pink-floyd wizard-oz-connection.jhtml The Pink Floyd/Wizard of Oz Connection."

74. Duncan Watts takes particular pleasure. Duncan Watts, *Everything is Obvious Once You Know the Answer* (New York: Random House, 2011).

74. Soldiers from rural backgrounds have an easier time adapting to military life. Paul Lazarsfeld, "The American Solider—An Expository Review." *Public Opinion Quarterly* 13 (1949): 377–404.

76. "Unproven start-ups with no profits." All quotes in this section are from chapter two of Phil Rosenzweig, *The Halo Effect* (New York: Free Press, 2009).

77. Her opponent, an aspiring physicist. Bill Flick, "Lexington Native

Crowned 'Rock, Paper, Scissors' Champ." Pantagraph.com, April 3, 2010. http://www.pantagraph.com/news/local/article_8de7435a-3ec8-11df-9aa3-001cc4c002e0.html.

77. At this, the worldwide rock paper scissors championship. Jeff Ruby, "Fist Fight." *Chicago Magazine*, April 2007.

78. "We really didn't know how things were going to turn out." From an interview with Graham Walker in the *Washington Times*, "Fists Fly in Game of Strategy." December 10, 2004.

78. It is impossible to define what is 'best'. There is a surprising amount of scientific literature on rock–paper–scissors. Both Michael Brooks, "Rock, Paper or Scissors?" *New Scientist*, December 22, 2007, and Ricardo Alfaro, Lixing Han, and Kenneth Schilling, "Classroom Capsules," *The College Mathematics Journal* 40, no. 2 (2009): 125–130 are fine introductions. If you are interested in a game-theory explanation of strategy see Avinash Dixit and Barry Nalebuff, *The Art of Strategy: A Game Theorist's Guide to Success in Business and Life* (New York: W.W. Norton and Company, 2008).

80. The auction house Christie's employed this approach. Carol Vogel, "Rock, Paper, Payoff: Child's Play Wins Auction House an Art Sale." *The New York Times*, April 29, 2005.

81. "Because things are lasting shorter." Phone interview by the author with William Fung on October 11, 2011.

82. "Will be outdated." Phone interview by the author with Randy Haykin on July 22, 2011.

CHAPTER 6

87. The story of where Diane Von Furstenberg got the inspiration for her wrap dress is based primarily on her autobiography *Diane: A Signature Life* (New York: Simon and Schuster, 1998) and an interview on the Bravo Show, *Watch What Happens Live!*, "Inspiration from an Unlikely Source," *Watch What Happens Live!*, http://www.bravotv.com/watch-what-happens-live/season-3/videos/inspiration-from-an-unlikely-source.

87. "I probably averaged." Email correspondence between the research team and Julie Nixon-Eisenhower, Oct. 12, 2011.

88. "The dress was nothing." Quoted from page 80 of *Diane: A Signature Life*.

88. "I remember in Minneapolis, going to a store on one side of the street." Ibid.

88. "I think she's peaked." originally quoted by Linda Bird Franckle, Lisa

Whitman, and Sari Gilbert, "Princess of Fashion." *Newsweek*, March 22, 1976.

90. But fashion is fickle. As reported by Tracy Rozhon, "The Dress That Saved Diane von Furstenberg." *New York Times*, September 5, 2004, 3.1.

90. They treated her like a has-been. Ibid.

90. "Today the wrap dress is simply iconic." Research team Interview with Rebecca Lay, August 14, 2011.

92. "The idea for the wrap dress." Originally found on page 79 of *Diane: A Signature Life.*

CHAPTER 7

97. "The most anticipated product in the history of the world." Originally referenced in James Wallace and Jim Erickson, *Hard Drive: Bill Gates and the Making of the Microsoft Empire* (New York: HarperCollins, 1992), p. 360.

98. They were catastrophic, bug-riddled disasters. Jennifer Edstrom and Marlin Eller, *Barbarians Led by Bill Gates* (New York: Henry Holt and Co., 1998), chapters 4–5.

101. Franklin had arrived in Philadelphia. Public Broadcasting Service. "Franklin Timeline: 1706–1790." http://www.pbs.org/benfranklin/ 1730.html.

101. That man turned out to be the crown prince of Sweden. Originally quoted by the Swedish Institute. "Monarchy: A Modern Monarchy." http://www.sweden.se/eng/Home/Society/Monarchy/Facts/Monarchy.

101. Angioplasty surgery was born. Morton Meyers, *Happy Accidents: Serendipity in Modern Medical Breakthroughs* (New York: Arcade Publishing, 2007), chapter 14

102. "Akin to pouring molasses in the Arctic." Erik Sandberg-Diment, "Personal Computers: Windows Are Open at Last." *New York Times*, February 25, 1986, C6.

103. It was to be everything. The hype for OS/2 was high and can be seen in the following articles: Peter Lewis, "The Executive Computer: Godot Had Nothing on I.B.M.'s OS/2." *New York Times*, September 6, 1987, and Andrew Pollak, "I.B.M. and Microsoft Promote OS/2." *New York Times*, November 14, 1989.

104. Microsoft wound down. Edstrom and Eller, *Barbarians Led by Bill Gates*, chapter 6.

104. Ballmer lobbied aggressively to have Windows killed off. Stephen Mahes and Paul Andrews, *Gates* (New York: Touchstone, 1994), chapter 28.

105. After two of the founders . . . Jim Hopkins, "Surprise! There's a Third YouTube Co-founder." *USA Today*, October 11, 2006.

105. "As I originally wrote it." Quote is from an interview: Paul Scanlon, "The Force Behind George Lucas." *Rolling Stone*, Aug 25, 1977, p. 41–50.

106. "It is difficult to comprehend the political motives behind Antony's conduct." Michael Chauveau and David Lorton, *Cleopatra: Beyond the Myth* (Ithaca, NY: Cornell University Press, 2004), p. 44.

107. He and his roommates. Peter Woit, Columbia University. "David Weise." http://www.math.columbia.edu/~woit/wordpress/?p=149.

109. Gates listened intently as Weise sketched out the details. Edstrom and Eller, *Barbarians Led by Bill Gates*, p. 92–93.

109. "Here was this little skunkworks." Larry Osterman, "Farewell to One of the Great Ones." http://blogs.msdn.com/b/larryosterman/archive/2005/02/02/365635.aspx .

110. "And as it happened." Author Interview with Murray Sargent, August 22, 2011.

CHAPTER 8

114. "They were on every street corner." This story is told in full in Howard Schultz, *Pour Your Heart Into It* (New York: Hyperion, 1997). The specific quote is on page 51.

114. "No one in America knows about this." Quotes appear in Ibid, p. 50–53.

117. The most famous psychological study. According to Google Scholar the article has over 750 citations.

118. Completely miss seeing a woman dressed as a gorilla. Daniel Simons and Christopher Charbis, "Gorillas in Our Midst: Sustained Inattentional Blindness for Dynamic Events." *Perception* 28 (1999): 1059–1074.

119. Spent a decade researching people's perceptions of their luck. Richard Wiseman, *The Luck Factor* (New York: Miramax Books, 2003), p. 10.

119. Unfortunately, by rigidly pouring . . . Rebecca Webber, "Make Your Own Luck." *Psychology Today*, July 28, 2011. http://www.psychologytoday.com/articles/201005/make-your-own-luck.

120. The subjects didn't notice. Wiseman, *The Luck Factor*, p. 44.

120. The "unlucky" woman. Ibid., p. 53–54.

121. "She looked sick. Her face looked, literally, like a ripe tomato." The story of the burkini and all quotes from Zanetti are from two interviews the team conducted with her in fall 2011 and winter 2012.

123. "Why would anyone pay five thousand dollars for a painting of a flower?" Interview between the author and Marcel Salathé, January 2012.

123. One thousand paintings of numbers, literally, numbered from 1 to 1,000. Daniel Pink, "Paint by Numbers." *Wired*, December 2006.

124. Number 1 would cost $999, number 2 would cost $998. "Frequently Asked Questions." One Thousand Paintings, http://www.onethousand paintings.com/faq.

125. "The fitness world [had] become so technical and lacked fun." Quotes in this section can be found in "The Man Behind Zumba Fitness." *Fitness First*, May 2011.

125. "I never thought it would be so big in Scandanavia." Interview between research team and Alberto Perlman, March 23, 2012.

126. "Usually animators, designers, and programmers sit in different parts of the building." Quotes from Dahl are from multiple conversations between the author and Tobias Dahl in 2011.

126. "We get hundreds of visitors every year just to see how the hell we do it." Interview between the author and Richard Sheridan, October 15, 2011.

127. "We want to put everybody under one roof." Steve Jobs in Leslie Iwercks, *The Pixar Story*. Recorded 2007. Disney/Pixar. DVD.

127. "What Steve realized." Jonah Lehrer, "Steve Jobs: 'Technology Alone Is Not Enough.'" The *New Yorker*, October 7, 2011. http://www.newyorker .com/online/blogs/newsdesk/2011/10/steve-jobs-pixar.html.

128. "He made sure of that by making the atrium." Conversation between the author and Ed Catmull, January 14, 2012.

128. "The main challenge for Pixar was getting its different cultures to work together." Lehrer, "Steve Jobs."

128. "I am a designer in my field of diversity and inclusion." Email correspondence between the author and Gina Warren, January 21, 2012.

130. One of the most successful toys. This document contains a wealth of information on sales data. Ray Hodges, Rubik's Cube. "Fast Cube Facts." http://www.rubiks.com/i/company/media_library/pdf/Rubiks Fast Cube Facts.pdf .

130. Rubik once wrote . . . Rubik is essentially a recluse, but he wrote an unpublished autobiography that John Tierney referenced in his article, "'The Perplexing Life of Erno Rubik." *Discover* 7, no. 8 (1986).

130. "Space always intrigued me." Ibid.

131. "But for me, it was a code I myself had invented." Ibid.

131. These moments. Steve Johnson, *Where Good Ideas Come From: The Natural History of Innovation* (New York: Penguin Group, 2010).

132. We create rigid rules. Webber, "Make Your Own Luck."

132. He gathered about a hundred thousand . . . The exact number of soldiers and horses is unknown, but most experts agree that Alexander was

overwhelmingly outnumbered. Debra Skelton and Pam Dell, *Empire of Alexander the Great* (New York: Chelsea House, 2009), p. 28.

133. While he was going through the selection processes to become the guest chef for President Obama's state dinner. Conversation between the author and Marcus Samuelsson, Fall 2010.

CHAPTER 9

138. He said he was a Russian programmer, and handed Eisenstat a floppy disk. The Russian/Apple intrigue is retold in detail by Jim Carlton in *Apple: The Inside Story of Intrigue, Egomania, and Business Blunders* (New York: Random House, 1997), p. 93.

139. Mark Zuckerberg placed a bet. David Kirkpatrick. *The Facebook Effect: The Inside Story of the Company That Is Connecting the World* (New York: Simon and Schuster, 2010), p. 24.

140. "The 1990s equivalent of the personal computer revolution." Originally reported by Rory O'Connor, "Apple's CEO Takes the Sweet with the Sour." *Baltimore Sun*, June 15, 1992, p. 10.

140. Sculley predicted a $3 trillion industry. As referenced in Owen Linzmayer, *Apple Confidential 2.0* (San Francisco: No Starch Press, 2004), p. 189.

141. 500 million had been laid down. Jim Carlton, *Apple: The Inside Story*, p. 281.

143. Several lists name . . . David Haskin, "Don't Believe the Hype: The 21 Biggest Technology Flops." *Computer World*, April 4, 2007.

143. Despite winning numerous industry awards. Pat Dillion, "The Next Small Thing." *Fast Company*, May 31, 1998.

143. Market share neared 80 percent. Robert Legge, "U.S. Robotics' PalmPilot Wins Hands Down." *PC World*, May 27, 1997.

144. Symbol of the new economy. Anointed a symbol by Rachel Konrad and Josh Borland in "Is Weakened Palm Ripe for Acquisition?" *CNet*, June 1, 2006. http://news.cnet.com/Is-weakened-Palm-ripe-for-acquisition/2100 -1040_3-267721.html.

144. Most influential technology products. Brian Heater, "The Most Influential Technologies, Round 3: Mobile Devices." *PC Magazine*. Last modified April 11, 2011. http://www.pcmag.com/slideshow/story/ 262899/the-most-influential-technologies-round-3-mobile-devices/2.

145. "Jumpers choose to land this way because it's exciting." "Skydiver Killed in Stunt after Trying to 'Skim across Pond at 60 mph' before Landing." *Daily Mail Online*, December 29, 2011.

145. "Accidents occur when parachutists start the maneuver too low." Ibid.

145. "Saw people I jumped with get killed right in front of my eyes." Author Interview with Vic Napier, January 2, 2012.

145. There were fourteen no-pull or low-pull deaths. Vic Napier, Carolyn Sara Finley, and Donald Self, 2007. "Risk Homeostasis: A Case Study of the Adoption of a Safety Innovation on the Level of Perceived Risk."

146. We each have our own level. Gerald Wilde, *Target Risk 2* (Toronto: PDE Publications, 2001).

147. The safer skydiving gear becomes . . . This is an old skydiving saying that is often attributed to Bill Booth, but we have not been able to find an original source.

147. ABS-equipped cabs increased their risk taking. Aschenbrenner and Biehl. "Improved Safety Through Improved Technical Measures? Empirical Studies Regarding Risk Compensation Processes in Relation to Anti-lock Braking Systems." In R. M. Trimpop and G. J. S. Wilde, *Challenges to Accident Prevention: The Issue of Risk Compensation Behaviour* (Groningen, NLD: Styx Publications, 1994).

147. Engaging in even riskier sex. Priscilla Alexander, "Sex Work and Health: A Question of Safety in the Workplace." *Journal of the American Medical Women's Association* 53, no. 2 (1998): 77–82.

147. Created a sense of invulnerability. Reed Albergotti and Shirley Wang. "Is It Time to Retire the Football Helmet?" *Wall Street Journal*, November 11, 2009.

148. It was too big. David Evans, Andre Haigu, and Richard Schmalensee, *Invisible Engines: How Software Platforms Drive Innovation and Transform Industries* (Cambridge, MA: MIT Press, 2006), p. 159.

148. The CEO of Andersen Consulting. "Webvan Pays Off Shaheen." *CNN Money*, May 16, 2001. http://money.cnn.com/2001/05/16/technology/webvan/index.htm.

149. The plan behind Webvan. Connie Guglielmo, "Can Webvan Deliver?" *Inter@ctive Week*, January 1, 2000, p. 26.

149. Today it is expanding. David Kirkpatrick, "The Online Grocer Version 2.0 : Forget Webvan, Say the Founders of FreshDirect."*Fortune*, November 25, 2002. http://money.cnn.com/magazines/fortune/fortune_archive/2002/11/25/332608/.

149. How often they end up writing excellent, groundbreaking papers. Dean Keith Simonton, *Creativity in Science: Chance, Logic, Genius, and the Zeitgeist*.

CHAPTER 10

154. Seventy percent of the town was leveled. Initial reports listed the death toll at two thousand. Historians now estimate that the death toll was between two hundred and two thousand.

154. The most widely discussed celebrated painting of its kind. Public Broadcasting Service, Treasures of the World. "Guernica." 1999.

154. "Did you do this?" Over the years the quote has become widely attributed to a variety of sources, but it can be found on p. 139 in Gijs van Hensbergen, *Guernica: The Biography of a Twentieth-century Icon* (London: Bloomsbury, 2005).

155. The most influential artist of the modern era. Robert Hughes, "The Artist Pablo Picasso." *Time Magazine*, June 8, 1998.

156. That translates into roughly two to four pieces *per day*. Picasso's career began around 1894; he was active until about ten years before his death in 1981.

156. "I don't think there is any." Told to Robert Hughes. "The Show of Shows." *Time*, May 26, 1980.

156. Collected dust in basements around the world. Among numerous examples of Picasso works fading to obscurity, here's one: Henry Samuel, "271 Picasso Paintings Discovered in Paris." *The Telegraph*, November 29, 2010.

156. The Virgin Group. All of these companies and people are prolific in their inventions. ENHS, "The Invention Factory." http://www.nps.gov/features/edis/feat001/inventionprocess/ENHS.html showcases Edison's work while Tom Taulli runs down's Branson's achievements. "Gevo: Richard Branson's New Age Chemical Company Goes Public." *Daily Finance*, February 10, 2011.

156. Failure rate of some 90 percent. Helen Walters, "Apple's Design Process." *Business Week*, March 8, 2008.

160. "Yet even the prisoners did not move voluntarily." From Wolfgang Braunfels, *Urban Design in Western Europe: Regime and Architecture, 900–1900* (Chicago: University of Chicago Press, 1988), p. 159.

160. "A low-risk action taken to discover, develop, and test an idea." Quotes from Peter Sims are from his book *Little Bets: How Breakthrough Ideas Emerge from Small Discoveries* (New York: Simon and Schuster, 2011) and multiple interviews with the Author during 2011.

161. "We should be more academic." As reported by Matt Cowen in "Fail Study: Jimmy Wales and Nupedia." *Wired*, April 1, 2011.

165. "News Corp's purchase of MySpace is looking like that rarest of rarities." Originally written by Marc Gunther, "News Corp. (hearts) MySpace." *Fortune*, March 29, 2006.

165. MySpace was the second most popular site on the Internet. Ibid.

167. Focus on calculating the affordable loss. Saras D. Sarasvathy, "What Makes Entrepreneurs Entrepreneurial?" http://www.semperprotinus. com/images/pdf/What%20makes%20entrs%20entl.pdf.

167–8. "If you place enough of those bets." Bezos was quoted in John Cook, "Jeff Bezos on Innovation." *Geekwire*, June 7, 2011. http://www .geekwire.com/2011/amazons-bezos-innovation.

168. "We can do quite large experiments without it having significant impact." Ibid.

168. "Started with us eating our way through every chocolate cake served in New York." Interview between the author and Naomi Josepher in spring 2009.

171. A fighter pilot by training. The entire Boyd saga is incredibly interesting. The definitive source on Robert Boyd is Robert Coram's excellent biography *Boyd: The Fighter Pilot Who Changed the Art of War* (New York: Little, Brown, 2004), p. 116.

172. "Once the air force understands what I'm doing." Boyd is quoted in Robert Coram, *Boyd: The Fighter Pilot Who Changed the Art of War* on p. 139.

CHAPTER 11

174. That morning. Lin Noueihed, "Peddler's Martyrdom Launched Tunisia's Revolution." *Reuters*, January 19, 2011. http://af.reuters.com/article/ libyaNews/idAFLDE70G18J20110119?sp=true.

174. His typical profit. Yasmine Ryan, "The Tragic Life of a Street Vendor." *Al Jazeera*, January 20, 2011. http://www.aljazeera.com/indepth/ features/2011/01/201111684242518839.html.

174. The scale was worth. Bob Simon, "How a Slap Sparked Tunisia's Revolution." *CBS News*, February 20, 2011. http://www.cbsnews.com/ 2102-18560_162-20033404.htm.

174. She slapped him. Kareem Fahim, "Slap to a Man's Pride Set Off Tumult in Tunisia." *New York Times*, January 21, 2011.

177. "More elk equaled less trout." Told to Michael Mauboussin in "Embracing Complexity." *Harvard Business Review*, September 2011.

177. It became one of the highest-grossing movies of all time. Box Office Mojo. "All Time Box Office."

178. "The shark not working was a godsend." Original interview appeared in, "Steven Spielberg and Quint Have an Epic Chat All About JAWS as it Approaches its 36th Anniversary!"*Ain't it Cool News*, June 6, 2012. http:// www.aintitcool.com/node/49921.

180. "It wasn't going as planned." From "Not Lovin' It: McDonalds' Twitter Campaign Hijacked by Haters." *Fox News*, January 26, 2012.

180. "Prevented from publicly criticizing the ruling regime." Analysis originally appeared in the Economist Intelligence Unit. "Country Profile: Tunisia." See http://www.eiu.com/.

183. The number of active users on eBay. eBay's user base was reported in its fourth quarter earnings report analyzed by Julianne Pepitone, "EBay Stock Pops 5% on Strong Sales." *CNN Money*, January 19, 2011.

183. In a famous paper. According to Google Scholar, the paper has over 2,400 references. Robert Merton, "The Matthew Effect in Science." *Science* 159, no. 3810 (1968): 56–63.

183. According to research by Brian Arthur. Brian Arthur, "Competing Technologies, Increasing Returns, and Lock-in by Historical Events." *The Economic Journal* 99, no. 394 (1989): 116–131.

184. If you could actually rerun history there might be different winners. Brian Arthur, "Increasing Returns and the New World of Business." *Harvard Business Review*, July 1996.

184. Asked fourteen thousand people to listen to a number of different songs. Matthew Salganik, Peter Sheridan Dodds, and Duncan Watts, "Experimental Study of Inequality and Unpredictability in an Artificial Cultural Market." *Science*, February 10, 2006, 854–856.

184. Watts and his team. The experiment is recapped on p. 76–79 of Duncan Watts, *Everything Is Obvious*.

186. Confused, Lorenz. The entire discovery is recounted by the American Physical Society in "Lorenz and the Butterfly Effect." http://www.aps.org/publications/apsnews/200301/history.cfm.

187. The average lifespan of a company on the S&P 500 was about seventy-five years in 1937. Arie de Geus, *The Living Company* (Boston: Harvard Business Press, 2002), Epilogue.

187. Intelligence agencies spent $125 million. Noah Schatman, "Pentagon's Prediction Software Didn't Spot Egypt Unrest." *Wired*, February 11, 2011.

189. *Half* of that billion came from porn. Merrill Brown, "Pay-TV, Film and Ad Industries Try to Tune In to World of VCRs." *Washington Post*, May 27, 1984, F1.

189. "Adult was a cash cow for VHS." Email correspondence between the author and Dan Miller, August 21, 2011.

189. "The adult-entertainment industry's preference." Sarah McBride, "The XXX Factor: Blu-ray or HD DVD?," *Wall Street Journal*, January 24, 2007.

189. "A wild card." Patrick Seitz, "High Def's Adult Situation Favors Toshiba." *Investors Business Daily*, March 2, 2006, A06.

189. *Macworld* concluded that . . . Lucas Mearian, "Porn Industry May Be Decider in Blu-ray, HD-DVD Battle." *MacWorld*, May 2, 2006.

190. "Is a sequel in the works?" Ian Rowley, "Next-Gen DVD's Porn Struggle." *Business Week*, January 22, 2007.

190. Were tons of lessons Sony had "learned." Michael Raynor, *The Strategy Paradox: Why Committing to Success Leads to Failure, and What to Do About It* (New York: Random House, 2007), chapter 2.

190. "We had the same demonstrations." Phone interview between the author and the director of the African Development Bank, January 5, 2012.

CHAPTER 12

191. "I had lost the feeling in my left arm." All quotes from Mr. Mahuad are from a phone interview between the author and Jamil Mahuad in March 2012.

192. "Won a standing ovation from investors." "Now for the Hard Part." *The Economist*, July 18, 1998.

195. "It took me a while." Conversation between the author and Yngve Bergqvist, April 6, 2011.

197. "It's the fastest takeoff of a new drug." Originally quoted by Bruce Handy, Edward Barnes, Lawrence Mondi, Wendy Cole, Greg Fulton, and Arnold Mann, "The Viagra Craze." *Time Magazine*, May 4, 1998.

198. Over four million prescriptions. Statistics were reported on page 112 of Jai Jack Li, *Laughing Gas, Viagra, and Lipitor: The Human Stories Behind the Drugs We Use* (New York: Oxford University Press, 2006) and Jack Hilt, "The Second Sexual Revolution." *New York Times*, February 20, 2000.

198. The fifth most profitable corporation. According to *Fortune*, "Fortune 500: 2002." http://money.cnn.com/magazines/fortune/fortune500_archive/profits/2002/ .

198. Second sexual revolution. Quoted in Hilt, "The Second Sexual Revolution."

198. "The drug did okay." Interview with Dr. Vera Strecher, October, 13 2011.

199. They knew that blocking PDE 5. For a detailed report on the discovery of Viagra, see Larry Katzenstein, *Viagra: The Remarkable Story of the Discovery and Launch* (New York: Medical Information Press, 2001), p. 11–12.

203. "The most innovative and devastating retailer in the world." Originally reported in "Zara, a Spanish Success Story." *CNN*, June 15, 2001. http://edition.cnn.com/BUSINESS/programs/yourbusiness/stories2001/zara/.

206. "Became the standard professional." Originally written by Horace Newcomb, *Encyclopedia of Television, v. 1* (New York: Fitzroy Dearborn, 2004).

206. "But all proved costly losers to Sony." Ibid.

207. "Sony logged nearly a billion dollars in profit." Passage appeared in Carl Howe. "The Wall St. Journal's Faulty Conclusion from The VHS-Betamax War." *Seeking Alpha*, January 26, 2006. http://seekingalpha.com/article/6178-the-wall-st-journal-s-faulty-conclusion-from-the-vhs-betamax-war-sne.

207. Compare that to Fox. Statistics for New Zealand's film releases can be found at New Zealand Film Commission, "Statistics." http://www.nzfilm.co.nz/FilmCatalogue/Statistics.aspx. Information on Fox's movie releases is from Aubrey Solomon, *The Fox Film*.

207. The movies cost over $310 million. Production costs and benefits can be found in Kristin Thompson, *The Frodo Franchise* (Los Angeles: University of California Press, 2007), p. 35–36.

207. Investment in the film industry in New Zealand went from . . . The New Zealand Institute of Economic Research summarized the film's economic impact in "Report to the New Zealand Film Commission: Scoping the Lasting Effects of The Lord of the Rings." http://nzier.org.nz/publications/scoping-the-lasting-effects-of-the-lord-of-the-rings .

208. Before long, tourism surged. Data for the economic impact of the LOTR films can be found in W. Glen Croy, "The Lord of the Rings, New Zealand, and Tourism: Image Building with Film." *Monash University Department of Management*, 2004. http://www.linkbc.ca/torc/downs1/Lordofthe RingsReport.pdf.

208. Due to the efforts of one pioneering director. The impact of the LOTR franchise was a large political issue in recent elections covered by Michael Field and Pattrick Smellie: "Thousands of Jobs, Millions of Dollars at Stake." *Stuff* 10, no. 21 (2010).

209. When I first started. As told to Joel Stein, "The Accidental 'Friend' Finder." *CNNMoney*, March 30, 2007. http://money.cnn.com/magazines/business2/business2_archive/2007/04/01/8403370/.

INDEX